Scott
Jaffe

BATTING
FROM MEMORY

BATTING
FROM MEMORY

Jack Fingleton

COLLINS
London and Sydney
1981

William Collins Sons and Co Ltd
London · Glasgow · Sydney · Auckland
Toronto · Johannesburg

Fingleton, Jack
    Batting from memory.
    1. Cricket players – Great Britain – Biography
    I. Title
    796.35'8092'4   GV915.F/

ISBN 0-00-216359-4

First published 1981
Reprinted October 1981
© J. H. Fingleton 1981
Photoset in Plantin by
MS Filmsetting Ltd, Frome, Somerset
Made and Printed in Great Britain by
William Collins Sons & Co Ltd, Glasgow

A tribute to the memory
of a wonderful mother,
Belinda May Fingleton –
1955 RIP

Contents

Illustrations

Foreword

The joy of being a true lover of cricket is that the season never ends. When winter comes we have its literature to sustain us, to carry us through the dreary days by reviving memories of seasons long burned out. We are lucky in that the game attracts and stirs the imaginations of creative writers; no sport has a more varied and rich treasury of poetry and prose.

The men who write about the game remind me irresistibly of the men who play it. A Cardus essay is an innings by Graveney, all elegance and silken flow. John Arlott is Len Hutton, superb technique and classic style. To read Robertson-Glasgow and Ian Peebles is to watch an over by Johnny Wardle at his most humorous and imaginative; while Jack Fingleton, the man who has set down his life story in this book, writes about the game in a way which Keith Miller played it, which is to say in his own inimitable fashion.

John Lovesey, the Sports Editor of the *Sunday Times*, and a friend and mentor to both Jack and myself, once told me that when he came new to the job and looked for the first time at an article by Jack Fingleton he wondered how he might edit it. To his trained eye the writing lacked form and structure, it did not conform to accepted patterns of journalism. He brooded a long time about the problem and then made a startling discovery: namely, the secret of editing an article by Jack Fingleton is to leave it alone.

Quite simply his journalistic style is unique. It's a combination of gossipy information, blunt judgement and telling anecdotes, all seasoned with a dash of humour. What Jack Fingleton illuminates (and has always done so) is what a lot of us tend to forget: that cricket is not only the loveliest and most difficult of games but also the most humorous. And, in doing so, he puts into proper perspective the fundamental truth that any sporting pursuit, whether it be as complicated and cerebral as cricket or as simple as soccer, is, when all is said and done, only a game.

Jack Fingleton knows better than most the certain truth of cricket's proper place in the order of things because, for most of his journalistic career, he has reported the doings of politicians in the Australian Parliament. And no matter how beguiling the sound of willow on leather, no matter how seductive the smell of new mown grass or the sight of flannelled fools flitting oe'r the greensward, he knows, more certainly than most, that these sensations are insignificant compared to the decisions that men make on behalf of mankind.

His years as a parliamentary reporter have also given him a sharp insight into both the foolishness and the grandeur of man. Of all my friends, many gifted with great perception, I am acquainted with no-one who can make a sharper and sounder assessment of his fellow man than Jack Fingleton. It was he who befriended Harold Larwood at a time when the majority of Australians believed him to be the Devil incarnate, discovering beneath the fearsome aspect, the simplicity, courage and essential niceness of the man.

It was he, in one of his best essays, who sensed that the traditional enmity between an Australian cricket team playing Yorkshire was not, as commonly supposed, caused by two conflicting and thereby varying philosophies. Rather, the conflict was due to two tribes of blood brothers competing for a reputation which, both truly believed, belonged to them. Moreover, each was agreed (but would never admit it) that if it didn't belong to one it belonged to the other, and the rest weren't worth bothering about.

I knew Jack Fingleton before I met him and, in truth, was a little hesitant in making proper contact with someone I admired so much as a writer and broadcaster. I needn't have bothered. The writer is the man. The image on the screen is not the disguise but the real person.

When, in 1979, I went to Australia to do a series of television shows, I was saddened how little his reputation mattered in his own country. Therefore it delighted me beyond measure when he came on my show and, simply by being himself, reminded his countrymen that he was a very remarkable and singular man. His television style, like his writing, is unique. And, as with editing his copy, the way to interview Jack Fingleton is not to try.

During the course of that interview, another one when I returned to Australia in 1980 and again in England later the same year, he told jokes with the timing of a comedian, rattled through 'On Ilkley Moor B'aht at', flirted with actresses, gave advice to trades union leaders and enraptured the audience with anecdotes about everyone from Bradman to Jack Kennedy, Trevor Howard to Douglas Jardine. But through it all shone his own distinctive humour. When I asked him to do the second interview in Australia he agreed, but worried about the wisdom of it. After all, his first interview had been little short of sensational, and he felt he couldn't top it. He said he'd go away for a while and think about what he might do on the show to make it different. For my own part I was perfectly happy for Jack to come on and do exactly what he had done before, namely be himself. The night before the show I had a call from Jack.

'I've been thinking about tomorrow,' he said.

'Come up with any ideas?' I asked.

'Think so. Tell me, have you ever had anyone croak on your show?' he said.

Just a couple more things I know about Jack Fingleton which I'll mention because I know he won't. Sir Robert Menzies, a fair all-rounder himself, described him as the best of cricket writers. Harold Larwood, not much given to excessive praise of anyone, particularly batsmen wearing baggy green caps whom he bowled at, told me that Fingo was simply *the* bravest of cricketers he bowled against.

I never saw him play, but I have come to know the man. He is a beguiling mixture: a humorist who is never flippant, a serious man but not po-faced. He is someone of deeply-held beliefs, but never censorious of others. He has walked with kings and commoners, fools and wise men, and never been anything but his own man. My only regret is that I might have met him sooner, and known him the better and the longer.

Michael Parkinson *June 1981*

Introduction

I could never quite believe that it was all happening to me. Like all boys in the Depression years I worshipped my heroes and dreamed my dreams, but knew that as a son of a Sydney tram driver who had died early, the only possible future was work – if I could get it. If someone had said to me then, when I was twelve years old, 'Fingleton, you'll grow up to work for some of the world's greatest newspapers,' I'd have been terrified. If someone had gone on to say, 'There will be a season in which you'll top the averages of the Australian eleven,' I'd have thought he'd strayed a little close to the flagon; but if someone had said, 'You'll be a trusted friend of Prime Ministers,' then I would have known the person speaking to me was going round the bend.

Even in my youth they used to say it's not what you know but who you know that counts. I knew nobody, so my expectations weren't high. Maybe it was a matter of reflexes – of grabbing opportunities on those rare occasions when I happened to be in the right place at the right time. I became a journalist because I started at the bottom and was prepared to put up with anything in order to stay in there and wait for a handhold on the next rung. I became a fair Test cricketer because I worked at it tirelessly. I coped, with some success, against bodyline, perhaps because I was too stupid to get out of the way. It wasn't until I'd finished, though, that I realized how I could have been much better.

But all this time things kept happening – people, now legendary, crossed my path; my cricket heroes became my team-mates; cricket and journalism took me round the world and into the company of fascinating celebrities. So to say that I have been more than fortunate in the people I have met and the many friends I have made in the cricket and newspaper worlds would not be an exaggeration. So many have helped and trusted me. One of the best homespun philosophers I've met in my life was Ben Chifley, once Prime Minister of Australia. The press gallery in Canberra looked forward avidly to Chif's press conferences; they were animated by his droll sense of humour. On one occasion I remember him saying to us, 'You haven't got to be a bloody genius to succeed in life. All you have to do is use the bloody brains God has given you.'

*

I had an extremely modest upbringing in Waverley, a Sydney suburb. My father's early death left a wonderful mother with six young children to rear and educate. We were often pushed for food. All of us would troop home for lunch from school and it was an event when one of us was given two shillings and sent to Charlie the Chinaman, on the corner of Cowper Street, as it then was, for some mixed fruit. There was no spare money for us to buy extras at school. I remember borrowing a shilling from a fellow-pupil, Len McWilliam, to buy a text book. I had no idea how I would repay it and when Len naturally pushed me for his 'advance' I was terror-struck. I didn't know how I would pay and even had visions of prison. I put the case to my mother; the shilling was forthcoming and all was well.

Brother Foran, a member of the order of Christian Brothers and headmaster of our parish school, took a father-like interest in me and gave me great encouragement. He had known my father and in many ways he stepped into my father's shoes after his death, helping me to gain some self-confidence. Brother Foran, whom we disrespectfully called 'Fat', singled out my friend Charles McCloskey and myself for English essay competitions, and he saw we had the right books for the subject. He gave me whatever love I have for words, though my father had been fond of poetry and would often read to us. When I left school at fifteen I could recite all of Gray's 'Elegy' and Goldsmith's 'Deserted Village' by heart.

It would be difficult to say who the greatest influences in my life have been; so many have been involved. But my first real break was due entirely to my jovial cousin, Jack O'Brien, who arranged a job for me on the newly started *Sydney Daily Guardian*, where he worked as a compositor. I was really a glorified office-boy but attached myself to A. R. B. ('Pedlar') Palmer, on the sports desk. When Mr Palmer found I was reliable he gave me more scope and I even had the power to engage casuals at thirty shillings a day to cover various events. Thus I was able to put some money in the way of my cricket club friends, Frank Conway and Jimmy Holm, victims of the Depression. They would bring in details of what they covered and I would knock it into shape. So I spent some happy years at the *Guardian*, serving my cadetship there; and when Pedlar Palmer moved on I moved on too, to the *Telegraph Pictorial*, where I was made a graded journalist. The *Pictorial* merged with the *Daily Telegraph*. That was a time of drastic changes in Sydney's newspapers but all the time I was able to play cricket during the week with our newspaper teams. We went to work on the morning papers at two p.m. and worked till about midnight, so we had mornings free for surfing, tennis, golf or cricket. I spent many of them in the company of Jack O'Brien, who was a very capable all-round sportsman. My only worry was whether the night work would damage my eyesight, but I have been lucky in that.

It was while working on the *Guardian* that I first came across file copies of the *Manchester Guardian* and from then on I was an avid reader of 'Cricketer' – Neville Cardus. Eventually I plucked up courage to write to him; that was the beginning of a correspondence and friendship which lasted till his death in 1976. He is the cricket writer I have most admired and he it was who always gave me the most encouragement in my own cricket writing.

The day came in 1944 when I moved into the press gallery of Parliament House, Canberra as political correspondent for Radio Australia. John Curtin was then Prime Minister, Robert Menzies the leader of the Opposition. Later, when Sir Robert was Prime Minister, it was no uncommon thing for Oliver Chidgey, one of his personal staff, to come to my room on the Senate side of the House and say, 'The boss wants to know whether you are busy?' Sir Robert was keenly interested in cricket and, if there was some controversy in the game, he would often want to discuss it. I wasn't slow, as a journalist, to take advantage of these meetings; I could ask him questions on political happenings of the day and he invariably told me his views, though more as background, not to be used as coming from him. One of his personal staff once told me Sir Robert had said he trusted me over this; he didn't trust many of any ilk, and particularly not journalists.

I was interested to read in Sir Robert's book *Afternoon Light* that the Menzies family, like my own in Waverley, had known tough times. Sir Robert's father had been a store-keeper in Jeparit, a small town in the Mallee district of Victoria. It was a district that knew well the droughts that so often blight Australia and there was a particularly bad one in the late part of the last century. A store-keeper would be one of the hardest hit in the district as the squatters, so-called from early days of occupancy in Australia when squatting was considered as good a way of ownership as the official seal, would run up gigantic bills and only settle when the rains came. Things would have brightened for his family when his father became a Member of the Victorian Parliament, as they did for my own when my father was elected a Labour Member for Waverley for the NSW Parliament in 1913. Sir Robert wrote in his last book that the education of both his parents was meagre but went on to observe: 'They both understood what many people with university degrees don't understand – that one's education begins when formal studies end.'

I had been writing for the South African Argus group of newspapers since 1936, when I was part of our cricket team touring there. When I took a journalistic jaunt to England in the mid-sixties I flew to Africa en route: Sir Robert had given me a warm commendation to Dr Verwoerd, then the South African Prime Minister. As a result of that, Dr Verwoerd gave me a seventy-five minute interview with no one else present. I'd made my own attempt at a good impression when, on meeting, I quoted an Afrikaan saying taught me by Rene de Villiers of the *Johannesburg Star*: 'Veels geluk met u verjarrsdag' – a greeting for Dr Verwoerd's recent birthday. I was listed to spend fifteen minutes with him and made several attempts to leave, but he motioned me to keep seated. I left at last and was pleased to note that I had kept a glowering Ben Schooman waiting for his appointment.

Politics and cricket seem to mix even in seemingly unlikely parts of the world. One of the places cricket helped me was, unbelievably, the White House in Washington. I had flown from New York to Washington after the England trip and met Pierre Salinger, President Kennedy's press secretary, soon after I arrived. Pierre had obviously enquired about me at the Australian embassy. 'I know all about cricket,' he told me. I expressed surprise. 'Yes,' said Pierre, 'I used to score for a team in Philadelphia.'

He said it was a pity I hadn't come sooner: the President was holding a press interview that afternoon and any visitor had to be vetted for forty-eight hours by security. Still, because of our mutual interest in cricket, Pierre said he would try to get the rule waived. He did the trick – I was admitted but told I could not ask any questions – details of these had to be submitted first so that the President, who pointed out which questioner he would answer, knew what to expect. A woman journalist in a big hat kept sniping at the President but he treated her kindly. He stood on a well-lit podium beneath the words 'President of the USA', looking magnificently fit, well-tailored, speaking quickly and musically, needing none of the trappings that seem such a feature of American politics. It was the last television interview he gave.

Just as it could be a help, cricket could also put you on the spot. I remember one occasion in England when I was asked to stand in at a Forty Club dinner for Lord Home – he'd been going to make the main speech but before then had become Prime Minister. Knowing that Lord Constantine was due to reply to my speech did nothing for my confidence and I decided to write to Lord Home, asking him for one of the stories he would have told. He obliged from 10 Downing Street. The story concerned a school match. The leading batsman thought he was a bit lucky to escape an lbw appeal. 'My word,' he said to the school umpire when he got down his end, 'I thought I was a goner then.' 'You would have been,' said the umpire, 'had you been on the visiting side.'

*

This book will have much about cricket in it and many well known personalities. I will always be grateful to the game for the opportunities it gave me to travel, to meet people out of the ordinary, and to advance my newspaper cause. I've been in newspapers since I was seventeen and it is possible there will be some exaggerations in this book, but they won't be malicious. Any journalist worth his salt doesn't think any good story can't be improved a bit. The Canberra press gallery, where I served most of my journalistic life, could prove the case. It might well be the quietest day of a peaceful recess, not a speck of news to be had anywhere; but next day's papers have to appear and columns have to be filled. The boys pass one another in the corridor with always the same lugubrious questions and answers. 'Quiet, isn't it?' 'Yes, dead.' Later they gather at a convivial spot and lament the lack of events and stories. They will have a drink on that to let it seep in. They'll have another few snorts and gradually the ideas will begin to germinate. Next day, when there hasn't been a single politician within a coo-ee of Canberra, devouring readers will learn that 'Informed opinion in the Canberra lobbies thinks ...', or 'Those in a position to express an opinion believe ...' And so it goes on.

Politics in Canberra have served me well and certainly having played cricket for Australia did me no harm with the politicians. On the day in 1978 when I retired from the press gallery there the Speaker, Sir Billy Snedden, announced the fact to the House from the Chair, drawing attention to my cricket career and wishing me well in semi-retirement on behalf of Parliament. Members of both sides of the House were kind enough to give a hearty hear-hear: it was the only time in a turbulent day (spent wrangling on privilege) that they showed any unanimity. It was the only time in the history of our Parliament that a press correspondent had been so honoured and farewelled. It would have made that twelve-year-old back in Waverley sit up and think.

Happy Days at Cullerin

It was on the last bitterly cold, grey day of June 1978 that we buried Winnie Hannan in the lonely churchyard of Breadalbane. Sweetwoodlea, an old home where I had spent many a happy country holiday, was a little down the road, nestling in trees. Otherwise, it was typically open Australian bush-land. On the other side of the old road was one of the two vast Breadalbane plains across which, in earlier times, the Melbourne expresses would belch and roar around midnight. The wind soughed even more sadly than usual through the thickly massed pines surrounding the churchyard where so many of Winnie's family lay. On the wire fence over the way that skirted a Sweetwoodlea paddock where sheep were grazing, I noticed four magpies but, in keeping with the occasion, they withheld their beautiful gurgle.

The district turned out in large numbers to honour Winnie because the Hannans were pioneers there, dating back to the 1860s, the time of the bush-rangers who had ridden the dense hills far to the south and west. Mourners came from Gunning, Goulburn, Gurrundah and Bungendore, but not on the horses or in the horse-drawn buggies, sulkies or phaetons of old that used to surround the church on mass days. They all came now by car and it was fitting that my younger brother, Wally, a Marist priest, should have driven up from Sydney to help say the requiem mass. My sister, Kitty, older than me by exactly two years as I was born on her birthday, was there from Goulburn. It was right that my family should have been present in numbers because the Fingletons owed a lot to Winnie and her parents, Frank and Theresa Hannan, who about 1883 had taken my father, Jim, an orphan, into their Cullerin home and family.

I blessed the urge that had taken me to visit Winnie in the nursing home at Goulburn. She was very frail but we knew each other immediately. I had wanted information from her on my father's early days but dear Winnie's mind had gone. She couldn't remember anything and thought hazily that her brother Gerald, who had died a few years before, was still alive. Realizing this, I didn't push her but just chatted along. I was glad I had taken her a bunch of red carnations and I was more than glad that I had, when leaving, given her an impulsive kiss good-bye. I reflected then that Winnie would not have had many kisses in life. She was a typical spinster of the Australian bush, one who sacrifices herself for her family. She was ninety-two when she died a few weeks later and I guess had had her fill of lonely life. She had never married and I doubt she had ever given it a thought. She had been a beautiful cook and I told her how much I had enjoyed her cakes. She smiled. There had been a strong link between my father and Winnie. Amy, at eighty-eight the last Hannan alive of a family of ten, told me how Winnie would go up the back of 'Wandella', the Hannan homestead, and bat and bowl with my father for hours. Dad was a very keen cricketer.

The visit to the nursing home had dejected me beyond measure because frail, old age is something depressingly sad. People are so helpless. One dear old duck asked me to call a taxi for her as she wanted to go home. A nurse came instead and tied her to a chair by a sheet to watch television; she fell to criticizing the programme most trenchantly. The nurses, kind and solicitous, called all the females 'darling'. I realized immediately that my old dear would never see her home again or, if she visited it, it would be in a coffin on the way to the cemetery. The matron told me how antibiotics now prolonged people's lives: once pneumonia used to take the aged off very quickly but now that science had overcome that with antibiotics, life was much longer. I pondered·on that and wondered on the value of sustaining the feeble 'life' to which we hold so tenaciously, eking out each lonely and repetitious day, merely awaiting the last one of all. I detected the click of death in the patients' dental plates, horribly ill-fitting, but nobody thought it worthwhile to do anything about it anymore.

*

The Fingletons came from Portlaiose, County Leix, in Ireland. When Lindsay Hassett and I played with the Australian team in Dublin in 1938, we accepted an invitation from Sam Roach, of Carlow, to stay on a few days with him. He told me that a lass, Brenda, who lived on the next farm, had been a Fingleton; borrowing the bike of the Roach's girl-servant, I cycled there one day and was immediately impressed by the likeness of the woman who came to the door to my sister, Kitty. It was Brenda, Mrs Bill Murphy.

In 1964 my elder daughter, Belinda, and I accepted an invitation from the Murphys to stay with them in Kilkenny, and one evening the Fingleton clan of Portlaoise turned out in force to meet their Australian relatives. There was no doubt we were related although, like many migrants, families had lost touch with one another. The resemblances, and the Christian names, were too much alike for it to be otherwise, and the manner in which one of the older ones sat and crossed his legs reminded me very much of my father. There was one rich old character there with a beard like our folk bush-ranger, Ned Kelly. One other who had had a bush beard like that was our Uncle Peter, who was very much a mystery man and, like so many of his countrymen, possibly because of their doleful existence, became addicted to the bottle. The story was told that evening of how one of their number returned one night to the bakery they had at Stradbally, locked it up, and went off to Australia. They said his name was Patrick but it could easily have been Uncle Peter; he was a rum fellow in many ways and could have changed his name. I would not have put it past him.

At all events my Uncle Jack, after whom I was named, was born in Ireland. As so many of the Irish did last century, with too many mouths to feed at home and little being produced from poor land, the small family set out about 1870 for Australia where my father and Aunt Kitty were born. They lived in Melbourne and one night my grandfather, who smoked in bed, burnt the place down. He died in the fire. It all made such a deep impression upon my father – that and the misery which followed it – that he promised himself he would never drink or smoke. Nor did he. He was not what we in Australia call a 'wowser', a person who lives a narrow and restricted life; he would go into a hotel bar with his mates but would drink nothing other than lemonade.

His mother died, too, soon after the fire and the three young Fingletons went into an orphanage. One wondered where Peter was at this stage but he never seemed one to accept responsibilities. Not unnaturally the three younger ones were not happy in the orphanage and a catholic organization, the St Vincent de Paul Society, sought homes for them. Despite her own large family, Mrs Theresa Hannan in Cullerin adopted my father and spoke of him as her 'favourite' son. Jack was adopted by the Sweetwoodlea Hannans, and Kitty went into the Mercy Convent at Yass, NSW, afterwards entering and becoming Sister Assissium.

Peter attached himself to Jack when he married, turning up at each home in turn and living, usually, in an adjacent bush shanty. Peter seemed to be content with life as long as he had a bottle of rum handy. At one period Uncle Jack ran the General Store at Cullerin and, Peter arriving shoeless, he gave him a pair of boots. The boots had gone next day and Peter was again barefoot; the rum had too strong a call. Yet, in spite of the rugged life he led, Peter lived until ninety-one, probably because he was well pickled. He knew all the native songs of Ireland and spent most of the day in his shanty singing them and accompanying himself with the 'bones' – ribs of sheep on a stick, that he would rattle and clack. One of my own son Jim's party tricks (he has many, particularly the rendition of our favourite bush poet, 'Banjo' Paterson's, 'Man from Ironbark' with its ' "Murder, bloody murder!" shouted the man from Ironbark') is to play the lagerphone, an unusual musical (*sic*) instrument: corks are taken out of beer bottle-tops which are nailed to a stick, so that they jangle in the manner of a tambourine.

Dad lived and progressed with the Hannans, going to the little public school on a nearby hill. The Hannans were steeped in their religion and the nightly Rosary was part of their lives. This habit stayed with my father and after he left with a bunch of his Cullerin mates to go shearing in the Queensland outback when he was twenty-one, he would drop to his knees in the communal shed to say his Rosary, despite the hurling of boots and abuse. Those must have been stirring times. My father took an active interest in union matters; he was a foundation member of the Australian Workers' Union, and loved to recount incidents of irate graziers chasing the uniting shearers out of their sheds.

The Rosary was always said at the Hannans'. Over the many holidays I spent at Cullerin and Sweetwoodlea, the ritual was always the same. We would have dinner and then gather around the comfy log fire, have a game of cards or a yarn, some music on the gramophone; and the evening always ended, for me, with a glass of hot, sweet milk and then the Rosary. I can still hear the steady tick-tock of the old grandfather clock as a charming family evening drew to its inevitable close.

On my stays at Cullerin I had a most comfortable room behind the Post Office, a part-time one which Eileen Hannan used to run. On the coldest, frostiest of nights, around midnight, I would get up, dress and slip out the front gate between the sweet verbena and japonica bushes, and cross the road and railway line. I made for a water-tank, some five feet high, that had been placed beside the line for the use of fettlers when their own tanks, supplied by rain-water off the roof, had run dry.

There was a hole in the top of the water-tank and into this hole I would firmly fasten my right arm and wait for the passing of the Melbourne express. Its powerful head-lights could be seen a long way off, across the Breadalbane plain. Then there would be twists and turns as it sped down past the property of the Evistons (relatives of the Hannans) and finally it would reach the straight run along Cullerin. It would come steaming at me, roaring and belching flame and smoke, and I would make doubly sure my hold with the right arm in the tank was secure. The strong head-light made it seem like day and the engine-drivers – there were usually two engines – must surely have seen me. But I would hold fast and the express, huge, high up on the line and rocking and jolting from side to side in an ominous manner, would flash past in a flurry of smoke, steam and noise. I was fearful, at times, that the engine-drivers would give me a burst of steam as they went by to let me know that what I was doing was highly dangerous, and that I was trespassing on railway property. But the only fright I had was one night when I could hear a broken coupling clanking along the line. A swish from that would have ended my vigils.

It would also have sapped my desire for 'kicks' but it was great fun, and exciting and romantic to see the rear red light of the train disappear swiftly down the line and around a bend. The memory of the belching and rocking engine, a few bare feet away, was to stand me in good stead in the thirties when Larwood and Voce came rocketing in with their bodyline, though they looked ferocious enough, especially my (now) friend Larwood. But my early training did me much good. What, I thought, were balls whizzing around one's head after facing the engine of the Melbourne express!

Sometimes, after the express had gone, I would linger on in the enveloping quietness of the bush. The tall gums would stand out grey and ghostly in the moonlight and the sounds of cropping by the stock would come clearly on the night air, portending the heavy frost that was bound to come with the dawn. At such moments I would ponder on the peace and majestic beauty of the Australian bush and nature, recalling the words of 'Banjo' Paterson: 'And at night the wondrous glory of the everlasting stars.'

That was one of the two tremendous hushes I knew in life, so quiet they shrieked. The other was to come when I was at the other end in the bodyline Test in Melbourne and Don Bradman, who did not play in the first Test, came to a tumultuous welcome from a packed ground. All Australia believed this was the moment of destiny in the bodyline series, that the great Don would soon put bodyline in its place. He played the worst shot I have seen from the other end. He was on the move far to the off before Bowes had bowled the ball, a rank long hop which Bradman hit into the base of his stumps. Never has an Australian crowd been so awe-struck! It was as if all had heard a voice from on high saying, 'Announcement, announcement. The sun will not rise in Melbourne tomorrow.'

*

I had mixed thoughts about the express one dismally dark night in 1934 when I set out to ride from Sweetwoodlea, where I had been visiting, to Cullerin, some six or seven miles away. On board the Limited that night were the NSW members of the Australian team chosen to play against England, and I had been missed out. I had set my heart on being selected; I had batted as best I could against bodyline, and it had left me with a nervous, queasy feeling. Despite this, I had made 655 runs during the season at 65.50, being above six of the batsmen who were chosen for the touring side.

I had put my all into that summer, jogging every day all the way round Centennial Park, plus a run up and down the long Birrell Street to begin and end; but I had over-trained for the final game against Victoria. My muscles were too tight and I suffered a bad attack of cramps, having to retire but coming back to make 135. It was after that game the touring team was picked. There is a story about Woodfull and an umpire's decision during it, but that will keep for later on.

Of all people, the man who nettled me most was Bradman. I had been in the same NSW side as him for several years and had played in the bodyline series with him. I was not a final success against bodyline – who was? It shook us all, but I had fought hard and made my share of runs, top scoring in four innings and playing a really good innings for NSW against bodyline the first time I saw it – going through the innings for 119 not out – when Kippax, Bradman and McCabe had all failed.

The press pundits that 1934 summer did not make the job any easier. I did not have much regard for most of them or their knowledge of cricket: the teams they were constantly picking were based largely on State preferences. An English tour in those times, in and out of flannels for six days of the week, knocked the love of cricket out of one; but I am sure I could have been a much better batsman had I been on that 1934 tour. Moreover, chaps I knew who didn't see bodyline or largely avoided it got the call, and they didn't have Larwood or Voce to face that 1934 year in England. I had my right of reply the following year when I was chosen for South Africa and had the distinction of heading the batting list by a large margin, in aggregate and average, in a team that included Bill Brown, Stan McCabe, Arthur Chipperfield and Len Darling, all good cobbers of mine who had made the 1934 tour of England.

But Don Bradman was the man I thought about most as I rode home that miserable night to Cullerin. On the very day the team was chosen for England he made a vitriolic attack on me in my own newspaper, the *Sydney Sun*. He gave me particular stick for my running between the wickets. I had had one bad fault that season as a runner between wickets: I would make to dash off as soon as I had hit the ball, and I can see now that this would have made my partner at the other end jittery. Young Darling, of Adelaide, has the same bad habit. Like Darling, I was fast between wickets but leading out did not mean I intended to run. Even Bill O'Reilly was admonishing me, only a few months ago, for allegedly running him out. In fact I was only twice run out in my career: once with Bill Brown when he called me against England and sent me back on a hopeless recovery task, and the other the first occasion I batted with Archie Jackson.

But this article from Bradman at such a time was, I thought, hitting a bit low. I saw him on the ground floor of the *Sun* just after the team was chosen. I shook him by the hand and wished him good luck. He said 'Bad luck,' to me and I told him, 'I think I have largely got you to thank for missing out.' Nothing else was said. In fact, I think he must have known that I would not be in the team, else he wouldn't have written so critically of a team-mate. Moreover I found out later that Bradman's opinion on the team had been sought by several of the selectors and that he didn't favour me. That probably was fair enough but, occasionally seeing his capers against bodyline from the other end, he wasn't top of the pops with me either at that particular time.

Looking at it dispassionately now I should not have been surprised that I was not selected in 1934. Kippax, McCabe, Chipperfield, Brown, Oldfield, O'Reilly and Bradman were chosen and they were all New South Welshmen. To expect an eighth such State-man was a bit rich. The team consisted of sixteen, and Woodfull (Victoria) and Dr Dolling (South Australia) would have been slaughtered on their return home had they agreed to so heavy a representation from the one State, and that NSW. What I felt most then was the hurt done to my mother and family.

*

However, cricket can wait. I have tried to give a general picture of Cullerin, a drowsy, secluded hamlet on the southern railway line. It greatly influenced my father, as it did me on my many holidays there. One vivid memory I will always have – the awesome smell of the spoon with which, each night, I would take a dose of emulsion and cod liver oil. I had an early fear that my lungs, like my father's, were weak and I took bottles of the emulsion to Cullerin. I was shy of this fear, wanted nobody to know anything about it, and so I hid my bottle and the spoon up a hollow log, like many an alcoholic in the bush with his bottle.

On hot nights, we would sit in the cool of the long verandah outside, yarning about this and that as Australians in the bush love to do, only interrupted by the puffing of some goods train as it steamed by just across the road. One night Gerald frightened the wits out of me by pretending that the rising moon, coming up in all its redness beyond a mountain, was a bush-fire. If there is one thing that gives Australians an apprehension of disaster, it is a bush-fire.

Life was always thrilling for me at Cullerin. I could ride early and well (I was thrown only once and that before noisy, cheering telegraph linesmen, who frightened the horse), but I gave Les Hannan, Winnie's elder brother just back from the war, palpitations once when he asked me to hold Whiskey, a fractious grey who had thrown most, while he went inside. Les emerged to find me sitting, foolishly, in the saddle. I guess Whiskey realized he had a novice on top. I knew all the gullies and creeks, where I used to wash hopefully for 'colours' (I imagined the mica to be gold – but there was gold in the creeks, washed down from the hills), and I would ride through the bush to Collector, bush-ranger country in the days of Dunn and Gardiner. The horses knew, however, that a 'mug' had come to collect one of them when I stalked them with the bridle hidden behind my back, while they cavorted up and down the home paddock.

Now and then I would ride out miles to the back of the Cullerin ranges, so rough and declivitous that I would dismount and lead the horse. The bush was so dense that it was pretty dark in there.

*

After Winnie's funeral and on the way to her wake, in the home of a nephew, I motored down the old road to what was now a deserted hamlet. It was tragic: the railway station had been blown up, the school which generations had attended had been demolished, and the old Hannan home was down to its rotting foundations.

I was almost tempted to go and search among them for the marbles which I often lost through the cracks when playing in the hall. All that was left of old was the shearing shed, in whose solitude I had spent many musing and thrilling moments. The stables, the hen houses which Winnie supervised, the geese sheds which she also managed – all were gone. The sound of the geese as they wended their way each morning to an adjacent dam and then returned at evening, in cackling line, had been as music on the still air. Gone, also, were the shearers' sleeping huts where Billy Burke, invariably in the DTs, would think somebody was after him to cut his throat in the full of the moon, and his shrieks gave everybody the horrors. There were always passing 'visitors' in those huts, many no-hopers, many victims of the bottle but more victims of the system.

What is now called the back road has given precedence to a speeding highway on the other side of the railway line, along which huge diesel trucks, spouting disgusting fumes to pollute the clean country air, roar their incessant and dangerous way to and from Sydney and Melbourne. Along the old road in other days would trudge an army of chaps, down on their luck, their swags clinging to their aching shoulders, asking for either 'tucker' or work. Most had been soldiers in the war to end war, and had returned home to seek this humiliating charity. During the Depression it was heartaching to see all those swaggies, but none called at the Hannans' in vain. If they couldn't be given a job chopping wood, they would be sent on their trudging way with food. Winnie had a soft heart and neighbours, too, who called for a pint of milk, would find their billys filled to the brim and no charge made. 'They have a lot of kiddies,' she would say.

It was the same with the meat the Hannans killed on their property. Legs of this and that, costing the earth today, would be given away, as were steak, chops and pork when a squealing pig went under the knife. They were warm, generous people and I admired them all, but none more so than the tall Leo, their youngest son, when he would summon his kangaroo-dogs (not the sheep-dogs) and we would go on a rabbit hunt through the bush.

There would be tumult as the lean greyhounds would first flush out and then pursue the rabbit. The poor bunny had no chance. Sometimes he would go to ground or up a hollow log but Leo, who had his mattock with him, would dig it out while the dogs whined and barked alongside him. They would try to get at the rabbit before Leo, but he was too fast for them: a tug at the feet with the head in one hand, and the rabbit's neck would be broken. Its body went on a pole to be taken home for skinning and the meat would be awarded to the dogs. There was money in skins in those days.

Life at Cullerin, away from the rush and bustle of the city, was sheer joy for me. I spent more time there than school holidays as father, no doubt due to his hard early life, contracted tuberculosis after the Spanish influenza epidemic of 1917 and was sent to the country for the dry air. It was the deep fear of that disease, which I believed to be hereditary, that made me take that horrible emulsion. The fear stayed with me all my early life. My son Larry tells me that TB would present no problem today and would submit to drugs; but those drugs were unknown then. Archie Jackson, the brilliant NSW batsman whose genius always seemed tinged with the inevitability of early mortality, died from TB in 1933.

Our family pinned its faith on (and the name recurs to me after all these years, so much did we believe in him) Dr Selwyn Harrison, of Macquarie Street, Sydney, but it was asking a lot of him. I can recall Dad coming home one night after a visit to Dr Harrison. He must have got the news then that he was incurable because he had a quiet talk with my mother in the kitchen. I remember him pacing up and down the hall thinking no doubt, not of his approaching death, but of leaving his widow with six young children: this was long before the days of widows' pensions. He can have had little comfort from his thoughts; I remember my father as a marvellous family man, and he and my mother were very close.

*

One other outstanding feature of the country of those days were the bush-dances, usually held in a shearing shed. Occasionally a piano would be loaned but mostly the music was provided by an accordion and a fiddle. The girls would sit on forms inside the shed, waiting to be asked to dance. The boys usually needed a swig of rum from a bottle outside to pluck up courage to ask; bush lads are generally 'girl shy' and the chance of a refusal before their fellows dimmed many an ambition. There was no conventional hour for ending the dance; it usually lasted as long as people wanted to dance and mostly ended with a sing-song outside, by a log fire, to the music of the fiddle and the accordion.

They were great days and nights. My greatest thrill, perhaps, was to see the passenger train each day, after tooting, steam on its way at one o'clock to sweaty, smelly Sydney, and to know I was not on it, that I still had some days to go. I am glad I knew those times because I fear the love and spirit of the bush is in danger of dying in

Australia. Horses and blacksmiths have gone, with their sweet music of hammer on anvil; markets have disappeared; and banks and finance companies, mainly through high-priced mortgages, are taking over land which has been in the possession of families for many decades. People, generally, are unable to cope with taxes and rates always going higher and higher, and with the ever-increasing costs of education in the cities to which they are forced to send their young. If something goes wrong now in the all-electric country home, a tradesman rarely will venture far out from the city; he will promise and promise, but rarely turn up.

Sixty per cent of the people now live in the cities along our vast coast line. The life of the average country town is too dull to interest the young; there is little for them to do at night but to congregate in the milk bar, and that frequently leads on to the other kind of bar. The saddest thing is the closing of bush-schools and the blowing up of railway stations. People in 'stopping hamlets', formerly on the railway line, have to travel miles nowadays just to make contact with a train.

As in England railway lines are continually being pulled up: Australian Railways lose 735 million dollars yearly. For me, the romance and thrill of a steam train have been poorly substituted by the ugly, smelling diesels. If this is progress, give me the old days of Cullerin where children would tramp or ride miles to the little bush-school, gathering mushrooms as they went.

*

The words of Oliver Goldsmith's 'Deserted Village' came back to me as I looked at the ruins of Cullerin:

> Ill fares a land, to hastening ills a prey,
> Where wealth accumulates and men decay;
> Princes and lords may flourish, or may fade,
> A breath has made them and a breath will make,
> But a bold peasantry, their country's pride,
> When once destroyed can never be supplied.

We had a good old-time Irish wake for Winnie. The parish priest of Gunning said he had not known Miss Hannan but

C

he paid an adequate tribute to her in speaking of death generally. I thought it sad he had not asked my brother Wally to say a few words. Wally had known Winnie and he could have spoken of the debt the Fingleton family owed to the kindly Hannan folk; it was a sizeable one.

Early Times in Ruthven Street

No. 112 Ruthven Street, Waverley, which I saw as 114 on a recent nostalgic visit, was a very humble abode. Our first home was one of two attached double-storey houses, with an entrance to the backs by an alley-way separating the two houses. It was a red-letter day when, aged about six and supporting myself by stiff arms and legs on the wall, I could clamber up to the roof of the alley-way. Another rich memory – I was five – was when Dad was elected a State Member of Parliament for Waverley in 1913. That was a red-letter night for the whole street. His tram-way mates carried him on their shoulders, a long trudge, all the way home from the Council Chambers, where the result was announced, and I can recall we four children being aroused from bed to go out on the upper front balcony where Dad made a speech to the assembled and cheering multitude below. His many tram comrades in the electorate un-doubtedly got him into Parliament. Waverley had long been a solid Liberal or non-Labour seat, and in taking it away from them Dad had beaten strong men in Charlie Oakes and George Beeby, later to be a judge.

Ruthven Street was a modest Sydney suburban street in all ways. It was pronounced as it was spelt by the in-habitants, although the English pronunciation is 'Riven'. We had a Sir Alexander Hore-Ruthven, later Lord Gowrie*

* Lady Gowrie provided Bill O'Reilly with one of his best stories, and he has many. Lady Gowrie was making an inspection of the wharves one day; she happened across a very muscular wharfie and commented on his biceps. The wharfie was not modest. He could lift a —— ton, he told Lady Gowrie. The escorting party was aghast. 'Eh, cut it out,' said one of them, 'this is Lady Gowrie.' 'Well, half a —— ton,' said the unabashed wharfie.

and Governor-General of South Australia at the time of the bodyline controversy in 1932–3. He took a prominent part in this upheaval with his private letters back to England, which were inspired by his Secretary, Leigh Winser. Knowing the game – he had kept wickets behind Dr Grace and Victor Trumper – Winser was bitterly anti-bodyline and what it was doing to cricket.

Ruthven Street ran from Birrell Street at the bottom to the busy Oxford Street at the top and it was peopled by humble and for the most part impecunious folk, many of them working at the nearby Waverley tram depot. Dad had been a tram-driver, as was Alf Creed who lived next door to us; but Alf cut himself off from his mates by not going out on strike in the big 1917 upset. That was the strike which began in the adjacent Randwick workshop and spread to all the tram depots and then to the railway. It concerned the introduction of an American system of timing. The unions said it was contrary to an agreement they had with the government covering the war period.

Thus the word 'strike' and its effects early permeated our home. The tram-way men on strike would meet each day in Centennial Park, and Dad was one of the speakers who would address them. It did his health no good; driving trams had not been beneficial to him, either: the weather would sweep into the driver's cabin, which was open on one side. Indeed, the trams of early Sydney (they are all gone now) were unhealthy and dangerous. The conductors had to walk footboards on the outside of the carriages with rails for support; they ran the constant risk of being swept off by the passing traffic as well as being continually drenched in bad weather.

This 1917 strike also involved Ben Chifley, later Prime Minister, who was an engine driver at Bathurst. Like so many others he was vicitimized when the strike finished, and at Canberra I always saw him as one of the last Labour men of his ilk – those who suffered for their convictions. Few politicians have in later years, but Chif knew all about the intense bitterness and hatred of those 1917 days. I don't think living next door to the Creeds made any difference to our relations with them although Alf, who found he had a higher position when the strike ended, got very cold treatment from most of his fellows.

*

Milton and Thelma were the Creed children and even now I can strum by ear on the piano the practising tune that Thelma played each morning. Grandma Creed lived with the family and she had about her some indefinable smell (perhaps of old age) which we detected whenever she kissed us. But as she also dispensed cakes and sweets we used to suffer her affection.

Next door to the Creeds lived the Dwights, with many children. The father was a gardener somewhere in the Darling Point district and Mrs Dwight was acknowledged to be *the* cook of Ruthven Street. She used to make magnificent meat-pies and would always send one of the batch down to my mother; the pie would be meticulously cut into small pieces for our family. Mrs Dwight's meat-pies were among my earliest recollections of Ruthven Street. The people there were so humble and poor that they had to be rich in something, and it was in good neighbourliness. Next door to the Dwights lived a Mrs Chaucer who had no husband but had innumerable young babies in her home. It was not until long afterwards that the secret of Mrs Chaucer dawned on me. The babies were from unmarried mothers and that is how, a splendid woman, she made her way in life as a widow.

When Dad was on the trams, we had lived pretty frugally. Mum was a good wife and on cold, wet days, I would take up a hot meal to my father in the depot. On the pay of a Member of Parliament things improved vastly in the Fingleton household. Around this time my eldest brother, Les, who was later to become the youngest Mayor of Waverley, got a prize for looking the most distinguished in a group photo of St Francis, Christian Brothers School, Paddington. I often thought later that Dad being a Member of Parliament might have had something to do with the choice, although Les wore a high collar and was the only pupil to have folded arms. He might have been told to do this so that he would stand out.

Ruthven Street was one of great friendship and company.

The neighbours were very close. Just recently I had a small snap of myself in a sailor's outfit sent to me by one of the Davies girls, a fine Welsh family that lived at the bottom of the street. She said they remembered the Fingletons as a close and popular family. There was also a dairy at the bottom of the street run, I think, by a family called Burrows; and there were always street singers, accompanied by a small organ, who would give us the tear-jerkers so popular at the time. They could not have been more different than the rock songs of today. Tunes of that time were always mournful; there was a pitiful one about Mary who, as the family sung it, 'was hup amon' the 'appy hangels'. Another was about Father, dear Father, who promised to come home, as soon as his day's work was done, but had stopped off at the local hostelry, and now the clock in the steeple was striking one.

If disaster struck a family the whole neighbourhood would fly to aid it. Benefit nights would be held in local halls and a little girl singing, 'Please give me a penny, sir, a penny to buy some bread' would bring a flood of coins to the stage and a flood of tears to eyes also. They were sentimental times.

*

I can remember the day that snap of me in sailor rig was taken, in Oxford Street, Darlinghurst. A more apt one would have been of me in singlet and short trousers with my beloved toy, a wheel attached to a long piece of stiff wire, that I used to take everywhere with me but particularly along the stone gutters where, always barefoot, I would stub my big toes. I was known to the neighbours, I believe, for my rendition, as I walked the gutters, of 'Chidley' – some poor misfit well known in Sydney at that time for taking off his trousers in public places and in consequence being in continual trouble with the police. The chorus ran, 'Chidley has no drawers, will you lend him yours, Chid, Chid, Chidley, Chid.'

The nights were magic when we were allowed out after tea, which was seldom. A large group would squat on the kerb-side under a gas-lamp and chat. The lamp never went out. A small pilot light constantly burnt, and the lamplighter would come with large pole each evening to turn it up. Most of the talk concerned the picture shows, then a novelty. Mary Pickford and Charlie Chaplin were our great talking points, each gesture being recalled with gusto and enjoyed over and over again. The whole street would still be crying next day after Mary played the part of the world's sweetheart; the whole street would still be gurgling next day after Charlie had been through his capers. The 'flicks', as they were known, were all silent and would be accompanied in the pit, mostly by a piano with sometimes a violin. These were accompanied in their turn by much whistling from the audience when a popular tune was played. The 'orchestra' then would switch very quickly to something extremely dull.

The yarns along the kerb were all of the films seen, and if the relater got his facts wrong he was quickly corrected. I recall vividly one evening when I – my family then could not afford the luxury of pictures – felt so out of it that I made up a picture of my own and spun it at great length until I ran out of 'material'. 'And that,' I said, 'was the end of the picture.' There were shouts of protest at this: no picture could possibly have such an ending, but I stuck to it. How I could have slain my little mates then had I told them that one day I would not only meet and converse with both Charlie and Mary, but that once, in England, Mary insisted on buying me a drink, and that I slept in the room next to hers. They would have howled me down, as they did the ending of my 'flick'.

Parents were keen that their offspring should not dally too long under the gas-lamp. Anon would come the sing-song call of some spiteful sister – we didn't think much of the female sex and they were never allowed to sit with us along the kerb at night – 'Billy, you're wanted.' Billy would try his luck and sit a little longer, and then would come the exultant call, 'Billy, you're going to cop it.' At which Billy would hurry off and his ensuing yelps convinced us that he had indeed copped it.

They were days and nights of intense community existence. After school we played a variety of games: cops and robbers, bus-rangers (both somewhat similar), rounders,

saddle-me-nag, egg-in-the-hat and tip-cat, a highly dangerous game with a small piece of wood like a bail but
sharpened finely at both ends: when you hit it on one end, it
jumped into the air and the knack was to hit it with the same
stick you had in hand.

We would, too, have our games of street cricket. One
never sees such community games today but they were part
of early Sydney and, I'm sure, of early London. Today,
after school and even before, the young fly to television for
entertainment, although traffic on the streets would not
possibly allow the many games we used to play. In some
parts of Sydney there used to be gang wars, with one crowd
throwing street metal at the other. Our school at Waverley
was often broken into by the Charing Cross mob, who used
to frequent the caves at Queen's Park. The rude messages
left on the blackboard about Old Fat (Brother Foran) left
the impression they could well have been former or even
present pupils of the school.

Walter Bone lived opposite us and Walter's family was the
first in the district to have a gramophone, its funnel, from
which the sound came, suspended from the ceiling. He was
the first also to have the miracle of a wireless. Walter later
became a tram-conductor and, whenever he met me on a
tram, would invite me to be the government's guest;
slapping his ticket-satchel and handing me back my money.
There was a very swarthy tram-conductor on Eastern
Suburbs lines, and many will remember him, who would
take your money, snap his book of tickets shut, hand you
back the change but no ticket. He never seemed to be
caught by Inspectors, who came on trams at odd spots. I
wonder how many cottages that chap finished up with after
years of skullduggery!

*

No. 112 Ruthven Street was not palatial and one day the
Premier of NSW paid a call on my father, who was ill in
bed. ' Be careful,' adjured Mum, as she led the Premier up
the stairs, 'keep away from the walls. The kalsomine is very
poor.' And so it was. NSW introduced the Fair Rents Act
and Dad, setting an example as a Member, was the first in

the State to appeal against his rent. He won the case and our rent came down from 15/– weekly to 12/6.

We saw out the early years of the war to end all wars, that is, the First World War, in Ruthven Street. Dad had come from the country to enlist in the Boer War but, meeting my mother, got married instead. He arrived in Sydney with a very pleasant reference from Miles Hannan JP, of Breadalbane, that he was a good horseman and bushman, attributes, no doubt, to impress his qualifications as a cavalryman for the Boer War. My mother's family, the Webbs, after whom I got my third Christian name, lived in Green's Road, Paddington, opposite the Victoria Barracks. Mother Webb, Catherine, was a fine spirited woman who had a hard life. Her husband was a surveyor and she followed him around the countryside (my mother, Belinda May, was born in Glen Innes, in the north of NSW). He was bitterly anti-Catholic but Grandma had all her family secretly baptized as Catholics. It didn't do them any good: Grandma and my mother were the only two who kept their faith, and this they did very strongly.

Dad lost his seat in 1917, regaining it in 1920, but during his first term, in 1916 when I was eight, we moved higher up Waverley, to Porter Street. There was a big soap factory near us, called 'Soapy' Allen, renowned for its smell of tallow. There was also a very big dairy, run by the fresh food and ice company, with many cows hand-fed and milked on the premises, and the district luxuriated in free manure. Milk-carts were the main traffic in what was then a quiet Porter Street; the milkman came twice a day, the postman twice a day, the baker always called – also in a horse-cart – and the garbage man came into homes to get the bin. Social behaviour in the Australia of the early days was interesting, to say the least. Mrs Tilyard, the society *grande dame* of early Canberra, laid it down that it was in order for ladies to come to tea at her Mugga Way home sitting on the seat of the baker's or milkman's cart, providing they wore gloves.

One of the family's greatest delights in Porter Street was when the Russian, Ally Regan, came to visit us. Ally had come to Cullerin as a swaggie and became a firm cobber of my father, who taught him so many things about the bush that Ally stayed on as a roustabout. Ally would recount how Dad taught him to cut down a tree. 'I would go jumpin' up and down, trying to cut the tree down from the top. But Jim taught me that wasn't right: I had to start at the bottom.' (Cullerin, in those days, had to be cleared of trees for the growth of grass, and so the trees had first to be ring-barked.) Ally was a bachelor and a very big spender. He would lead us off – and anybody else who might have been in the street – to the shops, and would feast us on icecream and chocolates. He was a lovely old man, full of kindness and love for 'my Jim's family', and he certainly knew the way to our hearts.

One of the Webb sons, Wally, was a very good all-round sportsman. He played football with Easts, Rugby League with the great Dally Messenger, now no longer even a name in that game but in those days depicted every week on the front of the League programme, leaping over an attempting tackler. Wal was manager of the 1933 Kangaroo side to England and I often wondered what the team thought of him. He had a violent objection to bad language and would not tolerate it in his presence. He was coming to my mother's funeral in 1955 in a taxi from town and the driver, coming around Centennial Park, let fly a few oaths. Uncle Wal made him pull up and took him into the Park to show his objections to bad language. There were no marks on Uncle Wal at the funeral and he was born in the last century.

One other son, Glen, was a classical batsman and scored many runs for Paddington and Sydney in grade cricket. Frank Conway, who bowled to him, gave Glen the highest praise, and Frank knew his cricket; Glen was said to be a beautiful stroke-maker. Another son, George, was also a good cricketer. He went to the war, came back a bad shell-shock case, as so many did, and not really in physical shape to play sport, although he did play occasionally for Glammis, a junior side on Centennial Park.

I had vivid memories of those First World War days. Les Hannan was in camp on Queen's Park and in addition to Uncle George, whose regimental colours were purple and white, cousin Jack O'Brien was also a Digger (as all were called who had gone to the war). George was in camp at the showground and the night before he left for overseas I spent with Grandma Webb in Rennie Street, Paddington. We were up before dawn to get a place among the crowd to try and glimpse George as the troops walked Anzac Parade (so called later) to Woolloomooloo and their ships. If anyone caught sight of his beloved one, he broke ranks and walked along proudly with the relative. The scenes and eventual farewells were pitiful.

More pitiful were the scenes when the first wounded, many of them blinded or on crutches without legs, came home through the Sydney Domain. 'Our' three got through the war and came home, but George was not well. His wife had gone elsewhere while he was away and I recall my mother breaking the news to him. What a home-coming! He was a broken man for the little future that was left to him, especially from shell-shock. Cousin Jack came back full of beans. Rennie Street was festooned with purple and white colours and I remember Cousin Jack in the front room with Cousin May. He was trying to nibble her ear and I recall her saying she didn't think much of what he had learned in France. Jack was Aunt Florrie's son and was to be a wonderful friend to me.

One other memory of that war I have: the troops from nearby camps were out for a march and their length ran the whole stretch of Birrell Street. It would not be long now, us admiring urchins told one another: with so many soldiers, we couldn't possibly lose the war. The war still had some years to run and all those troops would have been but a fraction of those killed daily on the Somme. One ghoulish trick we acquired during the time of Gallipoli: we would cut a hole in the bottom of a tobacco tin, put some wadding in it, daub a thumb with red ink, poke it through the hole and ask: 'Does anybody want to see a Turk's thumb?' Cigarette cards were then the vogue and many a one we got from cadging as the troops came up Barrack Hill to go on leave. 'Any cigarette cards, mister?' was a constant call. After what they had gone through, and after all the promises, a sickly jingoism permeated Australia (white feathers through the post were common and women thought nothing of asking fit-looking men in civilian clothes, 'Why aren't you at the Front?'). Many of the heroes came back to no jobs and no prospects of one. Down Rundle Street, Adelaide, in the twenties and thirties, long before it became a mall, ex-soldiers would stand in a long line playing all manner of musical instruments or singing, and all to get an odd bob or two. 'Spare a bob for an old Dig, mate?' was a common saying, and I well recall one poor old chap who used to come to our home in Porter Street with a basket of oranges perched on his head. Mum would give him a cup of tea and something to eat. He loved this break, sitting in the sun on our verandah seat, and he would gabble on. I did not realize then that he was a shell-shock case, like our Uncle George, and one day I said brusquely I would get rid of him. I told him we didn't want any oranges. The poor chap could barely believe his ears. No oranges, nothing to eat? No, that couldn't be right. I got rid of him, but have had the devil of a conscience about him ever since.

· 3 ·

The Strong Arm of
Brother Foran

St Charles's Christian Brothers School in Carrington Road, Waverley, no longer exists. It was a humble but very proud school. A few years after I had left, its choirs, under Brother Reid, were famed throughout Sydney and won prizes at many Eisteddfods. The headmaster in my time was Denis Benedict Foran; as a young man he had left his native Ireland to work in foreign fields; Australians of my generation owe much to such Irishmen. I, in particular, owe a tremendous amount to Brother Foran; he was a grand and inspiring teacher, with a love of his homeland and its history, of the English language and, in particular, of poetry and singing. He was renowned for his repartee and tall tales, a lovable and humorous character who used his strap with gusto but fairness. He was outstanding, too, in his knack of setting boys from under-privileged families on their way to bursaries, and many a prominent man in Sydney life owed his start to the Reverend Brother's remarkable facility in anticipating questions that would be set in such examinations.

I heard Mike Willessee say on the *Parkinson Show* one evening that the Brothers in Perth picked on him at a time of political crisis in Australia, and he copped more than his share of what we knew as the sock – punishment with a strap, a piece of horse-harness. I would say Mike was unlucky, although I also heard Mervyn Doyle, the Tommy Andrews of Waverley cricket, claim at a seminar that too much strap was used in his time. I worked alongside Mike for some years at the Press Gallery in Canberra, and some might say a bit more of the strap would not have gone amiss

45

with him. At all events, though we got plenty of it, I don't think we would claim its use was excessive.

Brother Foran was helped for a period in his training of the choir by Mr Leslie Hoffman, a cornet player. We had singing once a week in the big hall below our school, which was on the first floor, and it had a Gaelic inscription across the stage: '*Caed Mille Faithes*' ('A Hundred Thousand Welcomes' – which I was to see many a time in Irish homes and pubs). Mr Hoffman would bring his cornet to the school picnics at Balmoral and, just after the war, I remember him playing and us all singing on the top deck of the ferry, 'There's a Rose that Grows in No Man's Land' as the boat threaded its way across the wonderful Sydney Harbour.

Singing in the choir was generally regarded as a good lark to get out of school work. One day the headmaster severely weeded many of us out as he went with cupped ear from mouth to mouth. He coached us well and we were much in demand at the nearby church and at weddings. It was because of his teaching that I rank, for what it is worth, as the only Australian cricketer who's ever been to Ireland – not a great cricketing country – who can sing 'The Wearing of the Green' in Gaelic. Lindsay Hassett, who succeeded Don Bradman as captain, would act as my manager and conductor and never tired of asking me to sing 'To a Miniature' and 'The Exile'. Harold Williams, well known as a professional singer in England and a former Waverley cricketer, gave us polished tuition.

*

As a school, we were not pretentious. We were hot on sport, singing and study, in that order. Another Irish Brother, Paul Kearney (some wit spread the rumour when he came to us, his first school in Australia, that he was really a Sinn Feiner on the run) tried hard to introduce soccer into the school. A burly man, he would lead soccer games in the breaks, soutane tucked into his sash, with his famed yell of 'Hurrygee! Hurrygee!' which we thought was some form of Irish battle-cry.

Brother Foran had a gammy leg, the right one, and used a stick. Without his stick he came down hard on his right leg and could be heard from a long way off. This was both a warning to quieten the tumult in class and for the chap he'd left in charge, often me, hurriedly to erase the names of the errant written on the blackboard. To 'dob one in' is un-Australian.

In his temporary absence, also, someone would hide his straps; he had two, Doctors Brown and Black, as he called them. He was a swift and sure strapper and, the job done, he would put the straps on the top of his desk. While he was out of the room somebody, probably still smarting from a touch of strap, would hop out front and hide them. Brother Foran knew how to handle that. 'I will leave the room for two minutes. If, when I return, my straps are not back on my desk, you will all stay in for thirty minutes.' It never failed. If the miscreant didn't put them back, there were plenty of others who would. To be kept in for half an hour, especially in summer, with the surf or nearby Queen's Park calling, was pure purgatory. Sometimes, though, his reverence would get into a frenzy as he sought his straps. 'Ah, now,' he would say, 'somebody has hidden them on me. Have you hidden them, Pudden Meaney?' Pudden was the soul of righteousness. 'I haven't touched them, Brother,' he would protest. It was the highlight of any day when Pudden got the strap. Nobody had a liking of it but Pudden least of all. He would proffer only the tips of a tremulous hand and the tug-of-war would begin. Brother Foran would tug at his hand to get more purchase and so more hitting space. Pudden would pull it back and he would get a couple on the seat of his pants to encourage him to take his real sentence. Pudden would leap like a faun and so the comedy went on. Only those who had committed some bad misdemeanour, such as 'wagging' (playing truant), were invited into the spare room to straddle a desk. The chaps of my time didn't like the strap, especially on a cold morning if it came down on the wrist, but they regarded it as part of school and accepted it in good spirit.

*

One thing that helped our footwork at school were the four flights of stairs that led to the freedom of the outside world. We were adept at coming down them sideways, a necessity, three and even four at a time. It was incredible no legs were broken but I don't recall even any severe spills and, after school, we came down at full tilt. Not so fast going up.

In summer, we had one morning a week at Major Bond's Brontë Baths. There was a great race to get there, with the boys who went to Brontë by tram aiming to beat those who raced through the open bush and sandhills, now a mass of homes. In those days, sandhills stretched all along the Pacific coastline. I can see again the ones at Bondi, beginning from just behind the surf shed, as they ran for miles to the very tip of the Heads at Watson's Bay. One winter, Major Bond offered to teach us life-saving and once a week we would go down to the baths to mingle with the 'Icebergers', a nickname given to the mainly tram-way men on shiftwork who swam through the winter. The major also had a gammy leg but he taught us well and those sunny winter mornings, with the sun sparkling, are among my happiest recollections of school. When one got used to it, the water had a wonderful tingle.

We were tremendously blessed in having Brother Foran, who so encouraged us to play all sport, but we always let him down on St Patrick's Day. This was the day when all Sydney metropolitan catholic schools gathered at the showground for an athletic meeting. Before leaving we would be given a lecture about being a credit to our school and teachers and be told, in particular, not to indulge in water-melon wars. The water-melon season coincided with St Patrick's Day. Our special trams would draw up at Charing Cross and, amid a lot of noise and song, off we would go. Arrived at the showground it was not long before we were entrenched in a commanding position at the top of a grand-stand and were pelting those on the footpaths below with the rinds of water-melon.

We played in a schools' Rugby League competition on Saturday mornings. The best of referees were supplied by the NSW Rugby League. The grounds ranged from the Sydney Cricket Ground to far-off Birchgrove Oval and, meeting at the school in the morning, off we would go under Brother Foran's wing. He would be on the side-line hobbling up and down and exhorting us. One of his favour-

Above left My parents' wedding day. In those days the bride always stood, so as to show off her frock.

Above Ally Regan, a Russian friend of my father's: my brother Glen, Ally, brother Les, my sister Kitty, Agnes Haynes, (a friend of the family), and myself.

her Denis Benedict Foran, hom I owe so much.

Frank Conway, a life-long friend.

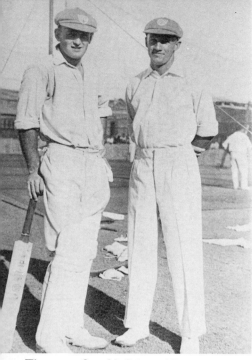

The young Stan McCabe and Don Bradman as the South Africans saw them at the Sydney nets in 1931.

Stan McCabe plays back: a classically correct back-defensive or forcing shot. Note the perfect footwork and right arm close to the body – also important for g

Wally Hammond forces off the back foot. It was this stroke which cut Hammond off from the productive pull. Fieldsmen are Chipperfield (slip), Seivers (gully), Bill Brown (at point), Jack Badcock (square-leg) having trouble with the sun, and keeper Oldfield.

ites, as he was everybody's, was Bill (Wobbly) Moran, who played in the front row. Bill would bring an onion sandwich to eat at half-time and this was regarded as the team's talisman. 'Have you eaten that onion sandwich yet, Bill?' would ask the headmaster, especially if we were being hard pressed. Whether it was that Bill's breath made him repulsive in the second-half scrums I don't know, but we did seem to get more of the ball. Still, as school teams went, we were rather good, producing David Brown, Ken McCaffery and Peter Bierschank, all classy players.

One day Uncle Walter, who was working at some job at the nearby showground, was persuaded by my cousins, Harry and George, to watch me through a hole in the fence. He wasn't impressed. 'He talks too much. He wants to shut up and play more football instead of yelling,' said Uncle Walter, who was a hard man. Though part of our tactics was to urge others on, one thing I really could do, in fact, was kick. I recall vividly when we got a free kick in front of the posts one day against Newton on the Sydney Cricket Ground and before I knew what I was doing I took a drop-kick at goal and put it over. Why I didn't place the ball, I don't know. Probably stage-fright. We beat Newtown 2–0. I really could kick. Some years later, playing with the Bellvue Fernleighs in the Eastern Suburbs Protestant Churches competition (we were nearly all catholics, incidentally) I put over a penalty on the half-way mark at Queen's Park. For three seasons running at school, I got over 100 points, our team twice winning by over 50–0. Our scores would appear in the Sunday papers and I would gloat as I saw my name in print and the tries and goals I had scored. Once, I remember, St Mary's had a big fellow, a lad of about sixteen, as a supporter. He didn't bring them any luck. We won just as easily and it was probably proof of my part in the win that he waited outside the SCG and gave me several beauties on the nose. My comrades ran for the tram. So did I when I recovered. He was a big chap.

I was no hero at school but rather the opposite. On my first day at St Francis' School, Paddington, excitement was intense. There was to be a fight after school and of all things to whet the appetite of young urchins, a fight after school was just the thing. Unfortunately, one of the combatants had second thoughts, cold feet, or some other excuse, and begged off. The disappointment was real. Nothing loath and not knowing how to throw a punch but obviously wanting to make a big fellow of myself, I offered to fill the breach. I stood high in public estimation and I can still hear the clamouring yells of the young cannibals as we wended our way the few hundred yards up the street to Centennial Park. I was a complete flop. I got an instant blow on the nose and buckled. This was not at all what I imagined a fight to be and I wanted none of it. I said so, was counted out by everybody there and left to make some lame excuse to the few who hadn't given me away in disgust. Ever since, at school and elsewhere, I kept out of trouble. I am a man of peace.

Paul Kearney left us to go to West Australia where his name and fame are legend. He took over the orphanage at Killarney there, and his building feats brought him State renown. Building materials were then so much in short supply as to be almost unobtainable but Brother Kearney, with his personality and soft Irish lilting voice full of blarney, would wheedle his way around Americans particularly, and Australian service chiefs, getting many a necessity for his orphanage. He had a rich sense of humour and delighted in greeting and scaring the wits out of a just-arrived countryman by dressing up as a dame and, flouncing into the parlour, would squat on the lap of a confrère who was party to the joke. The newly-arrived one thought he had come into a mad house and began to wonder how best he could get back to Ireland. Tragically, Brother Kearney died from a heart-attack as he was walking up the gang-plank of a liner at Fremantle for his first trip back to his homeland after coming to Australia.

Brother Foran also moved to the West and I would make a point of seeing them if I was going through Perth for a trip abroad. Brother Foran once proudly displayed me to his class at the Brothers' school on the Terrace, now no more. 'This,' he said, 'is one of my former pupils at Waverley. He is captaining the Australian cricket team to England.' This was pushing it more than a little, as Don

Bradman was our captain, which the boys undoubtedly knew, but I doubt that his reverence had heard of Don Bradman. Dave Brown, also a Waverley old boy, had just led the Australian rugby league team on a tour of England, and Brother Foran contended that he had a full hand in captains. Paul Kearney was always pulling the leg of Denis Benedict. He would ring him and say: 'Have you heard the latest now? One of your famous old boys of whom you are always bragging has been sent to prison in Sydney for a long stretch. I always had my doubts about that fellow.'

I must not give the idea that I thought all Christian Brothers were marvellous. Far from it. Some were pills who seemingly thought parents were unnecessary. Many years later a group of us one day took our own school lads from Canberra to Goulburn, providing transport that made the game possible, and when we got there we found the pavilion crowded by our hosts. We did the wrong thing by going on to the side-line and a very aggressive Brother threatened to throw us bodily off the field. We didn't think much of his Christian courtesy. 'And you, Mr Fingleton, will be the first,' he said.

One Brother everybody adored was Jimmy Lacey, once of Brisbane but in his latter years of Waverley, and of Strathfield (south of Sydney). He was one of the most charming and warm chaps I met in life. I first got to know him when, a powerful athlete, he walked up the many steps at Waverley on his hands. In 1939 he invited me to join him in running once a week with his polished Waverley Football side and that induced me to play in the Old Boys Match, in between my brother, Wally, who was the best-all-round sportsman at Waverley in his time, and Cyril Towers, an international. Invited by Jimmy Lacey to say a few words, I said that as youngsters at school we were all keen to know whether Cyril Towers would play in the Old Boys Game. Cyril did not have much humour and didn't like me trying to make myself out younger than he. Anyway in that Waverley Oval game I found many muscles that I hadn't known about for years and certainly hadn't found in the training runs.

*

I took a series of boxing lessons in the thirties from a Scot named Mills, who had won some title in his own country and taught boxing at Tom Langridge's gymnasium in George Street, Sydney. Tom was our masseur at the Cricket Ground. Mills did not let the fact that I was a paying customer interfere with what he handed out. He hit me with everything but the punching bag, and many a time I would totter out into George Street completely beaten up. But I kept at it and one day I got Mills with a beauty. I thought the fees had been recompensed. In later years, when dear Stan McCabe and I were getting into pre-season trim at Bill Henneberry's gym, I was photographed one day shaping up to Fred Henneberry, a lovely and graceful Australian boxer, whose fights with Ron Richards were worth going miles to see. This snap was just for publicity purposes but as it appeared in the window of Alan Kippax's Martin Place store, it made a big impression on my mates. Luckily, Fred never threw a punch at me.

In my early days of newspaper work, it was often my lot to cover fights at Sydney and Leichhardt stadiums. I think I knew enough about boxing to get by but the masses who cheered and hooted at fights never impressed me. They yelled for blood, ever more blood, and I would think that the sight of their own would cause them to faint. I recall the tragedy of a New Zealander, who was a very clever boxer, but who had become punch-drunk. Trams were in Sydney's streets those days and as they were starting, the driver would give his bell a warning clang. One day the tram bell rang just as this chap was passing in King Street and he 'came out' fighting, weaving and throwing punches. It was a sad thing to see.

*

With my family in straitened circumstances, as they say, there was little secondary education for me, which was imparted individually by Denis Foran. Les had a little but also had to leave school early and got his accountancy diploma by hard study at night. He was a marvel the way he used to stick at a very dry subject. While still at school we both became lolly-sellers at the Star Theatre, Bondi Junction, just down the road from our home. Les was efficient; I was a sucker. The 'bright' boys would cluster around me and while I was negotiating a sale with one, the others would steal things off my lolly-tray. I was always short in my takings.

They were the days and nights of silent films. We worked for Madame le Bruce, who had the sweet shop at Bondi Junction and the rights to sell at several picture shows. It was war time, and I recall how all the girls tittered when Madame told them what she thought DSO meant. Our beat was the Star Theatre in old Cowper Street. The sides and roof of theatres in those days were built of corrugated iron, as many buildings* were. Holes were drilled in the side of the corrugated iron at the Star and every night the holes had their avid watchers, strung along Cowper Street, now Brontë Road. Chaps from our school used to have dates with girls of the district at the 'flicks' on Saturday afternoons but I was too keen on sport to waste my Saturday afternoons ogling some girl. In the winter it was football and in the summer cricket, watching the Waverley teams on the local Oval.

My favourites in the Waverley side were Carter and Kippax, little realizing that in a few years' time I would be playing under the captaincy of both men. The most exciting innings I saw played there was by Carter, just after he'd come back from England with the 1921 Australian side. He gave Jack Scott, a fiery-tempered Marrickville fast bowler (and in later years to be a Test umpire) a terrific lacing, taking him repeatedly over his shoulder with his famed 'shovel' shot which we on the outer were inclined to believe he had learnt in his undertaking business. He was missed a few times, which didn't put Scott in a better frame of mind, but it was a delicious century Carter made.

*

* The story is told of a famous English bridge player who came to West Australia and went up-country. Hoping to entertain her, the owners of the hotel invited a friend who said he had played bridge. At one stage he excused himself and from outside, against the corrugated iron wall, came unmistakeable sounds. Very embarrassed, the host and hostess made profuse apologies. 'Don't bother to apologize,' said the Englishwoman, 'it's the first time tonight I have been certain what's in his hand.'

I sat frequently for the Qualifying Certificate and first passed it at the Patrician Brothers, Orange, in the west of New South Wales where we went as a family for a holiday after my father's death in 1920. He had just been returned again as a Member of Parliament but he didn't live long to enjoy his second spell. My last memory of him was coming up our street, almost bent double in the final stages of consumption. Jim Dooley was the Premier at the time and putting a large car at our disposal to take us to Orange was about the only thing the former colleagues of my father did for his family. Although a time of intense sadness for us, my father's death was responsible for giving me one thrill. It was the first time I stood next to Hanson (Sammy) Carter, NSW and Waverley wicket keeper, who had come to our home in his business capacity to make funeral arrangements. I was then twelve. My mother took a job and tried to run the home and the family as best she could. She was a remarkable woman, a wonderful protective mother, full of spirit. When we were grown up and Les first, and then I could support the family, she took on all manner of charity work in the district, being president of the new Eastern Suburbs Hospital and taking charge of the women's committee that supported St Charles's School.

We had to scout for jobs. My first try was depressing. I went to Robert Reid, a big warehouse in York Street, and I seemingly gave the wrong answer when I was asked which Sunday school I attended. I discovered it was a way of finding out to which religion I belonged. The practice of giving preference to certain religions was rife in those days, on both sides. A Mr Applegate, an Englishman (my mother was friendly with his wife), lived near us and he gave me a job as a messenger at the Australian Drug Company in Kent Street. Had I stayed on I daresay I would have progressed to the Storeman and Packers' Union. It was only a small drug company, supplying the needs of chemists who wanted many lines we didn't stock, and it was my job to go around to the various agencies and collect them. The firms didn't believe in providing tram fares and I was forced to fall back on a means of transport we had often employed going to school at Paddington. This was on the back of empty horse-lorries. Most drivers wouldn't worry if you took a free ride, but now and then some cad from the footpath would call out, 'Whip behind, Mister,' and if a driver was so disposed, a cut of his whip would send one off hurriedly. Jumping on was an art as one had to twist in mid-air to arrive right side up on the back of the lorry. To ride a lorry with many chemical supplies was no easy matter and one day the inevitable happened. Hopping off, I dropped a valuable bottle of drugs on the roadway and that didn't make me popular in a firm that was struggling. But what undoubtedly spoilt my career as a storeman and packer occurred one Friday: after crying off work that morning through an alleged illness I went to the Star in the evening. Mr Applegate was also a Friday night devotee and my excuse that I had made a quick recovery didn't convince him.

Then I got a job at the King George distillery at Redfern. I teamed with a taciturn Digger in a bottle-washing exercise. Jack and I used to purge them on washing sprays, smell them for kerosene or some such, and then he would toss them to me in twos to stack in crates. One had to have the knack of catching them very lightly: a broken bottle in the hands was not humorous. The job had one great bonus, though not for me: each employee was allowed one snifter daily of the good Scotch before it was broken down for bottling.

Scotty Campbell, a great friend of my father's and a staunch radical, thought that being a bootmaking clicker was just what I was meant for in life especially, as he said, as one worked with a tie on. Being a clicker meant cutting out the patterns of footwear. I might have qualified for that in time but was put to the cobbler's last and even now, I am sure, could make a good pair of shoes. But my main jobs were sweeping a vast floor just before we knocked off, and getting the lunches at midday. If we, the apprentices, were thought to have done a good week's work, we might find a bonus of anything up to 1/- in our pay envelope. I rarely got that much. It was a job I hated but I liked the chaps who worked there. Those I can remember were Pat McGroder, later to become the Mayor of Moree, Stewart somebody and a pleasant chap they called the 'Botany Mullet'. He was keen on sport and often brought a Botany team across to Queen's Park to play one I had organized from local Rugby League teams.

The firm was the Britannia Shoe Company and the boss would often take a place in the factory gang, which was spurred on by one named Tom Mills, generally regarded as a boss's man. The Stewarts, who owned the firm, were a grand family, of whom I recall Gordon the best. (My son Larry came up against him in hospital recently and he reminisced of me.) My own direct boss there was Bill Butler, a man with a sense of humour, who had a girl-friend working in nearby Sergeants'. We called her, disrespectfully, 'Frog's Eyes'. She often, surreptitiously, slipped something in my order for her Bill.

The Britannia had plenty of floor space, and during the lunch break we played cricket with a tennis ball. I could swerve it feet in the air by spin. One great character in the firm was Perce Burgess, who worked the press, a machine which came down with great power and a lot of noise to cut soles from patterns. Perce, judging by the number of fingers he had missing, often failed to get his hands out of the way. He was a man of rare humour who ran a jazz band at night in the Western Suburbs.

The Britannia made me my first pair of cricket boots, though in fact they were shoes. I got them at a good price and wore them that 1926 summer against Petersham and Sam Everett, chosen that year to tour England, but the shoes were no good for cricket; they gave the ankles no support.

Even the prospect of wearing a tie while I worked failed to keep me at the boot factory. It meant taking two trams to get to the factory in Bay Street (I was invariably running late) and it was not, as they say, a viable proposition. I left the boot factory with no misgivings and for some time worked at the bottom of our street making slippers. This place was run by a man named Trahan, who followed Waverley closely at cricket. All this time, our family was still struggling. Uncle Wal had a number of racehorses and I would occasionally go with the Misses Dunn to the pony race-courses to have a day in the catering business. At my own window I would sell Sergeants' Pies, normally three-pence, for 1/–. I remember one day seeing Wal getting a large wad of notes from a bookie and I pushed myself near him thinking he might say, 'Take this home to your mother.' But he didn't, and I learned that Wal was a bit stingy in giving the 'good oil' on his winning horses to his friends. 'They don't offer me a bag of chaff when I have losers,' he would say. Going to the races with the Misses Dunn was also not a paying proposition. I would gallantly stand the fares, which gained me great kudos as a Gentleman with the two sisters, but left me badly out of pocket.

Then Jack O'Brien, my cousin, luckily came into my life. Back from the war some years, Jack was courting a fine woman, Dorrie Hopwood, in Birrell Street, and they both took a liking to me, taking me to tennis, swimming and surfing and, when they got married, to their home at Randwick. I knew about nothing then of life. I remember telling them that Florence Webb, our cousin, was born in an incubator. I had presumably overheard the story of a premature birth.

Jack was the best thing, if I can call him that, that happened to me and I owe my newspaper life to him. He was a linotype compositor, at the Sydney *Guardian*, which had not long been started. 'How would you like to work at the *Guardian*?' Jack asked me and, being despondent about any future, I jumped at the suggestion. So Jack tried to wangle a job for me there and told me one day that Fred Coughlan, the turf man, would give me a start. Cog, as he was known, had done a year at medical school and had then dropped out. He was a genial man, prolific in his stories of good and bad luck at the races, and he had the odd habit of camping some nights in the big easy chair in Robert Clyde Packer's unlocked office, unknown to Robert Clyde (one of the three founders of the paper).

*

The prospect of newspaper work daunted me. My education had not been good enough for that, so back I went to school to have a yarn with Brother Foran. 'There's no reason in the world why you shouldn't be able to work in a newspaper office,' he told me, encouragingly. 'You wrote well at school and have a good usage of words. The one thing you must watch and re-watch are the rules of syntax,' and he sent me on my way with confidence and a whole list of books for required reading. One of them, *Pickwick Papers*, I had already read and doted on when I found it at Cullerin. Dickens' way of describing his characters, and his wonderful humour, impressed me deeply. His work should be every young newspaperman's Bible.

So I began work with Fred Coughlan and his offsiders, Lachie Melville and Alan Dexter, also a prolific turf writer and son of a famed Sydney newspaper family. I was really a messenger or copy-boy, to file every day the blocks of horses used in stories. But in no time I had left the Turf Room. One night Jack O'Brien asked Cog how I was doing. 'I wouldn't know,' said Cog, 'I never see him. He has joined up with 'Pedlar' Palmer.' Indeed I had. I found my way to A. R. B. Palmer's office, the sports editor, and I must pay tribute to Fred Coughlan for not making a fuss about my desertion of him.

I could talk sport with Pedlar – who was always Mr Palmer to me – and I thought him the most fascinating man I had met. He was an arts graduate of Edinburgh University and had been secretary of the NSW Rugby Union. He talked as well as he wrote and I don't think in my career I ever met a pressman who had such a grip on every sport. I used to stand, captivated, behind Pedlar and watch the words stream without effort on to the copy-paper in classical hand-writing. I was fortunate in that he seemed to like me, and he set out to teach me in all ways. I owe a great deal to many men but none more than to Andy Palmer. Pedlar set me to cut my teeth on a particular correspondent's copy. He was a scrawling writer and hopeless in expression. All his copy had to be re-written, but it was good practice for me. Later, when Pedlar found he could leave me with responsibility, this correspondent mentioned money to me if I gave his copy preference when making-up the page. That was the only time a bribe was offered to me in the newspaper world and it had the result of this chap's copy getting even a bigger run than usual in the over-matter, that is, unpublished material.

I had had a reference from Brother Foran that pleased me. 'The worthy son of a worthy father,' he had written. Pedlar gave me another reference I liked when I thought of playing football with Eastern Suburbs. 'If he is as good a footballer as he is a cricketer and a trier in life, you are lucky in getting him,' wrote Pedlar. No aspiring young pressman could help but try with Pedlar. He was encouraging and full of good advice. Taking me down to the machine-room with him to make-up, he taught me the little tricks of that trade so well that soon he left the make-up of pages entirely to me. That was a fascinating job, moving pieces of print about to make them fit, planning one's lay-outs, getting the picture-blocks to balance, juggling the various types, and then scanning the proofs of the pages to look for errors that, maybe, the readers had missed.

Being a cousin of Jack O'Brien was also mighty helpful. He was a clean, fast compositor and popular with his work-mates. Jack was more than a good cricketer, giving the ball a tremendous whack, and he had a prominent place in our mid-week *Guardian* team, which played in the Referee Cup. Through him, I made instant friends with his chums on the machine-room floor and they were always ready to help me in those formative newspaper years. Three I remember with affection were 'Bluey' (all Australians with red heads are called 'Bluey'), Chambers and Frank Johnston, the last two both ex-Diggers and good members of our cricket team. The wit of the floor was George Corkhill, who was an inveterate leg-puller. It was mainly because I was a relative of Jack O'Brien that they all went out of their way to help and advise me in the nicest way. I owe a great deal to the comps and the stone-hands of the *Guardian*. I was even friendly with the advertising men who had the annoying habit of snatching space for late ads from us at the last moment, and so disrupting the planned lay-out. Jack Sherwood, a promising tennis player, is one of those I recall well.

Oddly, it was in the *Guardian* office that I first met Don Bradman. He had come in one night to talk business, I think, with somebody and took the chance to learn how a newspaper was produced. I was introduced to him and remember telling him about a lad at school, Les Buxton, I thought would have been a champion cricketer only for running a nail into his foot. 'He was left with a stiff right knee; he had tetanus,' I said, only I mispronounced the word 'tee-tanus'. The Don quickly corrected me with the proper pronunciation and did so, I thought, with some scorn. But I didn't take umbrage over that. He was right and I was wrong and learning all the time, in all ways. I never stopped learning at the *Guardian*.

· 4 ·

Cricketers' Nursery

Waverley Oval was where the young cricketers of our district got their early training. The outside park, with its uneven bounce off the turf, and its one decrepit concrete pitch that yielded bouncers and shooters, was where we learned our defence. It stood us in good stead when we got on to Waverley Oval itself because it rarely knew a good pitch in the middle there in my time.

Looking back, I am sure the fault was that the various curators never gave the square sufficient water in preparation. Thus it was dusty and powdery, with uneven bounce, somewhat like the Old Trafford pitch in 1956 on which Jim Laker got his harvest of nineteen wickets, although it is to be noted that other spinners didn't do much on that. Alan Kippax and I did get fair runs at Waverley but it was, invariably, a struggle; and the pitch, especially when coming to it after one that was first-class, could run one out of form. Bradman, McCabe, Jackson and the brilliant Sydney rest in our day, all played at Waverley, but I never recall one of them playing a big innings.

The ground, the district club and the district were full of cricket activity. We had a long string of internationals from the early Gregorys, Carter, Kippax and Hendry, the later Jack Gregory and Arthur Mailey in addition to myself, in the thirties. I don't think anybody would claim Tony Greig or Geoff Boycott as 'home' internationals, although both played with Waverley when money and its attractions were coming into the game.

*

We had good club players aplenty. Ted Forssberg was a big hitter and he made a new ball do amazing things; Davis;

Caswell, who always said, as he came to the ground of a Saturday, that he had some ailment; Jimmy Holm; Davidson; Harry Savage, a class keeper from Centennial Park; Cox; Lewis and many others were very, very capable club cricketers. The club had a long string of successes, but threw away a first grade* pennant one year in a match against Glebe that must have drawn ten thousand onlookers; after Frank Conway and I had put it in the bag, the middle and tail threw it away.

I denied my old club another pennant, when Tom Conway was the skipper in the only season I didn't play for Waverley, by making a century against them for Paddington at Trumper Park. That glorious pitch, under a rich character named Paddy Ryan, was the attraction there and I don't think I ever played on a better one.

There were many Conway brothers, perhaps the best-known cricketing family in Waverley. Frank and I cobbered up at school and we continued the closest friendship through life until cancer claimed him in the early seventies. We were naval reservists together; we were inseparable, taking our holidays together in the country; and we had epic struggles at golf and tennis. We were both avid readers and Frank would get books by P. G. Wodehouse and C. B. Fry out of his local school of arts library. We devoured them and talked the language of Wodehouse, particularly. C. B. Fry was harder to follow, with his analytical approach to batting, but we stuck at it and 'nutted' things out for ourselves.

*

Waverley was steeped in cricket lore. Ernie Williams, by then retired, would dismiss those with pretensions and little ability as 'shysters' or 'grubbers'. He would give opinions with a finality that brooked no nonsense, his finger emphasizing every assertion out of a mouth which always drooped a cigarette.

Ernie, also known to us as 'Cocker', had known intimately all the cricketing greats. His name was one of the

* Grade cricket is district cricket with five grades that run from fifth upwards. First grade sides could be very strong, perhaps including a couple of Test players and two or three inter-State men.

first of many on the list for Victor Trumper's benefit match. Nobody could say a word against Trumper, whom Ernie adored. He just would not listen to a word of criticism against his hero and if someone started debating figures, Ernie would leave the huge throng of cricket enthusiasts who crowded the Bondi Junction corner (the police would often ask us to move on), cross to the other side of Old South Head Road and stop Sammy Carter, who would be walking home from his funeral business in Oxford Street to Bellvue Hill. Carter, who had been Australia's wicket keeper for many years, knew a thing or two. Ernie would return and deliver final judgement. 'It is no use you talking nonsense,' he would start off. 'The Old Man says . . .' – and that would be the end of that argument.

Ernie was truly the patron saint of Waverley cricket. Without any fuss he would pay the entrance fee into the club of any junior he thought worthwhile. The junior fee was only 10/6 but that was far too much for most of us in those days. Ernie paid my own sub for a number of summers and I, with many others, remember him with deep affection. Moreover, he would finance visits by our juniors to play the juniors of St George who were organized by Dick Jones, later an Australian selector. They included players later to become well-known in higher cricket: Alan Fairfax, Lennie Vaughan, Bob Louden and others.

Young cricketers of that era throughout the world owed much to the love of cricket and the support given by men such as Ernie Williams. Dr L. O. S. Poidevin, who had played a lot of county cricket with Lancashire (England) and Davis Cup tennis for Australia, used to run a weekly cricket clinic at the Waverley Pavilion at which he taught the young, a few years behind us, all he knew about the game, and he knew plenty. He later wrote most polished material on it for the *Sydney Morning Herald*. Freddie Grey was our President and, a chemist, had much to do with originating the flavour for a favourite ice cream. It was from our club that the Poidevin-Grey Shield originated for cricketers under twenty-one who had not played first-class cricket.

Frank Conway, who was a deep thinker about the game,

had the honour of leading Waverley to the first Poidevin-Grey win. Frank was a good performer with bat and ball and nobody could have had a truer life-time pal. He was best man at my wedding and I was pleased to recommend him to Alan Kippax as a worthy player to take on a tour of Northern Queensland. Frank, it could be said, missed out on the big pleasures of life but he had innumerable friends who loved his sense of humour, and that cricket trip, by ship, he enjoyed to the utmost. Jack Davis, of the then Sydney *Referee*, asked him as the ship was leaving to keep him posted on the scores and innocent Frank, seeing no harm in such a request, did it. When the tourists saw their figures in print they set up the howl, 'There is a spy in the camp.'

Frank was very embarrassed and admitted he had sent the scores to Davis. Archie Jackson, who was top of the averages, reassured him. 'You keep sending them, Frank,' he said. 'It is only those who are not up the top who are crying.'

*

Not only were there fine cricketers in all the Waverley grades but many wonderful characters. Two who kept us amused at twice weekly practice were Harry (called 'Cakes' because he was a caterer) and Dinny Kelly, a big, sunburnt man just back from the war. Dinny was a fast bowler; Harry a solid and most determined batsman who, oddly and sadly, featured every annual meeting of the club with a personal attack on Alan Kippax, why I don't understand, because Kippax was one of the nicest men I knew.

Harry would always put several florins (2/–) on the stumps when he entered the net against Dinny and Dinny would almost bust himself trying to knock them over and get the prize. Everybody was 'Brud' to Harry – short for brother. The two would argue all through net-time about luck or snicks, and when stumps were finally drawn in the gloaming there would be a challenge to a race around the Oval, Harry on foot and Dinny on a wobbly bike. Dinny would establish a big lead but soakage from the nearby reservoir left a part of Waverley always soggy and Dinny would slow down on this. The race invariably ended in an

Bill Brown (*left*) and myself begin our first Australian partnership at Durban, Natal. Each of us scored centuries. Our stands in the Tests were 12, 93, 105, 233 (a record opening stand against South Africa), 99 and 162.

Myself hitting Eric ...alton for six for ...ustralia against Natal ... Durban. It was in ...is innings that I ...ade my highest first-...ass score of 167.

...*elow right* In national ...lours for the first ...ne. I could not ...lieve my luck and ...irried off to be ...otographed as soon ... possible.

...pening the 1938 tour: I get one through the covers against ...orcester. Don Bradman, who got his usual double century, is in ...ns at the other end.

Billy Hughes, Australian Prime Minister between 1915 and 1923, to whom I acted as press secretary for a turbulent period during the Second World War.

Sir Robert Gordon Menzies, Prime Minister of Australia for a record term a close and helpful friend to me.

Dr Herbert Evatt, president of the United Nations, in all his glory. He was to become Leader of the Australian Labour Party but never achieved his ambition to become Prime Minister.

Gough Whitlam, Prime Minister of Australia in the seventies, who was concerned in a constitutional crisis.

argument about cutting corners and the like, but it was good fun and typical of the wholesome cricket kinship that permeated our club. There was about cricket in those days a sense of affinity which drew people close together. In the doleful days of the Depression many of the jobless would come to the nets to watch from the adjacent Bondi Beach, the sand still in their hair. The beach was where they spent most of their soul-destroying days, and often on an empty stomach.

There was no finer cricket gentleman in the whole club than Mr McNamara and I will write of him because he was the Victorian type so threatened in modern cricket today. I didn't know Mr McNamara's christian name and I don't think anybody did. He was always just Mr McNamara to us, and that with the utmost deference. He was English, silver-haired, silver-moustached, and he had his own preparatory school somewhere down Henrietta Street which ran off Waverley Park, near St Gabriel's School, now no more but then a college for girls.

In their crocodile weaving across the park the boys would come early to practice and Mr McNamara would put them through before the club practice proper began. He was the net-captain and did the job with great propriety, brooking no nonsense – not that anybody thought of back-chatting Mr McNamara, a fine old English gentleman, the essence of good behaviour. Mr McNamara always looked the part, dressed in immaculate flannels, with an MCC tie and a straw boater, also decked with the MCC colours. The modern 'sledging' was of another cricket world.

Club practice, in my time, was of the utmost importance and there was no suggestion of fooling about. Chaps coming from offices in the city would judge whether they could beat the tram to Penkiville Street opposite the Oval, hop off the wrong side and career at full tilt down Bondi Road, leap the picket fence and report in to Mr McNamara and have their names jotted down in his book. Those gained minutes were vital when the light was closing in.

There would be Alan Kippax to watch and field against in the open net on the off. There would always be a tribe of fieldsmen to pay him homage. Lyall Wall was a magnificent left-hand bowler; Bill Clark would send up his twirly

E

offbreaks and there would be intense competition among the second and third graders. One great identity of the nets was Bert (Brud) Jones. It was no exaggeration to say that Brud Jones moulded his game on defence; in short, he was almost all defence. He began with a wide-apart stance, which meant he didn't intend to move his feet for strokes. As the bowler approached, Brud would shuffle his feet even wider, which meant he was going lower to the ground all the time. When the ball arrived to him Brud was a good example of an almost horizontal batsman. When Brud finally retired from the game he gave a powerful interview to the local press in which he claimed vehemently that the modern batsman did not play enough strokes!

All three practice nets would come to a sudden stop when Bertha, a curvaceous blonde who lived in a flat opposite the Oval, emerged to walk down to the shops. Bertha was a 'hello' girl (manual exchange telephone operator) and when she hove into view, suitably clad or unclad in shorts (very daring in those days) to show off her superb lines, all cricket was forgotten. She was a surfer, had a lovely suntan, and was a vision for all eyes. Mr McNamara was human enough to take time off during these diversions and many were the wolf-whistles that went towards her. I don't think Bertha minded this compliment. It often seemed that she forgot some of her shopping and had to make a second appearance.

*

We had a multiplicity of spinners in the club. I can remember them all now but Bill Noonan, who has guided me on what I should put into this book, said they would be about as interesting to the average reader as the sexual habits of logarithms; and so I pass most of them by. But one could have seen at least a dozen twirling them up at the nets and this is interesting, I think, because modern cricket has killed that type off.

One I will mention was Ocker Stevens,* a generation up

---

* I think Stevens, whose Christian name was Horace, was the original Ocker, a name applied generally to extrovert Australians. Jim Bancks, who through Mailey, was very keen on cricket, used the name Ocker in one of his Ginger Meggs comics and I think that is where it originated. I had never heard of it before that.

on me and the biggest spinner of a cricket ball I knew. Ocker would run to the stumps and stop, and this abrupt stop would enable him to get greater purchase on the ball. It would fairly hum as it went down the pitch but he spun so much, including a beautiful bosie, that his length, like himself, was profligate. 'It is hard to concentrate upon length,' would complain Ocker, 'when one is keeping an eagle eye out for an irate father jumping the pickets.' I should explain that at night the Pavilion was a favourite rendezvous for spooners.

We, too, eyed suspiciously the military captain who would sit out front of the old Pavilion, which served as his office, checking whether those he watched playing cricket were on his roll. Compulsory military training was then in force but most of us, living in a seaside district like Bondi, were naval reservists. Three other spinners who spring to mind were Ossie Asher, Bill Bassett and Jimmy Randall, whom I was to meet in my first grade game. They would regularly get their hundred wickets in a season but none was a success when tried in a better class of cricket. I think it was because they could get a little turn on grade pitches which was denied them on better ones. In addition to these rich reapers of wickets, Sydney also had class spinners in Arthur Mailey, Bill O'Reilly, who was a holy terror on grade pitches, and Dr Reg Bettington.

Bettington, a very good all-round sportsman, was the one I exaggeratedly mentioned on the *Parkinson Show* as having swum from Crete to Alexandria, a fair stretch of water, with his bag of golf clubs between his teeth. He was a champion Australian golfer. The story is told of him that in between seasons in England he played cricket getting wickets and runs, then rugby in the long twilight, all in the one day, went to a ball that night (Reg was one to enjoy himself at a ball), did an operation early next morning and then gave several pints of his blood as the bank was running short. I had read in the *Manchester Guardian* an eulogy by Neville Cardus of Reg, who played for both Oxford and Middlesex, and wagered that he would play for Australia against Percy Chapman's English team. He didn't. Reg captained NSW in my first Shield game; in that Don

Bradman made 340 not out and could well have broken the world's record score (which he later did with 452 not out against Queensland), I came in late and made 25 not out (my colleagues from the press box high up in the Noble Stand gave me a noisy welcome, which was a little embarrassing).

I was in a city team that went once to Tamworth and when the guard, at a stop, came to our carriage and asked us to break the noise and festivities down a bit, Reg gave him a snifter of a whisky and sent him back to his van. Reg, at Tamworth, outfitted all the team with 'coloured' caps from his bag, relics of the teams he had played with in England. Reg was a man and a half. I met him for the last time in New Zealand at Hawke's Bay. I was the guest of the New Zealand government, and Tom Lowry was a bit 'stuffy' (as the best-worse Englishmen can be; he went to Oxford), about receiving me at the local races. Reg, who married one of Lowry's sisters (as did Percy Chapman), made up for everything in the grand welcome he gave me.

*

Those early cricketing days at Waverley were chockful of good companionship and sheer enjoyment though, to be true, there were a few shysters in our ranks. Anybody who rose above the ruck and achieved first-class or even Test status had his malevolent critics, usually little people of sour disposition. Medical people then had time to play cricket, although there is barely one anywhere these days. We had redoubtable performers in Dr Tim Lamrock, a mighty hitter, and Dr A. C. K. Yates, a good spinner who played much cricket in England. And there was, later, Dr Calov, who did much to encourage juniors and who diagnosed my antrum trouble one day at the Sydney Cricket Ground nets when I had a horrible taste in my mouth after a tooth extraction. That, together with its treatment – a hollow needle down the nose into the antrum and accompanied by blinding pain – was to give me much trouble for years. As I struggled to the nearest hotel for a brandy after the penetration my only consolation was that I had given the dentist, a slow left hander, a pretty good hiding one day at St Joseph's College.

Other good medicos in my time in Sydney cricket were
the Hogg brothers, Jim and Geoff, brilliant stroke-makers
from the King's School Parramatta; H. O. Rock, a lovely
batsman with superb square-leg shots, who hit a double
century in his only Shield game for NSW; Jimmy Garner, a
slow left-arm bowler from Sydney University; Mayes; Bill
McCristal (a very good friend); Otto Nothling, who played
cricket and rugby for Australia, once opening a Test attack
with Stork Hendry; and Alec Ross, as solid and reliable a
full-back as we ever saw in Australia and also a dashing
batsman for Sydney University. Dr Eric Barbour com-
pleted the list. He made good runs for Randwick and, later,
was a gifted writer on cricket for the *Sydney Morning
Herald*. There was also, of course, our own L. O. S.
Poidevin.

We had one terrific smiter of the ball in Goldie Thomas,
but Ted Forssberg was the biggest hitter of sixes I met in
all cricket. He often cleared our Pavilion and caused havoc
on the tennis courts behind. At Petersham Oval, once, he
almost put the ball into Parramatta Road. During the
Depression he had hopes of getting a job in Lancashire
League. Because of that I voted for him as Waverley captain
against Alan Kippax, my NSW captain, which was not a
sensible thing to do. Alan never bore me any grudge.

One good slow spin bowler I must mention, because he
only became a bowler after an eye had turned on him and
ruined his brilliant batting, was Noel Levy. I think Noel
had been a better batsman than his brother, Roy, who later
captained Queensland. On looking through my records in
Wisden's (which has robbed me, incidentally, of three
centuries – one in Tasmania and two against West
Australia) I find that Roy robbed me of another when he got
my wicket once in Brisbane, caught and bowled. I must
have lost concentration because nobody in Waverley
thought Roy could bowl. He would have claimed that he
'thought' me out.

Roy was a champion baseballer, one of the best in
NSW. He had a terrific throw and would fire them back
at our Sammy Carter from the shortest of ranges with no
chance of a run out. Sammy was too proud to tell him to

ease up. Another star baseballer with Waverley, Perc Wellings, came out to field for us one day as substitute and missed the biggest 'sitter' of a catch ever seen.

Johnny Moyes, who was a prodigious hitter, and Charlie Macartney, played some hurricane innings for Gordon, but very capable players abounded in all clubs. Gar Waddy and Mudgee Cranney were two Cumberland stars, but this club spoiled itself by possessing some of the most notorious spectator yahoos in Sydney who didn't think their Saturday afternoon complete unless they insulted every well-known cricketer who played there. Once, when I was playing for Waverley and got the 'treatment', I went out later to sit among those people to study them, but they seemed to be devoid of any knowledge of the game. I played my last season with Paddington, heading their batting: but when the time came to play Cumberland at Parramatta I was 'unavailable'. I could not see any merit in making the long trip to Parramatta, paying ground fees, and being insulted by hooligans.

Had they come in other times Norbert Phillips, Gordon Morgan, Roy Loder, Austin Punch, Albert Scanes, Des Mullarkey and Andy Ratcliffe could well have been internationals. I have seen many in Australian teams of recent years who did not possess the technique or ability of those men.

*

Every Saturday when we had a home match at Waverley my path from home in Porter Street would lead me across the top of the Waverley reservoir before descending the many concrete steps to the bottom; and on top one had the most glorious panoramic view. Sailing craft dotted the harbour, white beaches stretched endlessly, and by the time I got to the top the big liners that had left at noon for England would be standing well out to sea, coming down the coast with funnels belching. One could visualize the thrilled passengers unpacking in their cabins.

Planes to England are all very well for their quickness, and I have flown there thirteen times, by every possible route. But give me a ship every time, to Tilbury or Southampton, with its atmosphere, enjoyment and languid

days in the sun and the enthralling evenings of dance and
moonlight when the big liner would gently glide on the
placid waters. The most enjoyable thrill in a cricketer's life
went overboard when the big jumbo jets took over from
ships. Imagine a fancydress ball on a plane! A team,
arriving bearded and unkempt and much the worse for
being all night on a plane, has no chance of knitting together
in that one night.

I never think of Waverley without remembering Roy
Kippax, the blind brother of Alan, and a most loveable
man. He was a leading member of Sydney's blind community and died in 1979, well into his eighties. He would
come each Saturday to Waverley on the arm of his brother.
The whole Kippax family, mother and father, were
delightful people to meet with and converse. Roy, always
smiling, was one of nature's gentlemen.

I had one big thrill with Alan. He was on his way to visit
Mabs, not then his wife, and he invited me to ride in the
tram with him as far as Paddington. I was very awed and
recall asking him about his famous back-cut. I don't know
whether I expected him to demonstrate it as the tram
swayed and careered around Centennial Park, but his advice
was as clear as his cut. 'Forget all about it, son,' he told me.
From the other end at Waverley one day I saw him play the
most perfect off-drive I have ever seen.

One other big thrill I had as a boy. I was coming home by
tram one day, from one of my many jobs before I settled
into newspaper life, and at Regent Street Hunter L. Hendry
not only got into my tram but sat right opposite me. He had
been in the 1921 and 1926 Australian teams that toured
England, and played with Waverley through the twenties.
My eyes nearly fell out, goggling at him all the way to the
Junction. A few years ago 'Stork', as he was known, climbed
those many steps at the Lords' press box just to say hello to
me. I appreciated that.

We always had an intense rivalry with our next-door
club, Randwick. We had a marvellous new-ball bowler in
Harold Comber, who regularly headed the Sydney averages; and with Randwick was Ray McNamee, who swerved
the ball a prodigious distance in the air and could break

from the off, like Don Blackie, of Victoria, on glass-top pitches. Randwick had the three Ward Brothers playing at the same time; the Donnan twins, relatives of the old international, Harry; Alec Marks; and Jack Carter, a fine spinner.

Over the harbour at Mosman was a side that compared with any other in Sydney. It was led by E. A. (Chappie) Dwyer, one of my best friends in cricket and outside it. He managed a side to South Africa and would have charmed England also had the Board the wit to choose him. I have known many managers but the Lindsay Hassett–Chappie Dwyer combination that took the team to South Africa was far and away the best. Mosman also had the magnificent Stan McCabe, who gave our Waverley new-ball bowlers a terrific lacing at Mosman one day; Ben Salmon, a huge schoolboy scorer with Shore; Keith Carmody, who originated the Carmody field of close-set fieldsmen; Ken Gulliver, one of the best of fieldsmen; McCaffery; and a fine character and cricketer in Halford Hooker, who was 'Hook' to everybody.

It was Hooker who shared that unbroken last wicket stand of 307 with Kippax against Victoria at Melbourne in 1928. When they asked 'Hook' what was his most vivid memory of that epic, he replied, 'The way the bowlers managed to get the ball up to me between all those close-set fieldsmen.'

I would class Hughie Chilvers, a slow bowler from Northern Districts, as the best bowler I knew never to get a tour of England. Many leg-break bowlers are too slow to be of value in England but Hughie pushed the ball through. I would bracket Syd Carroll (Gordon) and Warren Saunders (St George) as the best batsmen never to go on tour. Bill Brown and I kept a very wary eye on Les Fallowfield, a gifted opener from the same club as Chilvers. It is interesting to recall, when mentioning these names, how an English tour was wasted on some others!

*

I learned one bad habit at Waverley which handicapped me in big games when I batted on pitches that could be trusted. Because of the uncertainties of the Waverley pitch, I allowed my bottom hand to slip down the handle, the better for defence and to counter shooters. Joe Hardstaff of Notts was one who, I thought, held his bat too high on the handle, not having complete control over it; but to let the two hands get apart on the bat handle is one of the worst mistakes in batting. Mike Brearley has done it all his cricketing life, in addition to not keeping his head and body still as the ball is coming to him, although Derek Randall is the greatest offender I have seen in not keeping his body still. Brearley is a very sensible fellow and I am amazed that he has not worked this out for himself, though admittedly there was much I learned about batting after I had finished with the game. In short, having the hands apart on the handle means they perform different swinging arcs, one pulling against the other. They must begin together, though it is permissible to shift the lower one down for different shots.

One other important point I learned after I had finished playing, and that through golf: it is the importance of the top hand. This is the dominant hand for the drive, which is much freer when the top hand is in control. I should have worked this out for myself. Kippax, Bradman and McCabe were there constantly in the middle or at the nets to watch and I could have studied and copied any of them. They all played the drive perfectly and, when it is examined, it is the easiest of strokes. All one has to do is judge the ball correctly, putting the left or front foot adjacent to the line of flight, swing through with the top hand dominant and the drive is Bob's your uncle, so to speak.

There is one further important aspect. The front foot, as Herbie Taylor, the Sprinkbok theorist, insisted, points side on, not pointing the toe up the pitch. This latter stance turns the shoulder, and the swing in consequence is not to and through the ball. It also throws the weight of the body back and away from the ball of the front foot, where it should be. These are simple rules but they are all-important in the drive, and no first-class batsman ever lived who wasn't proficient in the drive. It is the most paying of strokes and the least dangerous, as the full face of the bat is always looking at the ball. It was Don Bradman's best-paying stroke, I suggest, because no bowler likes to be driven and it is then that he drops short.

Batting is a side-on science but when I stress that the hands should act as one in driving, that doesn't mean that the bottom hand should not be moved down for defence, the hook, the pull and the square-cut. Syd Barnes, of Sydney, was the best square-cutter I knew and it was his bottom hand that did most of the work. When he was made into an opener he forsook most of his strokes in front of the wicket, and became very much a back-foot player. That is what opening can do to a batsman.

Cricket people talk of coaches as if they are indispensable, as if a boy cannot learn about cricket unless he is coached. That is absolute piffle. The first thing to be developed in a boy is ball sense and this can't begin too young. I took my two-year-old grandson, Forbes, out on the tennis court one day and began by getting him to hold his two hands together and then plopped a tennis ball into them. He thought it was a game and tried to hit me with the ball but this is the age to begin to teach ball sense. It is the first essential in any game and I recall how Bert (Punter) Tate, a keen baseballer who married Bill Moran's sister, tried my catching out on a lawn by having me diving and jumping in all directions. Bert passed me, and that was the best lesson in catching I had.

If a young chap is keen enough on cricket, he will work many things out for himself, but he will be fortunate if he has an elder who can put him on the right lines. What I lacked as a youngster was somebody to explain what was wrong with my grip and tell me, 'You are missing a lot in this game. You have to think positively. You can play all the strokes but you are afraid to let yourself go.' And that was true. I had a depressed, 'safety first' mentality. Against the good slow bowling of Frank Conway, soon after dawn in the dew of Waverley Oval, I would sparkle with footwork and strokes. Frank, the truest of friends, was full of admiration. I should have tumbled to the way I was going, had I the experience or somebody I trusted to tell me, when I was dropped from the Waverley side for the Kippan testimonial game. Alan had missed out (obviously, wrongly) in the 1926 team for England and Waverley gave him a testimonial match. Although he was the only one ahead of me in the averages, I wasn't asked to play. At that time there was a train of thought in cricket that the score on the board was all-important. It didn't matter how you got runs as long as you got them. I was indoctrinated in that belief and that was why I was snubbed for this particular game: I was too defensive, I didn't have the strokes for a game that was meant to have appeal.

Had I used my brains, I would have worked out this one for myself. The only virtue I see in one-day cricket lies in that it demands that a batsman play his shots, and many a batsman can play better than he thinks or tries. But it is also imperative that a youngster gets advice from somebody who knows what he is talking about. I had coached my youngest son, Larry, from a toddler and he was faultless, as I saw it, in all he did. A well-known coach from Sydney came to Canberra once and the first thing he tried to do with Larry was to change his stance and grip!

*

There were plenty in the various grades at Waverley with cars and we would be certain of a lift each Saturday. Frank and I would insist that we be put off at Bondi Junction on the way home. If we were in different grades we would get the latest paper at the corner and then go to Joe Ristuccia's ice-cream and milk shop to discuss every detail of cricket in the newspapers. In those days they not only gave the full first and second grade scores but also a little story on each match. The lower grades would also be printed and we would eat every detail, over many milk shakes and passionfruit ice-creams. If Mrs Conway or Mrs Fingleton wondered that their sons had no appetite for the evening meal after a day in the sun, petite Mary Ristuccia could have told them why.

*

I said good-bye to Frank Conway on the sunlit lawn of the War Memorial Hospital at Waverley. I had a long car trip in front of me back to Canberra but Frank, sensing his end was near, didn't want me to leave. 'Don't go yet, Brud,' he kept saying to me, as we sat on a seat in the sun and yarned and yarned and reminisced. I took his very frail arm and led him back at last to his room. That was the end of the best cricket partnership I ever knew. The day he died, a little nurse had said good-bye to him and said she feared she wouldn't see him again. 'What b . . .' said Frank to her, a fighter to the last.

His brother, Tom, gutsily read the lesson at his requiem mass. Tom said we were known as Hobbs and Sutcliffe in Waverley, so inseparable were we. For year after year, we walked together in the May procession at Waverley College. Nobody than he had deserved more the epitaph: *Requiescat in pace.*

· 5 ·

Memories of
Bradman

In 1931 I had been twelfth man against South Africa for
three Tests in Australia. It was a tremendous experience
just to be in the same dressing-room and atmosphere as the
mighty although, if truth be told, I would have been better
off playing in Shield cricket because it was a very formative
period in my game. I had played only five first-class games.
Being twelfth man for Australia brought its perks in a very
tough Depression year. The twelfth man was treated as
one of the team and it meant, moreover, that he was first
in line for selection if a vacancy occurred. And after looking
on from the dressing-room in Sydney, Melbourne and Adelaide, I got the call for Melbourne's final Test against
Jock Cameron's Springboks. Ponsford had taken ill and
an accident having befallen Don Bradman, Len Darling
was summoned from the MCC Staff to make up the twelve.
The accident to Bradman was a mystery. Nobody saw
it happen and the first we knew about it was when he was
seen on the dressing-room floor. He had evidently caught
his sprigs on one of the coir mats that covered the rooms
in those days. In no time our room, as was always the
case if the slightest thing happened to Bradman, was
chockful of medicos whose greatest thrill, which they could
pass on to their mates, was getting a hand on the Great
Man.

So leaving Bradman in the hands of the medicos, let us
pass to Len Darling, a tremendous character who was to
bring into Australian cricket both his favourite footballer,
Bobby Pratt (South Melbourne) and his sister, Violet, who

played women's cricket. Darling was forever invoking Pratt's name and ability. According to him, Pratt could drop kick a bag of cement fifty yards. Every bowler was judged on Violet's standards and in all the time I knew him, there wasn't a bowler who could get Len's Violet out. Len was a hard man on bowlers. To be true, Len hadn't impressed me very much when I first met him and I would imagine I had much the same effect on him. Darling was one of those strident football followers common to Melbourne and including politicians who, I was to notice over the years, pushed their viewpoint as noisily and vigorously as they could. They seemed to think that noise was 80% of the argument. We were wary of each other and it wasn't until we toured South Africa together in 1935–6 that I realized how big his heart and friendship were. He was a chap who would do anything for you. It was fortunate for me that F and D were not far apart – the berths, rooms and all else went alphabetically – and so we accepted a kinship that gave me the best mate I knew in cricket. He watched over me like a mother at the Centenary Test in Melbourne and tended to all my wants, which were then considerable.

*

But this was not the Centenary Test and, winning the toss, Woodfull put the Springboks in on a vile sticky pitch. Darling, not Bradman, took the field with us. Playing in one's first Test was a feeling I had never known before. The fact that it was a Test had an overpowering effect that left one wobbly in the knees. Woodfull put me at point and the first ball that came to me went right through me. I was in a daze. There was a time when a New South Welshman who did that would have been roasted by the Melbourne crowd. Reggie Duff played his first Test in Melbourne and he kept a Victorian out of the side. That was unforgiveable and Duff was roasted unmercifully as soon as he appeared on the field. Not even the fact that he got a century in his first Test spared him. He had kept a Victorian out and that was all there was to it. Luckily, I was not in a similar position and the crowd spared me, for which I was most thankful. I settled down after that.

The South Africans were hopeless on that pitch. Len Darling caught Viljoen off Ironmonger, who was in his element: a left hander on a pitch biting and kicking. It was odd that in neither South African innings were the stumps hit once. Only Jock Cameron (11) could manage double figures and the Springboks were out for 36. Ironmonger took 5 wickets costing 5 runs off 7.2 overs, 5 of them maidens. Laurie Nash, a very good type of all-rounder who could well have played for Australia more than he did, had 4 wickets for 18 runs off 12 overs. Stan McCabe was the only other bowler used, though Grimmett and O'Reilly were in the side.

Woodfull took me with him to open and it was a disturbing sight to see the skipper's stumps spreadeagled first ball by Sandy Bell. Keith Rigg, another good Victorian player, was next, and together we got past the South African total, taking the score to 51. Still Bradman did not come to bat. Alan Kippax came instead. Alan was one Australian who knew what to do on a sticky pitch and he made 42. I made 40 before Cyril Vincent caught me off Bell. McCabe was out for nil and Darling, of course, did not bat, being twelfth man. Neville Quinn had 3–29 off 19 overs. McMillan also had 3–29 but I felt thankful to the tall Quinn as I sensed he gave me one to get off the mark.

So Don Bradman did not bat at all. The South Africans, who had taken a terrific hammering from him in other games, had been anxious to get at him with conditions all in favour of the bowlers. Well, the South Africans batted again on the Monday and the game finished in quick time, the tourists faring little better than in the first innings, making only 45 with Curnow alone getting double figures. But the story of the match was that Bradman, though unable to bat in the first innings because of a strained ankle, took Darling's place in the field in the second and ran yards and yards at his top speed to catch Herby Taylor on the boundary off Ironmonger. That made us all wonder, and nobody more than the South Africans: they had fields out while he made 226 against them in Brisbane; 219 for NSW in Sydney; 30 and 135 again for NSW; 112 in the second Test; 167 in the next and a mammoth 299 not out in Adelaide's Test.

*

Alan Kippax, my club and State captain, was most comforting to me over my innings, which, under such conditions, had given me pleasure. 'You have done yourself a good turn to-day,' said Alan, 'Woody [Woodfull] will never forget anybody who gets runs when the going is tough.' It didn't take Woody long to forget – just exactly until the next summer when the team was chosen for England. But, in retrospect, it is interesting in view of the lambasting he gave me in my own newspaper for bad running between wickets – and that on the eve of the touring team being chosen for England – to recall the occasions when Kippax, who was not very fast at the best of times, was run out in Adelaide while Bradman was scooting for his 200th run, and Thurlow also run out when Bradman was trying to get his 300th run; and to reflect that a team-member should have acted in so mysterious a way in Melbourne after giving the Springboks such stick. As it was my first Test and this is my book, I am including the scores (per favour of the NSWCA librarian, Cliff Winning).

AUSTRALIA v. SOUTH AFRICA.
FIFTH TEST.
Played at Melbourne, Feb. 12, 13 and 15, 1932.
Won by Australia by an innings and 72 runs.

SOUTH AFRICA.

B. Mitchell, c Rigg, b McCabe	2	c Oldfield, b Ironmonger	4
S. H. Curnow, c Oldfield, b Nash	3	c Fingleton, b Ironmonger	16
J. A. J. Christy, c Grimmett, b Nash	4	c and b Nash	0
H. W. Taylor, c Kippax, b Nash	0	c Bradman, b Ironmonger	2
K. G. Viljoen, c Darling, b Ironmonger	1	c Oldfield, b O'Reilly	0
H. B. Cameron (Capt.), c McCabe, b Nash	11	c McCabe, b O'Reilly	0
D. P. B. Morkel, c Nash, b Ironmonger	1	c Rigg, b Ironmonger	0
C. L. Vincent, c Nash, b Ironmonger	1	not out	8
Q. McMillan, st Oldfield, b Ironmonger	0	c Oldfield, b Ironmonger	0
N. A. Quinn, not out	5	c Fingleton, b Ironmonger	5
A. J. Bell, st Oldfield, b Ironmonger	0	c McCabe, b O'Reilly	6
B. 2, L.B. 3, N.B. 3	8	B. 3, L.B. 1	4
Total	36	Total	45

Fall: 7, 16, 16, 17, 19, 25, 31, 31, 33.

Fall: 0, 12, 25, 30, 30, 30, 32, 32, 33.

AUSTRALIA

W. M. Woodfull (Capt.), b Bell	0
J. H. Fingleton, c Vincent, b Bell	40
K. E. Rigg, c Vincent, b Quinn	22
A. F. Kippax, c Curnow, b McMillan	42
S. J. McCabe, c Cameron, b Bell	0
L. J. Nash, b Quinn	13
W. A. Oldfield, c Curnow, b McMillan	11
C. V. Grimmett, c Cameron, b Quinn	9
W. J. O'Reilly, c Curnow, b McMillan	13
H. Ironmonger, not out	0
D. G. Bradman, absent, hurt	0
L.B. 3	3
Total	153

Fall: 0, 51, 75, 75, 112, 125, 131, 148, 153.

F

AUSTRALIA—BOWLING.

	O.	M.	R.	W.		O.	M.	R.	W.
Nash	12	6	18	4		7	4	4	1
McCabe	4	1	4	1					
Ironmonger	7.2	5	6	5		15.3	7	18	6
O'Reilly					9	5	19	3

Nash, 3 no-balls.

SOUTH AFRICA—BOWLING

	O.	M.	R.	W.
Bell	16	—	52	3
Quinn	19.3	4	29	3
Vincent	11	2	40	—
McMillan	8	—	29	3

Umpires: G. A. Hele and G. Borwick.

· 6 ·

Ups and Outs in Newspapers

My newspaper career could have been very short-lived. I have written in my Trumper book how I was sacked one day by the *Guardian* editor, Vol Molesworth. Pedlar Palmer, having found that I was reliable left me, while he went out on various rounds, to handle telephones, take messages and do the filing. Our room was a favourite rendezvous for the copy-boys; the girls in the office used to make their afternoon tea there and they were generous with their biscuits. That day I decided the time had come to get down to work.

'Clear out,' I said to the copy-boys, my slight meed of authority exceeding the none of theirs. They answered me back and, light-heartedly, I picked up a paste-pot and tossed it to Jack Hopwood, brother of the girl Jack O'Brien married. This Hopwood was a very good sportsman and should have taken the paste-pot catch with ease. Instead of doing that he slipped aside, and the paste-pot broke with a terrific noise on the concrete floor that separated our room from that of Robert Clyde Packer.

The copy-boys did a quick disappearing trick and I was left standing forlornly when Robert Clyde emerged from his room, deathly white. 'Who did this?' he demanded to know. I was not quick enough to think of an excuse. 'Please, sir,' I said, 'I did.' 'Go in to Vol Molesworth immediately and tell him I said to sack you,' said Robert Clyde. The world scrambled apart. This was not only the best job I had had but one with definite prospects, and I loved it. I went in very chastened to the editor's room.

I was not one of Mr Molesworth's favourites, indeed he had told me once that I should try to smile sometimes: life, he said, could not possibly be as difficult as I made it look. He regarded me with some disfavour. 'What do you want?' 'Please, sir,' I said, as if I were well disposed to the fate in store for me, 'Mr Packer has sent me in to you to be sacked.' If the thought entered Mr Molesworth's mind that a blight was descending on the *Guardian* with my sacking he managed to conceal it. 'Alright,' he said, breezily. 'I'll ring upstairs. You buzz up and get your money.'

Upstairs was the place we visited once a week to get our money, but this was not pay day. However, the pay office was equal to the call and in no time I had bailed out of the *Guardian* with the heaviest heart ever, with my pay in lieu of notice, holiday pay and the rest. The *Guardian* was nothing mean in my dismissal and Pedlar Palmer would have returned to the office to find that his disciple had moved on.

I spent succeeding days disconsolately at Bondi Beach but, coming home one afternoon after a day in surf and sun, I was told there was a telephone call for me. I answered to hear a voice say: 'Is that you, Fingleton?' I admitted identity. 'It is Vol Molesworth here,' said the voice. 'Where have you been lately?' It was an interesting question which I could have answered with 'Bondi and the surf,' but it seemed to me that something had escaped Mr Molesworth. 'Please, sir,' I said, 'you sacked me.' 'Don't be a bloody fool,' snapped the volatile Vol. 'Nobody takes any notice of the sack at the *Guardian*. You come in here immediately.' Pedlar, good friend that he was, must have spoken up for me and made it seem that for him newspaper life without me was something unthinkable.

I caught the next tram and resumed my duties at the *Guardian* but, to be on the safe side, I kept out of Mr Packer's way, though I doubted whether he would have recognized me again. Whenever my path crossed Mr Molesworth's I would summon up the happiest of smiles, but I didn't feel like smiling. Life was a pretty serious business for me.

Still, it was a fact, as Vol said, that nobody at the *Guardian* took any notice of the sack. I recall the religious editor of the time had been on a binge for several weeks, and wasn't seen at the office. Eventually he decided that he would front up like a man and take his medicine. He knocked, tremulously, at the editor's door. 'Ah,' said Vol. 'Come in, Mr . . . I want to see you.' The guilty one thought he could well understand that the editor wanted to see him. 'I want to tell you, Mr . . .' said Vol, 'that we have been so pleased with your work lately, we have decided to give you a rise.'

*

The *Guardian* was a happy newspaper office with no pretensions to be like its English sister, the *Manchester Guardian*. We were like our editor, jazzy and erratic, looking for the sensational in everything. Labour was in government in NSW at the time and the newspaper was constantly spilling caucus secrets. Vol had been an MP of the Labour Party and would come into a room near us to take private telephone calls. 'Yes, Bobby, and what then?' he would say, and though I was a green-horn as a newspaperman I did not need two guesses as to the identity of Bobby. He would have been Robert Emmett O'Halloran, a member from the Eastern Suburbs, and later a member of the Sydney Cricket Ground Trust.

If somebody senior was missing from the office, it was a safe bet he could be found in the hotel next door on the corner. Hotels used to close in those days at six pm and the *Guardian* seldom began to function until after then. Not surprisingly, the atmosphere that enveloped the office was a light-hearted one. Mrs Palmer set me back on my heels once when she rang for Pedlar and I tried to cover up for him, saying he was at some important meeting. 'You liar,' said Mrs Palmer. That rattled me more than a little.

About once a week we would make a blistering attack on Catholics. Robert Clyde Packer would come in from his club some afternoons and call out to Molesworth: 'Vol, sack all the Catholics!' Vol never did. Clyde Packer years later said he would have loved to walk into Consolidated Press one afternoon and cry: 'Sack all the Protestants,' then hurry outside to get a taxi to take him to South Head Cemetery to hear his grandfather revolving in his grave. Clyde is Kerry's brother.

Pedlar Palmer was a magnificent boss and was always teaching and encouraging me. He gave me the messenger ticket for the Cricket Ground and that opened a fascinating box for me. The ticket took me into the Members' Reserve and I could walk around the Pavilion and the nets as I wished. To that stage, my big cricket experience had been limited to one afternoon on the Paddington Hill in 1925, when I saw Bertie Oldfield make his sensational catch of Jack Hobbs off Jack Gregory on the leg-side from a genuine leg-glance. That was Clarrie Grimmett's first of many Test matches; he took 5–45 in the first innings and 6–37 in the second. Mailey bowled only five overs in the match, none at all in the second innings, and while his fellows crowded around Grimmett to hail his triumph as he left the field, Mailey held back. It seemed that Clarrie had put Mailey's nose out in several ways.

I would not have believed, sitting quietly on the Hill, that soon I would be a Test team-mate of both Grimmett and Oldfield, and I would both be playing with and against Jack Gregory in club cricket. Jack did not have a great opinion of anybody in the newspaper game and always regarded me, I thought, with some suspicion. Players and writers were by no means as close then as they became in after years. Indeed, one sensed a big barrier between them although Billy Ponsford, in the bodyline year, was the first I heard to say, 'Nit, the press is about.' In 1934, after the bodyline tour, an English journalist, Trevor Wignall, sailed out to Colombo to return with the Australian team to London and to file stories about them. The players wouldn't assist. They refused to talk to him, let alone give him stories, and Wignall, whom we termed a poison-pen writer, described them as the 'silent, sneering sixteen'.

*

But all that was in the future. I have my own progress to trace in the game and it began on concrete pitches in Moore

Park, in the juniors. The Irish National Foresters, a lodge, had been good to my parents in lending them money to buy the Porter Street house and they were also very good to my mother after father died. It was only natural that when I began to play competitive cricket, at fourteen, I should join with them. I would use my brother Les's bike to ride the several miles from Waverley to Moore Park, a hive of junior cricketers on a Saturday afternoon, with constant cries of 'thank you' for the return of balls that came from adjacent fields.

Bill O'Reilly played on Moore Park also, but in the morning competition; he would go off in the afternoons to do athletics with Botany Harriers. Jim Cope, Speaker of the House, once told me that he had made a big score for Randwick Workshops against Bill, but the bowler had no recollection of the happening; he had a pretty good memory for batsmen who made big scores against him and I wouldn't think there would be many of those on the matting wickets of Moore Park.

I made some useful scores for INF and scored a half-century once on the pitch near the SCG, at the time a big match was going on there. That ground, at the foot of Mount Rennie, has gone now and swells the city council coffers with parking for cars. One Sunday when INF had a match against Holy Cross College at Ryde, a fair distance out of the city, my only part in the game apart from fielding was to collect balls that were hit over the boundary so that time wouldn't be lost in our chase for an outright victory. We got that win, but I thought I would go elsewhere for more chances next summer.

*

Bob Holm, who became one of my greatest friends, invited me to join Woollahra Alberts, a team on Centennial Park. I first met Bob when I was wicket-keeping as a boy on Waverley Park: I didn't sight a ball on the leg-side and stopped it with my face; the blood was plentiful and Bob gave me first aid. That was how one of my greatest cricket friendships began. Bob invited me around to his home in

Bondi Junction, where I would listen in awe to his many cricket stories. Bob's son, Jimmy, was one of the best batsmen in Waverley in my time. He was the club's most prolific scorer in second grade, consistently scoring centuries, but he didn't prosper as well as he might have done in first grade. He was a lovely stroke-player but looking at him in retrospect, he had the habit of trying to pick the ball square off his legs and his stumps. That got him into much trouble.

As well as the supper which was always produced at the Holms', I used to lap up the cricket atmosphere. Bob must have thought me the best audience he had met. I would swallow everything, especially how he held the ball for different dismissals, with appropriate gasps of wonderment. He would put his finger around the ball this way, for instance – and a ball was always on hand for demonstration – to get a batsman lbw, or this way for a catch, or this way for a c. and b. I would gape in amazement at his many wiles; it was natural that I should go with him to Centennial Park.

The nights at his home would be enlivened by a chap we called Long Tack Sam, a comedian of that time, and Bill Beaumont, whom we called the One-Eyed Gunner. Bill had lost an eye in an accident but was a very competitive third grade bowler and one of the nicest, mildest men I met in life. Bill and Long Tack Sam would keep us amused with their string of comical songs, without any music. The nights among such good company at the Holms' were magic ones to me. Outstanding in their simplicity, but unforgettable.

*

I had had experience of the Park some years before. My father had played an occasional game with Glammis but was not a regular member of the side. When the Waverley Guilds began he had linked with them, and as I always went to the Park with him on a Saturday afternoon it was but natural that I should change my allegiance to the Guilds. One day – they were invariably short – I was asked to field substitute against Glammis, of all teams.

Uncle Wal was the captain and stalwart of Glammis. He was a splendid junior cricketer and would have done well in grade, but good cricketers preferred to play in the juniors with their mates, and also grade meant much travelling. So there I was fielding against Uncle Wal, whose word on sport was law in the family (hadn't he played football with the great Dally Messenger?) and he adopted an immediate air of aggression towards my father's bowling. Dad used to walk just a few yards and then send down slow off-breaks. Uncle Wal, to show his contempt, hopped down the pitch and tried to hit him into the faraway tram-shed at Oxford Street.

He miscued and the ball went up a steepling height. I circled under what would have been a tough catch for anybody and Uncle Wal didn't help me, or intend to for that matter, by bawling out, as he saw me under the ball, 'Come two, he'll miss it.' But I didn't and had much satisfaction that afternoon, after helping to gather the boundary flags, in looking at the score-book and seeing W.W.W. (for his Christian names were Walter William Wallis!) Webb, c. J. Fingleton, b. J. Fingleton. I think Dad was proud of me as we walked home that evening.

Uncle Wal was being unsportsmanlike in calling out, 'He'll miss it,' something that wouldn't be done at Lord's, but it must have been a blow to his fame on the Park to fall in such a way. Even if I say it as shouldn't, I didn't miss many catches in cricket. I gathered them in at cover, the boundary, slip and short-leg in eighteen Tests, never missed one, although in somebody's book recently I read a caption 'Fingleton misses Barnett off O'Reilly.' I don't remember it.

Uncle Wal was to get his revenge when I batted against him for the Alberts. In my third game on ant-bed pitches under matting (we were to play on such a pitch at Bloemfontein in 1935–6) he deceived me with a change of pace and had me lbw, roaring his lungs out for it. Most umpires on the Park deferred to Uncle Wal, but the decision was good enough and led him to promote the idea in family circles that I was a sucker for lbw. No doubt I was, but I got a bit back on Uncle Wal in the Referee Cup a few years later when, in a match against the Beaufords at Trumper

Park, I picked his change of pace and hit him for several sixes. Hans Ebeling, a member of the 1934 tour to England, told me once when I hit two sixes off Syd Barnes at the same ground, one could hit a six off the knuckles at Trumper Park. A sardonic man, was Hans Ebeling.

*

I never got accustomed to Centennial Park pitches. I only had three games there. The advice was that I should move on to turf with Waverley, but two subscriptions in the one summer were beyond me. Generous Ernie Williams took charge of that for me and so I went to Waverley as his guest, and for several more seasons after that. I was put into the seconds as a start (something which did not endear me to the many sour-grapes in the club) and I succeeded at once, getting runs and wickets, and thus I never played third grade. It would have been better for me to have done so and become accustomed to turf pitches. They were strange to me and I had to concentrate upon defence, keeping the ball out of my stumps.

At that time, Bob Holm put down a concrete pitch in his back-garden, with a net. As the pitch was on a down slope the ball would scoot through, but to play on it meant that one was accepted by the Waverley cricketers. Leaving the Alberts never affected my friendship with Bob and he was to remain a constant supporter and friend in my cricket career. In after years, however, I often wondered about all those wickets Bob would take by holding the ball in a certain way. Still, he deserved a good audience.

In 1924, aged sixteen, I was picked to play in the firsts against Manly at Manly Oval. Bert Collins, Australian skipper at the time, also did some book-making and one Saturday he preferred the Randwick races to grade cricket. So I got the opening batsman's place and went in last, making 11 not out. Sammy Carter was our skipper and, as we followed on, he told me to keep the pads on. This time I made 52 not out and was to keep my place in the firsts always, until that time I was dropped for the Kippax testimonial. Later in life I wanted to interview Bert Collins for a chapter in *Masters of Cricket*. He was marvellous copy. The interview, in a King's Cross night club, was interrupted when somebody tried to bounce Bert about paying him more money on a bet. Bert didn't waste too much time on the malcontent or the argument. He came with us on one Australian tour to write it up for some newspaper, and didn't mince words.

*

It was always a happy hour when the first edition rolled off the press. The subs would relax, reading and commentating on the paper or, under the splendid bass of Bob Harper, start community singing. Their best number was 'Jerusalem', which they would specially direct to Eric Baume, who was a Jew. 'Jerusalem, Jerusalem,' they would bellow, 'Lift up your hearts and cry.' 'Shut up you b——s,' he would yell back. Several would stay on as late stop, just in case something broke, but most went home.

One night Eric Baume instructed me to stay back and to teach him cricket for the office game at Rushcutter's Bay Oval on the morrow. That was a tall order as he was slow and bulky, by no means a natural athlete. He never got the chance to show off my coaching. Fielding first, he was on the boundary and lumbered after a ball. Failing to get there he oddly tried to kick it, and it hit him a whacking blow on the shins. Eric, with his leg in a splint, took no further part in the game.

I continued at the *Guardian* for several more years but my interest in that newspaper lessened when Pedlar Palmer went to the *Sydney Morning Herald*. Johnny Moyes, then sporting editor of the *Telegraph Pictorial*, offered me a better paid job with him and I took it. This newspaper later merged with the *Telegraph* at a time when the Depression was at its worst, entering the thirties. I recall Campbell Jones, a big man who looked over his glasses, calling all the staffs into the Common Room one day and telling us: 'Gentlemen, we now have two staffs but only one newspaper. Soon we will need only one staff. Gentlemen, go to it and I wish you the best of luck.'

The door was practically jammed as the two staffs rushed out and began to prove their indispensable worth. I was one to fall by the wayside but I was given the consolation of being made the district man for Redfern-Newtown. This meant that I kept an eye on all things for that district, and as there were two important courts and councils in the area I had much scope for lineage that was paid 2½d a line. I made more money than most senior men and in no time I was put back on the staff again.

Eric Baume was by then the editor of the *Telegraph*, and a very good one, too, being full of imagination and ideas. Tommy Dunbabin was editor-in-chief. He had been a Tasmanian Rhodes scholar and was a magnificent historian. He was not the best shaver in the world, possibly one of the worst. It was apparent that he used a cut-throat razor and also apparent that he didn't waste much time looking at himself in the mirror after the job was done. His face was often amazing in its dried blood, which had sometimes run on to his collar. This never seemed to worry Tommy, who had the odd habit of referring to everybody as 'Fish' and another odd habit, which Samuel Johnson had, of tapping each post he passed by. Tommy would go back if he missed one. He was an oarsman in his youth and would scull around Sydney Harbour before he came to the office of a morning.

Tommy never stood upon ceremony. At a big Sydney dinner, which he attended as editor, he asked the waiter for a siphon of soda. That obtained, he took out his set of dentures, put them in a glass, squirted the soda at them, and said: 'I feel better now. Those damn teeth are very uncomfortable.' After his newspaper days Tommy joined forces with the Australian government. In London once, he was one of many listening to a talk by a certain High Commissioner. This man went on tediously long and then asked another high official to say a few words. The few developed into many. Finally, the High Commissioner said, 'Mr Dunbabin will now add a few words.' And Tommy said, 'To what?' The meeting ended on that note.

★

I had been chosen in the 1935-6 Australian side for South Africa, the happiest tour many of us knew. Jack Ryder was also taking a private team to India and wanted Kippax and Chilvers. The Board wouldn't give them permission to go, contending they were wanted for inter-State games in Australia. I think the Board's view was a reasonable one, in the circumstances. Eric Baume didn't see it in the same light. He took the view of the afternoon press that the players had been victimized. Eric was always dramatic. He strode into our room and said to me: 'You will tear strips off the Board. This will be a front page story. No punches will be pulled. You will go for them.'

'Just a minute, Eric,' I said. 'You know I have been chosen for the Australian team of South Africa?'

'Yes, I know that,' said Eric, 'and that's the point. One of the Board's own men attacks the Board. That will make it all the better.'

'Eric,' I said, 'I will write anything you want me to write but it won't be under my own name.'

Eric stood there, brow thundering, his status at stake. He struck a pose.

'I suppose you realise what the alternative will be,' he said.

Eric stood there, brow thundering, his status at stake. He struck a pose.

'I suppose you realize what the alternative will be,' he said.

I knew that well enough. The city of Sydney was crammed with unemployed from the Depression. The best work the government could offer the men, debilitated and near starving, was to dig a trench along Moore Park, with more unemployed following up behind to fill it in. But having missed the English tour of 1934 I didn't want to miss another. I would take my chance.

Eric stamped out of our office back to his editor's den. I was wondering how it would all end when the telephone rang. It was Tommy Dunbabin and he had a kindly voice.

'Oh, Mr Fingleton,' he said, 'I understand there has been a little trouble tonight between you and Mr Baume?' I admitted that.

'I wouldn't worry too much about it, Mr Fingleton. Mr Baume is an odd fish. He is apt to get a little over-excited

at times, but I would not worry about it if I were you.'
The editor-in-chief had obviously taken my side.

Eric took it like the man he was. It was a complete defeat
for him: his stance had been taken in front of some of my
workmates, but he never bore me the slightest grudge and
newspaper life went on as of yore. He often told me that
when I was playing in a Test he would go into St Mary's
Cathedral and light a candle for me.

*

The old *Telegraph* newspaper was the finest I worked on.
There was a great spirit among the journalists. Adam
Mackay was a brilliant columnist whose work daily was a
treat to read on the front page, with the odd classical
quotation, clever verse and wise comment. 'Dum' was a
noble type. He would buy his vegetables in the city and sit
stringing beans or shelling peas as he travelled home across
the Harbour. He got into trouble with the journalists club
in Philip Street on one occasion when he was found rolling
a full (he was also) barrel of beer down the street.

Brian Penton used to write vitriolic articles on the
politicians in Canberra and the joy of Sydney was Lennie
Lower, who turned out a daily humorous column which
used to have people laughing openly in trams and ferries.
Being funny didn't come easy to Lennie. He would sit at his
desk for hours, crumpling up sheets of copy-paper, and
would often duck next door to the Leagues' club for
inspiration and stiffener. He came once to Melbourne for a
Test against England, and wrote about everything but the
cricket.

*

I was moving up in the newspaper world when I went on the
South African tour. Things had happened to the Sydney
papers when I returned and I went back to the *Sun*,
belonging to Associated Newspapers, the company I was
with when I went on tour. Frank Ashton was the editor and
I was sent to cover Philip Nel's 1937 Springbok rugby tour

around Australia. The Argus group of South Africa also wanted a cover from the Australian viewpoint, and I was asked to do that. They sent a highly complimentary letter to Frank on the service I gave.

One of the Springbok newspapermen put one over me that tour. He was privy to the players' common room and there was a notice there before the final Test, enforcing a curfew. He couldn't write the story but gave it to me and when it appeared he was then free to cable it. I remember Johnnie Wallace there also. He had been captain of the much-famed Waratahs (the NSW rugby side) on their home tour in 1927 and to show his disdain – he was an Oxford rugby blue and had played for Scotland – he gave us three pressmen a sardonic talk one night on the rules of rugby. We didn't take it too seriously. It was Johnnie's way of saying he didn't agree with what we wrote. As the other two pressmen were Sid King, one of his Waratahs, and Ken Hardy, who had also been a keen rugby player, I think Wallace's lecture was aimed at me. A pressman learns to live with these things, and always has the last word.

There were still trams in Sydney during my time at Associated Press. They could be slow and cumbersome, cluttering up the traffic, but they encouraged one great art – that of hopping on and off – and the boys selling newspapers were incredible in their dexterity. They would hop on a moving tram backwards, do their sale, slip the change, and hop backwards, a perfect feat of balancing, and be back at their selling spot in a trice.

All the youngsters in my day learnt the art of tram-hopping. My own greatest feat was to hop off the wrong side at great speed between King and Hunter streets, to time my arrival at the office, a resplendent building, swish through the revolving front door, catch a waiting lift, go to the seventh floor and, looking out of the window, catch a glimpse of the tram I had just left still at the Hunter Street stop. That would make my day, but all had to coincide. I think my best feat in hopping on was at Regent Street, Paddington. Coming from a night event at the showground, I was on my way back to the office to write my copy. The driver saw me shaping up between stops to board his tram but he accelerated. I still 'went' for the rail, got it, and such was the momentum that my body hit the side of the tram a resounding whack. The wheels were not far away and I still shiver when I think of it.

· 7 ·

When Sydney Was
Really Bohemian

Sydney journalism in the twenties and, to some extent, in the thirties, exemplified the age of the individualist. Regimentation had not yet stifled original thought and enterprise; there were no computers or vdt's; the only radios were experimental 'cat's whiskers' wireless sets; television was hardly a scientist's dream.

The only popular means of news communication was the newspaper. For this reason, a certain glamour, even adventure, was attached to being a journalist (or a press-man, as he was known in those days). This is not the case today, when petty criminals or traffic violators, in search of an identity, are prone to describe their vocation as 'journalist' or 'labourer'.

The twenties were the age of such brilliant young journalists as Brian Penton, Brian Fitzpatrick, Hugh Buggy, Syd Deamer and Cyril Pearl. All were individualists who fiercely retained their individualism after they became editors and executives. It was an age of give-and-take on newspapers. Star writers and artists were given extraordinary latitude by their editors and management. Reporters could be absent without leave for hours, sometimes days, and escape with only token rebuke. On the other hand journalists found a rare excitement and a sense of achievement in their work. They were prepared to work long hours, without thought of overtime payment, in pursuit of a good story and the satisfaction of seeing it in print (a by-line being the supreme accolade). The competition between newspapers was fierce, extending to the journalists them-

G

selves. The height of the Depression saw the ironic emergence of the song 'Happy days are here again'.

Meanwhile, at the top, things were much the same as they are today. The proprietors played with newspapers and magazines like toys; buying them, selling them, closing them down, amalgamating them and generally tossing them around. The big boys included Robert Clyde Packer, Sir Joynton Smith, Hugh D. McIntosh, the Nortons and Herbert Campbell-Jones, hatchet-man for Associated Newspapers.

Campbell-Jones, an ebullient and likeable man, was universally known as 'CJ' and, at the height of his power, as 'JC'. There must also have been a Beckett to have produced the scurrilous *Beckett's Budget*, a sex and scandal weekly. The Fairfax dynasty sat back snugly and disapprovingly in their *Sydney Morning Herald* headquarters in Pitt Street, but their time to play the take-over game was to come.

Those were the 'roaring twenties', the Jazz Age, the days of flaming youth, air heroes galore, Rudolph Valentino, Mah Jong parties, Coué-ism, Freud-ism and a world revolution in manners and morals. Girls suddenly began to wear short dresses, bob their hair, use lipstick, flatten their breasts to look boyish and smoke cigarettes in public. The cigarettes were ordinary cigarettes; marijuana was not known to young people then. Although alcohol flowed freely and there was a thriving sly grog trade, a 'drug scene' did not really exist. Any drug smuggling was confined to opium to be used in sleazy dens in Sydney's Chinese quarter. They were wild, light-hearted days, reflected in the newspapers and the blithe mood of the journalists who reported it all. It was as if everybody in some mysterious way knew that the Depression was just around the corner, and that life would never be the same again.

A lot of the action took place under the sign of the Golden Ball, the Associated Newspaper building between Elizabeth and Phillip Streets (now the Government Insurance Office). There actually was a golden ball on top of the building to represent the *Sun* newspaper. A variety of other newspapers and magazines were produced under the

Golden Ball, including the *Sunday Sun* and the *Daily Telegraph Pictorial*.

Next door to the Golden Ball was the NSW Rugby League Club, described by Bill Tonkin, editor of the *Telegraph Pictorial*, as 'The Menace'. Searching vainly for staff in the reporters' room he would cry angrily, 'Send somebody into the Menace!' Sure enough, staff would be hurried away from the bar and the snooker tables.

There were other menaces in blocks adjacent to the Golden Ball. There was the Balfour Hotel (where customers drooled over a blond barmaid named Zillah); the Phillip; the Assembly (the watering place for the *Daily Guardian* and *Smiths Weekly*); Belfields; the Durban Club; and Ushers (with gold miners, patrol officers and air pilots in its special New Guinea Bar just inside the door). Farther afield were Aarons, the Euston and the Star (the *Bulletin* pub). In the Wintergarden of the Australia Hotel you would be likely to find Charles Kingsford Smith, Hugh J. Ward and other great figures of the theatre, business and social worlds. In the upstairs bar of the Tudor, you might find the morose and moody Lennie Lower, the greatest humorist Australia has produced. His *Here's Luck* must surely be one of the funniest books ever written anywhere in the world. Alas, all these marvellous pubs are gone forever.

*

One of the best stories to come out of the Golden Ball concerned Sir Hugh Denison, chairman of Associated Newspapers. A man of high repute and standing in the community, Sir Hugh was a prominent racing man and won a Melbourne Cup with Poseidon. One Friday afternoon old Tom, one of the liftmen at the Golden Ball, was taking Sir Hugh up to his sanctum on an upper floor. The lift was crowded, mostly with employees returning from lunch, with a respectful and awed silence for the Big White Chief. Suddenly old Tom said, in a supposed-to-be confidential tone, 'Tell me, Sir Hugh, will the little horse be trying at Randwick tomorrow?'

The Damon Runyon of Sydney in the twenties was Hugh Buggy, a crime and sports writer on the *Sun*. Everybody loved Hughie, including the criminals and madams of Sydney's many bordellos. His face and name were an open sesame to the most notorious houses of ill fame and sly grog joints in the 'dirty half-mile' of King's Cross. It should be emphasized that Hughie's visits to these dens of vice were strictly in pursuit of crime stories, though he was not above sharing a bottle of beer with the inmates. A brothel was about the only place beer was obtainable after licensed hours in those days. The crooks trusted him and revelled in the stories he wrote about them. He got many a scoop that way.

If you were with Hughie on those after-dark excursions into the underworld, no harm would come to you. The protection was certainly needed. Those were the days of the Darlinghurst razor gangs, when vicious thugs roamed the streets with safety razor blades embedded in pieces of cork. The face slashings, especially of prostitutes, were horrific, to be gaudily embellished by Hugh Buggy's purple prose.

You did not have to understand what Hugh was saying to like him – in fact, very few people understood what he was saying half the time. But a kind of Esperanto broke through his quick-fire mumbles and you could pick up a word here and there. His long-time copy-taker at the *Sun* was Owen Hoy, the reason being that he was the only person on the paper who could interpret Hugh. They were a great team, and great drinking mates after hours. If you were with them on those occasions you could always ask Owen, 'What did he say?' if you were in real doubt.

The story goes that Hugh once telephoned a big-shot bureaucrat in Melbourne for a story and mumbled, 'Buggy here.' 'And bugger you, too!' the angry bureaucrat is supposed to have replied. Hugh also reported wrestling and cricket, his writing style consisting of an absolute avalanche of illiterative adjectives. It is generally conceded that he coined the word 'bodyline'. At first, Harold Larwood's attack on the leg stump was known as 'leg theory'. Hugh drew the parallel of a ball in line with the body, hence bodyline. Others say Jack Worrall, the all-rounder who had played for Australia in 1897, coined the word. Claude

Corbett of the *Sun* was also mentioned, but Claude never claimed the honour for himself.

Hugh had an astonishing encyclopaedic memory for cricket statistics. You could ask him the score of any match or any player over the past hundred years and the chances were he could answer it off pat. He would have made a fortune on cricket mastermind quiz sessions – that is, if the quizmaster had been able to understand what he was saying. Hugh lived, mostly in Melbourne, into his nineties.

Two of my most helpful friends in newspapers I met at the *Sun*. They were identical twins, Izzy and Alec Brodsky, who were magnificent men and citizens. They put themselves through a medical course at Sydney University with their earnings from contributions to the paper, mainly on athletics; and apart from their friendship, they gave me much encouragement. They induced me to attend the English classes at the university under Professor Le Gay Brereton. Dr Izzy was later to become a noted writer on early Sydney history. They were models in all things, their behaviour and meticulous dress contrasting in the newspaper corridors with that of the Bohemian pressmen.

*

All Australian newspapermen have been hard men. Denis Hamilton once asked me in the *Sunday Times* office, if I would like to meet Roy Thomson (Lord Thomson of Fleet). I said I would and Denis took me into an office where his lordship sat with his little eyes bubbling behind huge, strong glasses. Thomson told me that this was formerly the office of Lord Kemsley. 'When I took the paper over from Kemsley, I said to him "I feel sorry for you, Lord Kemsley, here I am taking all your office, the paintings and so on." "You needn't feel sorry, Thomson," he replied, "these are all my private possessions and are not included in the sale."' Thomson told me he thought all Australian newspaper proprietors were buccaneers, which I thought pretty rich, coming from him.

Lord Thomson came once to Canberra and I showed him around. With pride, I took him into the newspaper filing room and pointed out the recent editions of the *Sunday Times* and the *Times*, just a few days old. Thomson turned to the back of the *Sunday Times*, noted the page number and said 'That's about as much as they can do.' He turned to the back of the *Times* and said, 'They should be doing better than that.' He never bothered to scan the pages: what was in them did not concern him. He then walked across to the *Montreal Gazette*, saying: 'This isn't one of mine but it is a good newspaper.' He turned the pages to read the ice hockey scores and that was that. Despite all his money I was told that Lord Thomson flew from Canada to the United States sitting in a cheap class, so he could get a cheaper fare to England. His editors travelled in style, first-class. I sat beside him on one occasion at a huge lunch he gave the *Sunday Times* staff in his board room. He told me his ideas for changing cricket to avoid drawn games. 'Each team should leave the field when a wicket falls,' he said. He would have had them dizzy in the Long Room.

*

Massey Stanley, one of Sydney's political journalists, was supposed to have ridden an elephant up the steps of Parliament House in Canberra for a wager, biding his time for the arrival of a circus in those parts. Massey insisted to the day of his recent death that the story was just a legend, but anyone who knew him well was quite certain he would have ridden an elephant right into Parliament House had the occasion demanded it. Anyway, anything could have happened in the early days of the small Canberra press corps, whose hectic forays from the 'dry' ACT into the nearby village of Queanbeyan in search of grog have become folk lore to older inhabitants of the district. One day at that time a man named Andy Cunningham rode a horse into the public bar of a Queanbeyan pub. That's how small the place was in those days.

Nobody knew why Jack Hatch gave up playing a cornet in a Royal Australian Navy band about 1926 to become a journalist under the Golden Ball. For that matter nobody knew, many years later, why Jack suddenly gave up journalism to run a duck farm. Jack had a heart of gold and everybody liked him. But he was a compulsive ear-basher, at his most dangerous when cornering a victim to explain why he could not understand his reputation as an ear-basher. A group of drinkers would hurriedly disperse when they saw Jack approaching. One day, with a captive audience in a club, Jack was in full ear-boring flight when an exasperated listener exclaimed, 'Jack, I'll give you two quid to stop talking for ten minutes.' 'Don't take it, Jack,' cried another voice, 'you can do better!'

Another character of the day was New Zealand-born Stan East, a top sub-editor. A man of many parts, he had been a professional actor at some period of his career. He had taken the stage name of Owen Hardy because, he explained, he was usually owing money and cracking hardy about it. Then there were the other Easts – Stan's wife, Milba, Tibby, Kenneth ('General Jackson') and Kura. They eventually settled in a cottage at Bondi. Parties at 'the Easts'' became legendary, lasting for days and nights and attended by journalists, artists, actors, postmen, milkmen, sometimes the police by urgent invitation of irate neighbours. The laundry tubs were refilled with bottles of beer throughout the night as new waves of guests arrived.

Stan maintained the perpetual drama of his life by winning £25,000 (a vast sum in those days) in the Queensland Golden Casket. The Easts quickly departed for England, presumably to escape a horde of spongers and/or creditors. In London they rented a mansion in St John's Wood, near Lords cricket ground. There Stan fulfilled a life-long ambition by hiring a real live English butler named Watson. Gilbert Mant described a visit to the Easts at St John's Wood in *Nation* magazine, after Stan's death at eighty-one in 1965:

'My first encounter with Watson was a baffling experience. In chauffeur's uniform, he turned up at our West Kensington flat at the wheel of a magnificent car. He drove us to the house at St John's Wood, quickly opened the car door, then without a word, sprinted away to the back of the house. In some bewilderment we walked to the front door and rang the bell. It was almost immediately opened by Watson, dressed this time in immaculate striped trousers and a frock coat.

'"Please come inside, sir," he murmured respectfully. "The master is expecting you."

'The master, also playing his part to perfection,

ushered me into his library (another fulfilled ambition) and flung open the door of a cupboard containing every conceivable type of alcoholic beverage.

'The parties at St John's Wood were frequent but not quite so hectic as those at Bondi. But I recall one in particular. For some reason I can't remember, a team of gigantic South African Rugby Union footballers attended. In the early hours of the morning they suddenly burst into some kind of Boer song.

'This greatly incensed Stan East, who was a veteran of the First World War. With bulging eyes, he bellowed angrily, "I will not have German songs sung in my house! Out of the house, all of you, before I throw you out with my bare hands!" There was a stunned silence among the guests. Then the South Africans meekly looked for their hats and coats and disappeared into the night. Watson showed them out.'

· 8 ·

Don Bradman
as I Knew Him

This won't be an easy chapter to write but it must be faced, even if only to attempt an analysis of Sir Donald Bradman, undisputably the greatest and most publicized batsman in the history of cricket. I have received much criticism over the years, mostly from sycophants, I feel, for having an occasional 'dig' at the Great Man; but no pressman had the chance of batting with him, travelling, touring and living with him as I did, so I consider myself equipped to write dispassionately of him as a batsman, as a legislator who had a tremendous influence on the game, and as a person, observed at close quarters.

After meeting Bradman for the first time in Adelaide our war-time Prime Minister, John Curtin, said that he would have liked to have Bradman in Canberra, that he would have made a wonderful politician. By this Curtin meant that Bradman was a sound thinker, who expressed himself well. Yet Bradman had other attributes to qualify him as a wily politician. He had a cool and incisive mind. He was a skilful exploiter of his name and fame: once, when chairman of the Australian Board, he went into print to extol the virtues – not apparent to many – of a team he had helped choose to play the West Indies. On the other hand, saying he wanted to avoid publicity, he was equally skilful over three to four years observing a steely silence on the biggest upset known to cricket, the World Series Cricket breakaway. He resisted any attempt to interview him – above all on Packer cricket. Michael Parkinson twice did his best to get Bradman on his programme when, undoubtedly, his probing style would have portrayed Bradman as he had not been seen before. But even Parkinson finally had to admit defeat.

Bradman finally broke his silence in a much-trumpeted article in the *Sydney Morning Herald* in March 1980, but he managed to spread himself over four-and-a-half pages of broadsheet without once mentioning the name of Packer. Bill O'Reilly, who had been a colleague of Bradman's in many Tests and who wrote for the same newspaper, was invited to comment on the comments. In his usual forthright way, O'Reilly said Bradman had fallen well short of the mark. He said what most people wanted to know about was the sacrifice of spinners in the game, wholesale appealing and the incredible slide in the behaviour of players on the field. 'To the dyed-in-the-wool cricket enthusiast,' wrote O'Reilly, 'no present feature of the game is more depressing than the disgusting displays of larrikinism that seems to have taken melancholy control of field tactics in recent years.' O'Reilly wanted to know what Bradman thought of players kicking the stumps over, a nauseating habit introduced by the Australian, Rodney Hogg, and allowed to go unpunished by our Board of Control. He wanted Bradman to write another article and expatiate on the many aspects of the modern game. Bradman ignored the invitation. To me also, the significance of the article lay not in what Bradman wrote but in what he didn't. The avoidance of Packer's name was a considerable feat, because I would think Packer has had as much influence on cricket as Bradman himself.

Obviously, Bradman had his own reasons for not referring to Packer and one can only guess at these. Then, too, Bradman might have put himself in an invidious position had he reflected tartly on players throughout the world who had defected to Packer mainly for reasons of cash. Bradman was, arguably, the first superstar in any sport who manipulated his fame to his own ends. In the thirties, for instance, when his fame was at its height, he made a pop record in which he played the piano. It sold well. Bradman, thus, was early cognisant of the value of his name and of capitalizing on it. No one could blame him for that; but a person acutely aware of what was what in 1930 could hardly criticize players of a later, and more money-conscious, generation who did precisely the same thing. Moreover, the Chappells, who never saw eye to eye with Bradman in Adelaide (possibly a legacy from their grand-father, Vic Richardson) might well have retaliated. This is particularly true of Ian. When he was last 'carpeted' in Adelaide and had to appear before Bradman, he showed his disdain for him by sallying off to his inquisition armed with a fat cigar and a big beer. He was let off with a 'caution'.

*

In a critical review of a book I recently wrote on Trumper, which extolled the virtues of Trumper on a 'sticky' pitch to the detriment of Bradman in such circumstances, one Gerald Pawle had this to say in the English *Cricketer*: 'More apposite are Fingleton's views on Bradman, not entirely unknown to aficionados of a long-standing rivalry but revived here with intemperate zest.'

Never, in my extensive cricket days throughout the world, have I known anybody guilty of 'rivalry' with Bradman. He was freely criticized by others for being a loner, but that was his own business. Every cricketer I have known the world over gave Don the fullest credit for his amazing ability. His early critics, the Englishmen Percy Fender and Maurice Tate among them, expressed varying ideas of how the puppyish unorthodoxy of his early days could lead to problems for Bradman on English pitches. Don noted these criticisms and dealt with them in the best possible manner – with the bat.

In whipping himself up about 'rivalry', Pawle omits to say what all this was about. In that book I related, for the first time, how the Warner–Woodfull story from the dressing-room of 1932–3 leaked to the press. 'Plum' Warner and R. C. N. Palairet, the two English managers, came to the Australian dressing-room to express sympathy with Woodfull, who had been hit a dreadful blow over the heart by Larwood. Woodfull, still shaken and lying on a table, sent them scuttling from the room with the remark: 'There are two teams out there. One is playing cricket, the other is not.'

That story leaked to the press and for years I was given

the blame. Claude Corbett, now dead but then of the *Sydney Sun*, got the story exclusively and told me that Bradman had rung him at his hotel, arranged a rendezvous in Bradman's car on North Terrace at night, and there Don gave Claude a splendid account of the incident and the words used. Claude thought the story too hot to use on his own and after having first cut at it, gave it to his fellows. Warner jumped very quickly to the conclusion that I was responsible for the leak. He offered Larwood a quid if he could dismiss me for another duck in the second innings (which he did!) and in a subsequent book Warner wrote: 'Unfortunately, there was a journalist in the Australian team and next day the story was blazoned all over the Australian newspapers.'

'Plum' very much pointed the bone at me. Bradman would have saved me a lot of backlash in the game had he admitted that he had given the leak. Part of his job was writing for the *Sydney Sun* and he had every right to leak such a vital story. Warner was being more than naive, in the tumult and tenseness of those times, if he thought a story like that wouldn't surface from the Australian room. One other of our team had a strong press affiliation. I might have been able to take this particular reviewer more seriously as a critic had he been balanced enough to quote the story as I wrote it and not dealt in balderdash about 'rivalry'. No one ever rivalled Bradman on a good pitch and no one would suggest it. I would have been the last in the world to pit my meagre talents against his glittering ones.

*

There were those in cricket who were jealous of Bradman's great name, his fame, the business spin-off he enjoyed, and went looking for faults in him, real or imaginary. Bradman's success in business earned understandable envy from many fellow-players. In his book, *Farewell to Cricket*, in which he seemed to answer every criticism made of him, he wrote of the occasion in 1930 at Headingley when he made the then-record Test score of 334 and of how he was criticized for remaining in his bedroom the night of his epic. Bradman preferred to listen to music rather than submit himself to the gaze of his admirers by going down to dinner. He would have hated entering the dining-room that evening with everyone standing in clapping adulation and the band playing an appropriate tune. But what influenced his team-mates against him and gave rise to later claims against them of jealousy was the gift to Bradman by an Australian industrialist named Whitelaw of a cheque for £1000 (sterling) to commemorate that score. Bradman never bothered to stand his team-mates a pint (many would not have had one) to acknowledge their part in aiding him or to toast his good fortune. £1000 was big money in those days. Bradman was then, in many ways, an immature lad; he was not quite twenty-two. Had this happened in later life, I think he would have been diplomat enough to quell any feeling against him. But he didn't help his cause with those avid to carp at him by cutting himself off from his fellows on returning to Australia, and making 'See The Conquering Hero Comes' appearances at various theatres, or by writing that he had no objection when some who had criticized him stayed late at the ground, drinking. These team-mates avoided public fraternization as much as Bradman, and to suggest that they would stay behind drinking at public bars was nonsense. They would have a beer in the dressing-room, and a song too, but that was their way of life and of cricket, even if it wasn't Bradman's.

Still, the path of a successful sportsman is never a smooth one and Bradman knew that however he reacted he would have his critics. Looking back, I don't think anybody could blame him for making the most of the greatest publicity known to any cricketer. Besides, it generated interest in the game. Boiled down, it meant that Bradman was just too proficient and successful in whatever he did, cricket or business, so far as many of his fellows were concerned. Bradman had not had a happy introduction to the NSW side or to Kippax. He came in the transition from the First World War era to that of the Depression. The brilliant Australian Imperial Force side had kept NSW and Australian cricket going for years, but time had taken its toll and men like Collins, Bardsley, Macartney, Taylor, Andrews (though he played a little longer than the others), Kelleway, Gregory and Mailey were departing the game, and in their stead came the Portuguese Army, self-designated as such because they were most happy-go-lucky, unconventional chaps, typical of an Australian way of life. Inter-State trips were then made by train and many were the jokes indulged in by the 'oldies' of the team to pass the long hours. Bradman had his leg pulled unmercifully on his first trip to Adelaide. It was harmless fun, no doubt, but the Don wasn't too happy about it. He soon gave his team-mates another view of his character by making 118 in his first big innings. There were no more jokes about him. In 1927 he came into the NSW side and next summer he made the Australian team. He was never again a figure of fun.

Bradman never allowed success to inflate his ego, he was too modest and sensible for that. In a country tour our NSW side made in 1933 he patiently made himself available to thousands of kiddies who queued up for hours to get his autograph at the various towns we visited. I never saw him refuse anyone, signing in a beautiful flowing style. He dealt meticulously with his pile of correspondence in the dressing-room, often reading to us extracts which amused him. He did everything with care and detail. I recall him most vividly when, not out at lunch, he would ask dear old Walter McGlinchy, who looked after our room, to bring him a batsman's lunch from the dining-room above. Walter, a player of old, would bring a tray with a glass of milk on it, some rice pudding, cheese, roll and butter. Bradman would sit, cooling off, at the long table, his pants off and a towel wrapped around him, his bat, pads, gloves and box nearby. It was a lesson to watch him, masticating each mouthful slowly as he planned the afternoon ahead. 'Let me see now,' he would ruminate. 'I am so many now. By tea, I should be so many. By stumps so many again.' The thought of dismissal never came into his head. Always enormously confident, he set himself a time-table which he rarely failed to keep.

It was no easy matter to bat with him. Bradman was all the crowd wanted to see, and they became more than impatient with the opening batsmen who kept him too long from view. Then, it was not possible to have much of the strike while Bradman was there. He was such a fleet and superb runner between the wickets that he always managed to manipulate the strike; this was fair enough, as he could do so much more with it than anybody else. The batsman in runs who failed to fall in with his call had invective poured on his head from over the wickets. He scored runs almost by stealth. An opening batsman might have managed 40 or more struggling runs when Bradman came in. In no time the Don, who made it a fetish to score off the first ball, his piercing call of 'Right' resounding around the field, was soon into double figures and away. He would leave his partner far behind in quick time. To bat with him was an exercise in embarrassing futility.

I knew and recognized some pretty good strike manipulators in my time. Sid Barnes, like Bradman, was outstanding. Once at Old Trafford against Lancashire, when Bradman called for 3 from the last ball of an over, Barnes ambled for 2 and kept the strike. Bradman summoned Barnes at the end of the over and was obviously castigating him for not running a 3. Johnny Ikin overheard the conversation and told us about it afterwards. 'All right,' Barnes had said, 'you have the bloody lot and I'll have none.' Bill Brown – and no-one could have had a better running partner than Bill – ran into trouble with Barnes when, at Southend, the Aussies made 726 in a day. Bill, who had scored a century, rightly refused to be a running hack for Sid. At the day's end Bradman summoned them both and told them if anything like that happened again, he would stand them down for two matches – which was hard on Bill.

*

While I played cricket in Australia, I was sadly astray in my attitude to the game. I played consistently with the great Bradman, the brilliant Kippax and McCabe, and never learnt from them. My best cricketing friend, Len Darling, fielded out while Bradman was making that huge score against Victoria in 1928. What impressed Len was Bradman's pull shot. Darling made note of it and on his return he practised every evening at the Melbourne Cricket Ground nets (where he was on the staff) and had the bowler pitch short to him while he concentrated on the pull shot. He became a splendid puller of the ball. It wasn't until I had finished with the game that I knew why I couldn't pull – but that later.

My first experience of big cricket had been against Archie MacLaren's team of amateurs at the Sydney Cricket Ground, when injuries hit the team hard. I used to frequent the SCG on my press-messenger's ticket and it was known that I could be easily contacted. I got my flannels and sat, suitably awed, in the NSW dressing-room. I wasn't called on to field but keenly appreciated being at such close quarters with the 'Great', Woolley and Duleepsinhji among the visitors and all my NSW heroes. That would have been in the late twenties. The game against Victoria was my first first-class experience, but I tasted blood in more ways than one against Grant's West Indians at the SCG in 1930. No doubt some good players were absent for me to get a game for NSW but I loved it, getting, I think, some 50-odd for once out. But I was over-eager in the field. The outfield was wet after rain and chasing a ball unsuccessfully to the pickets, I dug my sprigs in but they didn't hold; I careered into the fence, splitting my brow on the lower bracket. That earned me several stitches and a bent little finger.

In time I had several long partnerships with Bradman. I batted first with him in that game against Victoria. My most vivid impression of that was the flow of obscene words wicket-keeper Jack Ellis used behind his back. 'Haven't you had enough yet, you little – ?' Ellis would say, as he bent down behind Bradman's back. Ellis was a florid, knock-kneed character who went to England with Collins's 1926 side, but so far as Bradman was concerned that Sydney day they could well have been on different planets. We both got centuries in 1931 for NSW against Cameron's South African team and we had a record sixth wicket partnership of 346 against Allen's English team in Melbourne. 'You keep your wicket up,' he told me, 'I'll do the scoring.' There was a certain English bowler not too popular with us and when I was over the century I tried to straight hit him for six. It landed on the pickets and led to a great lecture in the middle from the master. 'No, no, no. I want you to keep your wicket up.'

writing a cricket book for Pat Murphy,
the *Sunday Times*' editor, hence the
-plume.

A happy picture of Sir Neville
Cardus, to whom I owe much
for his guidance and
encouragement.

Woodfull does a duck to
Larwood. This is a good
picture of a leg-side field:
Leyland, Allen, Jardine,
Sutcliffe, Voce and
Hammond; Eddie Paynter is
the lone man on the off-side.
I am in runs at the other end.

Herbie Taylor of South Africa, a noted theorist and, with the MC, the only decorated man in the four sides I would choose for an imagined series (*see* Postscript).

Harold Larwood in full flight as he looked to the batsman. He and I developed a strong friendship and I later helped him settle in Sydney with his family.

Clarrie Grimmett sending one up. Note his front foot pointing up the pitch, thus turning his body to give top and not side spin.

In 1932, Bradman and I had travelled across the Nullabor Desert in 1932 to play for an Australian Eleven against Jardine's Englishmen in Perth. The enthusiasm over Bradman was incredible. At lonely outposts on the long, straight railway line children clustered and called: 'Bradman, Bradman,' as the train rushed through the night. Not even royalty attracted such a large crowd as Bradman did at the Perth railway terminus.

It proved not a very happy match for the Don, and I wondered once when he called a mid-pitch conference and asked me to take Allen. 'I think they are going to have a pop at me,' he said. The composition of Jardine's team clearly indicated to Bradman what the English intentions were but Allen would never agree to bowl bouncers. He could afford to be aloof – he was an amateur. It seemed odd to me at the time that Bradman should want me to take Allen. Bradman would have been the first batsman chosen in an Australian team of any year; I would be bracketed with about four others for the final batting position in 1932. I finally got the place on the strength of my innings for NSW against England in Sydney, when I had my first unpleasant taste of bodyline and went through the innings for 119 not out.

*

I had a short period out of the NSW team after an operation for, of all things, a football injury. When I returned to the side in the early thirties the line of demarcation on Bradman was clearly defined: One either liked him or didn't. I was in an awkward position. Alan Kippax, our NSW skipper, was also my club captain and I liked him as a man and as a wit. He certainly had no personal liking for Bradman. I had much in common with Stan McCabe and Bill O'Reilly. We talked a similar language. Although they had no enmity or 'rivalry' with Bradman, they had no real comradeship. They were not on the same wavelength. The lines, then, were formed when I returned to the NSW team and no doubt Bradman thought I lined up with my mates against him. I see now why he would have thought so and how I could have been more diplomatic with him. We disagreed openly one day in the dressing-room over some trivial matter. I should have had more 'nous', realizing what influence he

H

had in the game, and kept on the right side of him. He never dallied in the dressing-room after play to have a sing-song or glass of beer with us. He never worried about drink though he was not averse, on social occasions, to a sweet sherry. I think once I saw him smoking a cigarette. After play, he would be dressed and away, the first out of the room, to meet, as we thought, some business acquaintance. He always had a sound head for business. Maybe because most of us were of his generation he never, as captain, came the heavy hand with us as he did with the 1948 team when he meant to get an unbeaten record; and this he did. Most of our team called him Braddles. I called him Don and the whimsical Arthur Mailey called him George – not because Bradman's second name was George but because Arthur had no memory for names and called everyone George. That back-fired on Arthur, who was called George in turn.

*

I have written elsewhere of the press part I played in 1934, when I missed selection for the tour and England. I worked back late at night at my *Telegraph* newspaper office. As a press-man, I went out on the launch at early light and came up the harbour on the *Orontes*. I spoke with many of the team and Alan Kippax tried to sell the theory that Stan McCabe, and not Don Bradman, should be the next NSW captain. Much as I liked McCabe, I did not come at that line. Bradman could have the captaincy if he wanted it and I was not going to put my cricket-neck on the chopper over that. Bradman solved the problem later by moving to South Australia.

In Harrogate in 1938, the night before the vital Test at Headingley, somebody procured a football and we all proceeded to a playing field opposite our hotel. There we indulged in the most bizarre game of touch football anyone could imagine, and nobody enjoyed it more than Don Bradman. Our team was split 50–50 between Australian Rules and Rugby enthusiasts, and everyone thought it imperative he should do his best for his code. It was the roughest, toughest game of Rafferty Rules imaginable on the eve of a Test. Injuries and muscle-tear were not far away but nobody seemed to think or care.

When we were at Grindleford, in the Derbyshire hills, news came that our Board of Control had refused Mrs Bradman permission to come to England when the tour had finished. The Board said it was in conflict with our contract, an odd situation to visualize today, when wives and children travel with an English team in Australia. We thought this appalling, held a team-meeting and told manager Bill Jeanes what we thought. I played the part of what would have been shop-steward today and also told him that if Mrs Bradman were not allowed to come to England, he could play the final part of the tour on his own. The Board capitulated. Not only Mrs Bradman came, but other wives too.

*

I had reason to be thankful to Bradman in 1938 when he would have been well justified in carpeting me. The occasion took place in Nottingham, where we had never been too popular since bodyline. We were fighting time for a draw, and Bill Broan and I had understandable orders from the Don to sit tight and play for it. Stan McCabe had just ended his epic innings, and as they saw a win slipping away the Trent Bridge spectators gave vent to their feelings with a slow hand-clap.

Mervyn Waite came out with a message from the Don. 'The skipper says you are to draw away from the stumps if this slow hand-clap continues while the bowler is running in.' 'It is not worrying me,' I told Waite. 'Well, those are the skipper's orders,' he said. The clapping intensified. Wisden's man, who surely could not have been to the ground that day, said it was only 'spasmodic'. When it continued, I did as my skipper had told me to do and stood aside from the stumps. This angered the Notts crowd all the more. Umpire Frank Chester called down the pitch and asked me what I was doing. 'Don's sent out an order that I am to do this,' I explained to him. Wally Hammond, the English skipper, chimed in, 'That's all right by me.' The clapping grew worse and then I did a stupid thing, more out of devilment than anything else. I not only drew aside but sat down. It was only for a moment, but the crowd went into a fury. It was sheer bedlam. (Next day, humour restored at least in some areas, a race reporter said, when a horse sat down at the barrier, that he had 'done a Fingleton'.)

A pressman named Bill Pollock, of the Daily Express, engaged me in conversation that evening, and as we were all friendly with him I discussed the incident. I almost fell out of bed next morning when I saw my talk translated into a big story, quote for quote. Pollock had badly betrayed my friendship and confidences: he knew we were not supposed to talk with the press – only manager Bill Jeanes and skipper Bradman were empowered to do that.

I rang Bradman immediately and told him Pollock had let me down. Bradman could have carpeted me, given me a 'blister' or had me fined for a breach of contract. He did nothing of the sort, said he understood how it had happened, and I never heard another word of an incident that reflected my gullibility. As a journalist myself I should have known that not all pressmen can be trusted. Pollock got no talks after that and I said a few blunt words to him at our next meeting.

The Don showed much good faith in me in the early sixties when the South African cricket tour of Australia was cancelled. Don was then chairman of the Board and after the Board meeting he came out to talk to the press. I asked him the pertinent question: 'Do you think this tour would have gone ahead had Coloureds been included in the South African side?' He replied 'Yes.' I had my story and, as I had a dead-line to meet with my cable, I excused myself and left the interview. A little later, to my great surprise, Vorster, then Prime Minister of South Africa, denied my story and said Don Bradman had never answered 'Yes' to my question. I rang Don and he expressed surprise that a private letter to an Ambassador in Canberra had been sent on to the Prime Minister. I told him that was why ambassadors were in countries, to send everything back. 'If you say I said "yes",' said Bradman, 'then I accept your word unreservedly. I have no memory of saying that but I was flustered at the time and could easily have answered as you said I did. I accept your word.' That was a gracious and generous gesture.

· 9 ·

More Memories
of Bradman

If I am permitted to be critical of Bradman's influence
in cricket, I would dwell on the manner in which Lindwall
and Miller were allowed, under his captaincy, to bowl so
many bouncers against England in the immediate post-
war period. Nobody had lobbied more than Bradman
against bodyline in 1932–3; he and Kippax expressed
their antipathy towards it to our Board members. Our
Australian team for the vital Fifth Test of 1936–7 in
Melbourne had been held up for days while Allen, the
English skipper, and Bradman tried for an agreement that
no bouncers would be bowled in that Test. They finally
agreed that there would be none. Bradman, ever suspicious,
had Laurie Nash included in our side as a precaution; he
was a good cricketer who had the odd distinction of never
playing a Shield match in Australia. There were no
bouncers!

After the bodyline series, in which the English tactics
sometimes induced Bradman to bat 'hysterically' (his clear
aim being not to be hit by Larwood, and I don't blame him
for that) I thought the Don would have been the last in the
cricket world to foster bouncers again; but I never got the
impression, in England in 1948, that Bradman did anything
to dissuade Miller and Lindwall from bowling so many
bouncers, and particularly against Len Hutton.

Innumerable bouncers were bowled against Compton and
Hutton at Trent Bridge, Old Trafford and Lord's.
Compton had stitches put in a brow hit by Lindwall at Old
Trafford – off a no-ball admittedly – and when he returned

to bat Lindwall gave him a further surfeit of bouncers, as fast as any Compton had known. Lindwall jokingly told Compton he was anxious to hit the plaster off. Compton didn't see the joke! To that extent then, Bradman, who could have been expected to tell his two speedsters to put the brakes on because of his own knowledge of bodyline, could be held responsible for bouncers becoming so prevalent in cricket after the war. England had no fast men to retaliate: this was before the days of Trueman and Tyson.

Keith Miller was batting with the Don at Bramall Lane in 1948 when Aspinall, who wasn't built for fast bowling, sent Bradman along three balls in succession that pitched half-way. Bradman curled into a ball of energy and thrice pulled Aspinall hard up against the legside railings. 'I hope, Nugget,' grinned Bradman between the wickets, 'that nobody complains that Aspinall is bowling too many bouncers.' When many thought that Lindwall and Miller were allowed too many bouncers against Compton and Hutton in England that year, a press-man put this very point to Bradman at Trent Bridge and he made the strange reply: 'They have a bat in their hands, haven't they?' We hadn't thought much of that when it was said to us in 1932–3. Len Hutton was batting against Ray Lindwall in Sydney in 1946 when a roaring bouncer nearly decapitated him. Len got his head out of line just in time and looked across to cover at Bradman; he was smiling hugely. The Don, it appears, had two views of bouncers – one when they were bowled against him and the other when bowled by his side with no fear of retaliation.

There was a suggestion in a benefit game in Sydney that Bradman didn't think much of it when a bouncer was bowled at his head. Miller was opposed to Bradman. He bowled him an innocuous bouncer which Bradman pulled imperiously for 4. Miller tossed back his mane, as was his wont, and walking back to the spot he looked up to our press-box as if to say 'Keep an eye out for this.' The next was a rip-roaring bouncer which nearly took Bradman's head with it. Bradman was then the most influential of three selectors, and when, a few days later, the Australian team to tour South Africa was announced Miller, despite being the leading all-rounder in the world, was not in it. South Africa specially asked for him when Bill Johnston was injured later on. Miller went.

Miller was a mercurial type of man, most popular in England where he was fighter-pilot during the Second World War. He proved a magnificent skipper for NSW and some of us thought he would have reacted to responsibility and made an outstanding Australian skipper had he been given the chance, but it was always apparent he wasn't favoured at the top. Ian Johnson, a mediocre cricketer whose off-spin bowling action always seemed suspect to me, was given preference and there was reason to think that Bradman favoured him over Miller.

Miller had no two opinions of the merciless side of Bradman. He told Keith Butler (who wrote *Owzat*, a book published in 1979 by Collins) that when he, Miller, played his first Test against England in Brisbane in 1946, everybody was happy to be alive after the war. The players met the worst 'sticky' pitch Miller knew and Miller was scared of hurting someone. In his colourful language, Miller described his feelings to Butler: 'I got seven wickets on that track but Blind Freddie could have got wickets. I remember hitting Hammond and Edrich, a gutsy little player with a DFC, from bloody pillar to post. They were holding us up and Bradman came to me and said, "Bowl faster, bowl faster. When you play Test cricket you don't give Englishmen an inch. Play it tough, all the way. Grind them into the dust." Those were his words. I thought to myself, a war has just passed, a lot of Test cricketers and near Test ones have been killed and here we are after that war, everybody happy to be alive, and we have to grind them into the dust. So I thought b—— me, if this is Test cricket, they can stick it up their jumper. Don kept up this incessant will-to-win but it just wasn't my way of playing cricket.'

Lindwall and Miller plastered Everton Weekes with bouncers when John Goddard led his West Indies side in Australia in the fifties and there was never any hint that Australian officialdom, of which Bradman was a senior member, so eager to cable and complain to the MCC in London when Larwood was sizzling around our ears, seemed to be concerned at what our two fast bowlers were doing. One night in Sydney, when the tour had ended, Goddard complained bitterly to O'Reilly and me about the Australian tactics which, he said, were contrary to all the promises made to them.

*

The West Indies now is a country of unlimited fast bowlers. One would never imagine that they had produced such wonderful spinners as Ramadhin, Valentine and their off-spinner Lance Gibbs, the world's record taker of Test wickets. Holding is a perfect running specimen but I don't go to a Test to see running; if I wished to see that I would go to Crystal Palace to see Coe and Ovett. I was greatly dismayed and depressed at the Oval in 1980 by the manner in which their fast bowlers were permitted to bowl bouncers at Boycott's head. Frank Worrell, for one, would never have permitted it, but in their disregard of anybody being hit and hurt some West Indians appeared callous and reminded me of bully boys. It seemed to me, as an impartial observer, that some black men didn't like white men, for all that cricket and particularly English cricket had done for them in life. They seemed to be intent on proving something, something I didn't like. Basil d'Olivera told on Parkinson one night of a stand he made against India: one of the Indians bumped into him at the crease and said 'If you get out, we'll beat these whiteys.'

The worst feature of the bouncer, which panders to that element of the public which lusts for violence, is that the bowler often, in a desire to intimidate as much as possible, will wittingly bowl a blatant no-ball to get nearer his human target. I saw Croft hit Boycott on his helmet and stand aloof yards away, seemingly not caring a fig about Boycott's condition. I thought the two English umpires were very lax; he should have been warned at least. Also I didn't think much of those of the television commentators who wouldn't speak out and condemn the tactics. Richie Benaud got near it when he said he felt a warning to the bowler was imminent but Jim Laker was the most outspoken when he said near-murder was going on on the field. I didn't pull any punches in the *Sunday Times*. I saw the tactics for what they were, sheer intimidation, and I further offered the opinion that the West Indians, in the field, were the most boring team I had seen, with their super-abundance of fast bowlers who bowled so many bouncers (and therefore unplayable balls), their slow over rates with their incomprehensively long run-ups. The English tour of the West Indies hasn't started as I write this, but I will be amazed if there isn't dire trouble of one sort or another out there.

They have got more than tit for a tat over Everton Weekes. When Australia had in Lindwall and Miller the two best fast bowlers in the world, nobody warned them to go easy on the bouncers. Bouncers one summer have the habit of bouncing back the next and bring nothing but ill-feeling into the game. They are, too, a negation of the art of strokes.

*

Bradman was angry with me when, in England in 1948, I first toured as a journalist. I had long realized I had to finish playing and get on with my job of writing, with much leeway to make good. I went to England on a strained pittance, working only for my Argus group of newspapers in South Africa and for the *Hindu*, Madras. I was thus eager for more work and when Noel Monks, a distinguished war correspondent and an Australian, suggested a leader page article from me for his *Daily Mail* on the eve of the tour, I jumped at the idea. Knowing the Don's avid appetite for all records, I made a strong point in the article that Bradman would want an unbeaten record and would be merciless to achieve it.

I thought what I wrote was a fair interpretation of Bradman as I knew him but the maestro, in his book *Farewell to Cricket*, took strong exception to it, and said many who thought poorly of the article had come to him and apologized for it. I had my reputation as a writer to make and it did me no harm. At all events, I was asked to write many special articles after that, including another editorial page article for my favourite *Manchester Guardian*; and in a country where writers of anonymous letters don't bother to spare a writer's feelings I didn't get one such letter.

My dealings with Bradman were not all niggardly. He came to me after the 1948 tour and said how much he admired my *Brightly Fades the Don*, a book I wrote on the tour. He once sought me out in Adelaide to thank me for a broadcast I made on the ABC when he was caught off-guard at a luncheon and gave his opinions (he was a selector) of who should go to England. Back in 1938 in London, when we were going to a welcome at Australia House, he asked me to walk up the Strand with him. We chatted amicably enough. It was Friday, 13 April, and a press photographer had set up a picture for himself with a ladder under which he wanted us to walk. Much to the photographer's disgust, we were both too superstitious to oblige him, especially at the start of a tour. Bradman was most generous, also, when I wrote to him in the fifties and asked him for some opinions for an article I was asked to do for the now defunct *World's Sport*, an English magazine. He went to much trouble to give me considered opinions on sport during the ages and drew many conclusions in his deliberate manner. So there were times when I wasn't off-side with him.

The Don was a brilliant after-dinner speaker who captivated English audiences, but he didn't do himself justice when he made the main speech at the Board dinner for the Centenary Test at Melbourne in 1977. I thought he spoke too long and tried to cover too much ground – the whole history of Test cricket between the two countries. At the end of it the many assembled cricketers, with a few exceptions, rose in ovation to him. Two who didn't stand were Voce and Larwood, sitting at our table and I noticed Ian Chappell and Stackpole didn't budge either. There might have been others. An ovation is an interesting sight. It is easily started by several 'claquers' giving the lead, and before they know it others feel obliged to stand and clap. The person who deserved the standing ovation that evening was Hans Ebeling, who conceived the Centenary Test idea and went ahead with it, despite much opposition. Ebeling received a lowly MBE from the Victorian Government for his services while others, who belatedly got on the bandwagon when the game looked like being the success it was, got higher distinctions. The game was a tribute to Melbourne's civic pride and spirit.

*

No one, and particularly I, who saw so much of him, could doubt Don Bradman's genius on a good pitch. Nobody came near him. While I considered he didn't rate at all highly on rain-affected pitches – and that this was the fundamental difference between Bradman and Trumper – Bradman reasoned, obviously rightly, that such pitches were few and far between and that as there would soon be another good pitch to show his mastery, he needn't lose any sleep over sticky pitches. Nor did he.

When the English were in Australia in 1979, Bradman's unbeaten team from 1948 in England celebrated with a commemorative dinner. Glimpses of Bradman batting were seen on television. It warmed the cockles of one's cricketing heart to see once more his flashing footwork, his dazzling stroke-play, the audacity of the man, a cover drive and then, magically and murderously, his paralysing pull. This vintage glimpse of his departed glory showed up starkly in a summer when the Australian batsmen wouldn't use their feet.

Some moderns think Bradman would not have been so brilliant in present-day cricket. I will agree with that only because present-day cricket is negative – it slows down anybody who looks like succeeding with the bat simply because it won't give a batsman a chance to display his wares. I recall an over Norman Yardley bowled to Bradman at Trent Bridge in 1948. The whole over was down the leg-side and Bradman maintained his posture and stance watching the ball from Yardley go by. Today's tactics would certainly have negated Bradman's skill; they would curb anybody, because they make a mock of the game, refusing to give the batsman a chance to hit and also the bowler to get a wicket. The negative field-placing, also, would have circumscribed Bradman, as they would any batsman who faces bouncers with several men in the deep for a catch. Otherwise, I could not visualize any bowler of the modern age keeping Bradman in check. He was much too versatile, too gifted and innovative.

*

I have discussed Bradman pretty closely as I have the right to, being so near to him over the years and observing him long at close quarters. He was the greatest personality to walk a cricket field and it was fortunate for the bowlers of South Africa and the West Indies that he didn't tour there. On such perfect pitches and fast grounds he would have re-written the records book again. His consistency was incredible and his sharp mind was shown in all he did. He showed the full face of the bat to drive and pull and though some of his contemporaries complained that he got more loose balls than they did, this was not difficult to explain. His superb judgement, his swift and unerring footwork down the pitch gave few bowlers an appetite for the job against him and they realized there was no such thing as a good length to him. He converted an ordinarily good-length ball into something else and if, in the hopelessness of their task, they blundered into short-pitched balls or long hops, that was understandable. The Don was just too supreme and anybody who saw him bat would scoff at the suggestion that modern captaincy is now so gifted it would have nobbled him.

As a skipper he was merciless, determined from the outset in 1948 to get a record which meant as much as any to him – that of leading an unbeaten Australian team in England. No doubt too much could be made of that side of his nature. Herby Collins, a former Test captain, passed him one day in the Adelaide pavilion, and told him he had just written that he, Collins, thought it would have been a good thing for cricket had Bradman not returned to the game after the war. 'You play the game too hard,' said Collins. Bradman could have replied that Collins showed no mercy as skipper and moreover, Bradman in his career met many Englishmen who played Test cricket just as hard as he did.

I only knew one of his players openly flout him and that was his vice-captain, Stan McCabe, in Adelaide back in 1935–6. McCabe had batted gloriously for a near-century and was caught on the boundary off a long hop. Bradman, disappointed that his side had not built itself into a stronger position, grumbled in his dressing-room about McCabe playing such a shot at such a time. McCabe could be prickly, and bridled at being rebuked in front of his fellows. 'Well, Braddles,' he said, stubbornly, 'all I can say is that if a similar ball comes along in the second innings, I will try and do the same thing with it.' No answer. It was also to McCabe that I heard Bradman give his seldom-used words of praise at Trent Bridge, when he was playing one of his three brilliant innings in Tests. I was sitting alongside the Don on the balcony seat when he called inside to those of our fellows who were doing odd jobs: 'Come and see this,' said the Don. 'Don't miss a minute of it. You will never see the like of it again.'

*

I'd like to be able to recollect vivid examples of the Don's leadership. Apart from the instance of McCabe at Nottingham I never heard him praise a player unduly, or motivate his team with discussions of tactics. Perhaps his main resource as a leader was the example he set his men in concentration and the relentlessness of his attack. His humour inclined to the sardonic. He was much too realistic to worry about humour and I remember his high-pitched call from cover of 'Catch it, catch it,' when Percy Santall, a massive man, caught a long hop from Waite in the meat of his bat and put it almost squarely on my forehead in an ordinary county game at Edgbaston. Had I not ducked I would not be writing this now. I lapsed semi-conscious to the ground – my fellows caught me instead and off I went to hospital for X-rays. I had a headache for days.

The Don had never bothered about seeking the company

of his fellows on the 1938 tour; no doubt he was well occupied elsewhere. In 1948 he was fortunate to have a vice in Lindsay Hassett who took the entertaining out of his hands. I can see Hassett again, an elfish grin on his Irish face, standing on high in the lounge of the Himalaya and leading the whole lounge-full in community singing, conducting with a pencil and doing actions when needed. But Hassett was the complete extrovert. That was just not in Bradman's make-up. Neither was a night out with the boys in his conception of things. Yet he was not a prude. He never tried to stop anybody else from enjoying himself.

I had a good experience in comparative values at the Oval in that 1938 tour. After almost two days of fielding out against Len Hutton I pulled a muscle in my leg. It went off like a bullet shot. This was unlucky for me because the Don had told me I would be bowling a dozen or so overs if we got held up. We certainly did get held up. I often wondered what our score would have been had we won the toss instead of Hammond, as Don was in the mood for one of his very big scores. My team-mates carried me to the Oval fence and deposited me with appropriately rude messages, but not one Oval member offered a hand to me up the steps and up the many steps again inside the pavilion. I hobbled into our room in great pain to be greeted by dear Doctor Pope, who made so many trips with us. 'My dear Jack,' said the Doc, as we called him, 'what have you done?' Don saw me in my room that night and told me I would bat next day, if needed, if I had to come out on crutches. Wobbling along I was at the Oval next day when Hutton created his record, and I saw Bradman go over on his ankle when bowling. Our team-mates did the same for him and deposited him at the boundary. Innumerable Oval members rushed to lend a hand in carrying him up the steps and one could barely move in our dressing-room for all the members of the medical fraternity who wanted to be in on the act with him. Neither of us batted.

There was a time when I thought Bradman could have stuck by his players more than he did. It was after the Third Test in Melbourne in 1936–7 season. To that stage we were two down against G. O. Allen's side, and had we lost at

Melbourne the series would have been finished. We happened to win. I was showering in the next cubicle to Bradman at the game's end. The rest of the team were chaffing McCabe, O'Reilly, O'Brien and Fleetwood-Smith, all, incidentally, of Irish extraction, who had been summoned to appear before a Board sub-committee on some unstated charge. The news that trouble was brewing was not news to O'Reilly: a friend of his in the postal office at the Sydney ground told him he had sent telegrams to various Board members, saying the players were to be charged.

Bradman asked me what it was all about. 'Surely you know?' I said. 'Four of the chaps have been summoned by the Board.' 'I know nothing about it,' said Bradman. 'I think you ought to go along with them as skipper,' I said. 'No, not at all,' replied the Don, 'you know what I think of the Board.' After his epic 1930 tour of England the Board had fined Bradman £50 of his bonus for allegedly breaking his contract in England by having book material published. He bitterly resented that fine. As it turned out, the Board laid no charges and did nothing against the four named players. I think Board members had the view that the players were not giving Bradman full support as skipper. I thought, as the four did, that Bradman should have gone along in support of them.

*

Don never missed the slightest newspaper criticism of him. Somebody once wrote how Mailey, a slow bowler, had got his wicket a few times. Mailey had seen the press clipping and knew that Bradman would be sharpening his blade for him in a friendly game we were playing that afternoon at Callan Park, Sydney (Mailey had taken me to his home for lunch). 'They shouldn't write stuff like this,' he complained. Bradman cut him into small pieces.

Similarly somebody noted that Fleetwood Smith, a slow left-hander who toured England in 1934 and 1938, had got Bradman's wicket a few times. It was the kiss of death for 'Chuck'. In the game against Victoria in Sydney in 1934, when I retired early with an attack of cramps, Bradman came in and gave Fleetwood-Smith the biggest trouncing he knew in cricket. He waltzed yards down the wicket and hit him repeatedly over the fence; Bradman did not usually worry about sixes, being content to keep the ball on the ground. It was a point of honour with the Don to show utter contempt for all bowlers and he needed little urging. An exception was the bodyline series but that was based on a menacing, dangerous theory that was conceived specially for Bradman and was another story. I wrote it as I saw it, in *Cricket Crisis*, and see no reason years afterwards to amend it.

Apart from the instance of McCabe, which I have written, I don't think players of my era differed strongly with Bradman in his views on the game. Bradman did not think much of O'Reilly's double leg trap, which originated by accident under Vic Richardson in South Africa. For NSW, I had always fielded at short-leg for O'Reilly but Richardson took over the position in South Africa. I loved fielding and once did a whinge to Vic that I would like more fielding to do. 'Would you like to come up here and join me?' said Vic and while he stayed at silly short-leg I went to silly square-leg. So was born a tactic which Bradman did not hold in high regard. He tried to induce O'Reilly to do away with it and I think Bradman was right about this in England: the trap never held the same fears there as in South Africa. The Englishmen, and Hammond in particular, took leg-stump guard to O'Reilly and as his attack was directed at their legs, they gave themselves an advantage against him.

*

My last playing experience with Bradman was in Adelaide in 1939 and I did not enjoy it, thinking him unnecessarily boorish. Stan McCabe had been injured in a Testimonial match in Melbourne and I was appointed NSW skipper in his stead for the southern tour. I conferred with O'Reilly and we decided that Bradman was sure to get a hundred but we had to try and close him off from a huge score.

Darling. We didn't think much of each
er at first but he later became my best
nd in Test cricket.

ht Not quite the right background for a
ler but Wilfred Rhodes shows his
on at delivery to the camera. He was
of the world's best all-rounders of all time.

iglas Jardine, in his famous Harlequin cap which used to exasperate Australian
ackers, plays one carefully to the off against India. Paynter is in runs at the other end.

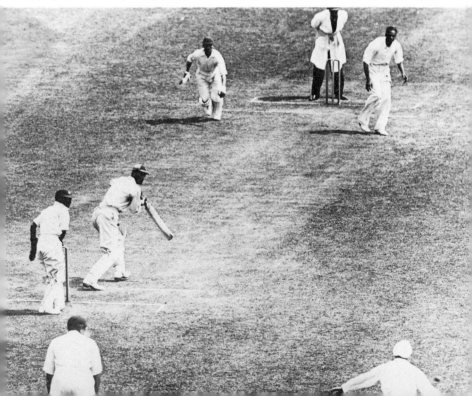

The greatest of all cricketing time: Bradman, playing his famous and payable pull shot.

Below left

West Indian Sonny Ramadhin, the famed spinner. His arm looks strangely bent as it comes up to deliver. I should doubt whether Ian Peebles, expert on bent arms, would have approved.

Roaring Wes Hall lets one go. His action is perfect, with a fluid follow through.

Bradman got his century, with more singles in it than usual, and statistics might show it was the slowest of his glittering career. It was the cheerful, smiling Jack Badcock who slaughtered us with a double century. We were mostly a young, inexperienced side and in the afternoon we were greeted with a voice over the tannoy: 'Announcement, announcement, the South Australian captain has now declared his innings closed.' Anybody could get to a tannoy, although I recognized the voice of the SA secretary, Bill Jeanes. No doubt I would have been justified in refusing to leave the field. The polite custom is for a captain to make an appearance and a gesture. However, I knew it would have been hopeless to stay on the field. Jack Scott was one umpire and Scott, as I found out, then considered himself very much part of the Adelaide establishment. At the end of the game, in which we were well whacked, Bradman did not come to our room, as is the custom of home captains in Australia, to thank us for the game, to bid us farewell and wish us good luck for the summer. Bradman could be ungracious when he felt like it.

There is a bad arrangement in Adelaide by which the umpires share the facilities of the visiting room. Scott tried to bait me into an argument about decisions. I shared the view that Scott was not a great umpire. I ignored him. Some time later he saw fit to attack me for some criticism I had made of Bradman and said that I had been in trouble with umpires. It gave me the chance to say that in no country had I been reported by an umpire. Records would show this, and he was obviously confusing the principles. When younger, Scott himself, playing with Marrickville in Sydney, leapt the fence and got involved physically with some barrackers. This earned him suspension from the NSWCA. But I daresay in my obituary this will be dug up against me from some newspaper file, although Scott made no reply to me. The triumvirate of Bradman, Jeanes and Scott was a big power in Australian cricket in my time. Cecil Pepper, a slow bowler, who said a few warm words to Scott when he refused to give Bradman lbw to him once, knew this and saw the writing on the wall when he refused to apologize to Scott and Jeanes. He lifted his roots and went to England where in time he became an umpire himself. My last playing contact with the Don was thus an unpleasant one. A gesture by him would have meant much to the young NSW players. The footnote to this is that I told Bill Brown in Melbourne about the field-placing plan against Bradman. Bill was on his way with his Queensland side to play in Adelaide. 'All right, Brownie,' called Bradman from the batting crease, 'I see what your little game is. I was going to get out after getting a hundred. I will get two now.' And he did!

Oddly, there was a period when Adelaide was the home of a clutch of chuckers but once it was determined to rid the game of these, they quickly faded there. I often wondered whether Ian Meckiff was caught up in this movement. The mystery of how he was called out of Test cricket by an Adelaide umpire who had previously seen nothing untoward in his action has not yet been fully explained. One got the impression that selectors Ryder and Seddon, now both dead, had chosen Meckiff over Bradman's wishes. Bradman and Benaud, the Australian captain, were seen constantly together in Brisbane before the match. I asked Richie once whether he was surprised that Meckiff had been no-balled. He looked hard at me for a moment and then replied 'No'. Perhaps the full story will be written some day.

*

There were several peculiarities about Bradman in his batting. He had his top hand, the left, more around the handle to the right than most batsmen and I think this aided his pull, enabling the bat face to close quickly over the ball and send it to earth. Then, too, his stance was unusual in that he rested the bat on the ground between his feet. He was the first batsman I noticed to stand out thus. Keith Miller stood likewise and Keith told me he copied Bradman. Another to stand thus was Graeme Hole, but the stance induced him to swing his bat out wide to clear his feet, whereas the other two lifted their bats up immediately and never swung across the line as Hole did.

Bradman never acted the fool in batting. It was much too

serious a matter for that and his resolution and co centration could not be tempted. It was, however, another case in fielding. Some thirty, forty or even fifty yards from the stumps he would hold the ball, poised to throw, and tempting the batsman to run if he dared. Bradman had such a strong, straight throw that nobody could be tempted to run. It was playing to the gallery and Bradman knew it was but, never mind, it was the only play-acting I saw him do and the crowd loved it. When I write that he never acted the fool in batting, this excludes times when he thought he had made enough and it was time to get out. Then, and only then, would he act the fool with the bat and play fancy strokes. He once, in a book, described me as a 'know-all'. I didn't mind that. If that was his opinion he was entitled to express it.

*

There were many aspects of Don Bradman and I have done my best to depict them all, as I knew him. It was historically interesting that his dominance brought the bouncer prominently into the game to quell him (our Jack Gregory and Ted McDonald had been known to bounce a few). To me he was an enigma, for it was he who was responsible for the bouncer, although never into a leg-field. Of his batting there could be no possible doubt whatever and certainly no 'rivalry'. To those who would read of his fabulous career, I warmly recommend my friend Irvine Rosenwater's *Sir Donald Bradman* (Batsford, 1978) which was compiled in a manner reminiscent of one of Bradman's huge scores.

England adored him and bore no resentment against him for what he did to the country's bowlers. He was, if anything, even more popular there than in his native Australia. He was cheered to the echo whenever he appeared on a ground, and the people's faces lit up as if they had seen a miracle when they recognized him in the street. He was seen for the last time on an English field at Lord's in 1948 and thousands stood on the field for him to make an almost Royal appearance on the Australian balcony. But he never came again nor was seen there in flannels. There comes a time when the Pavilion swallows up all players for the last time, but the thousands at Lord's did not comprehend that Bradman would come no more. That seemed unbelievable.

· 10 ·

The Victor Trumper
of Writing

I received many letters from Neville Cardus. From his last residence in London – 112 Bickenstall Mansions, Baker Street – he wrote me this quite typical example:

My dear Jack,
It was a great pleasure to get your letter this morning, a morning of rain and incipient winter, with cricket far away. Frankly, I didn't enjoy English cricket last summer; too much standardization, not enough individual identity. Your Australian boys, especially Lillee and Marsh, brought back a flavour of the old gutso and involvement in *cricket*. I loved our evening together, and only wish we could have seen much more of each other. We are on the same wave-length; we share the same vintage humour and experience. We have been friends for nearly *forty* years! In fact, you are the only man for whom I have acted as best man at a wedding. [Neville was a little off the pitch here. My best man was Frank Conway – Neville proposed the toast at our wedding.] Also you are just about my favourite writer on cricket. I am happy, then, to have your assurance you are really going to get into an autobiography. I am certain you will produce a book to be cherished. And I shall be proud to write the preface to it. So keep at it – every day, even if you turn out only five hundred words. The great thing is continuity of rhythm and mood . . . and remember me to all the boys

in the Cricket Club in George Street and to everybody who remembers me. And, of course, give my love to the beauteous Philippa. Again, Jack, warm thanks for the lovely evening you gave me here. Look after yourself – and God bless,

Ever,
Neville.

Neville Cardus was romantic in everything he did and wrote. I first met him in Perth in 1936, on his first visit to Australia, but I had corresponded with him for many years before that. One of the great joys of working at the Sydney *Guardian* had been to discover in our file room the *Manchester Guardian* and the lovely, lyrical works of 'Cricketer'. I devoured every word he wrote, never thinking that some day he would become one of my greatest friends.

I remember writing to him for the first time in 1926 and, spare my blushes, it was a critical letter. He hadn't thought much of the batting ability of Jack Ryder, then with Herby Collins's 1926 side in England, and waxed critical of him. I was prompted to write to Neville, saying how often Neville had criticized his own men, Hallows and Makepeace, and suggesting that Ryder could certainly smite the ball. Neville undoubtedly realized my youth but, possibly recognizing also my enthusiasm, answered me in the nicest terms and invited me to write again. I did so repeatedly over the years and we built up a very strong friendship. He wrote the foreword to my first book, *Cricket Crisis* and he did me proud. I threw into that book just about every piece of poetry I knew and Neville, in a neat comment upon such presumption, wrote wryly that he would have to look to his laurels.

There is a book published by John Murray called *The Lyttelton–Hart-Davis Letters* which gave me immense pleasure. It abounds with rare stories in the letters of the two friends which were obviously written with a view to publication. George Lyttelton, one of the famous English cricketing family, tells how he first tried to induce Cardus into a correspondence with him. Neville would not rise to the bait and I can understand why. George Lyttleton was a cricket enthusiast but not such a one as to attract Cardus to swop letters with him. Cardus wanted 'characters' who had something to offer beyond the pleasantries of the game, not somebody who indulged in the usual guff. Cardus liked those who had tales to spin and who, in turn, would listen to his. I don't suggest that I fitted into that pattern but, as he wrote, we had been friends for over forty years. I think he liked my audacity in writing to him from far-off Australia and he continued to be a faithful correspondent. 'There is no transaction which offers stronger temptation to sophistication and fallacy than epistolary intercourse,' runs a quotation from Dr Johnson. Innumerable letters from Neville Cardus are among my cricket treasures and he never failed to give me confidence, support and advice, suggesting books I should read for refreshers.

*

I once termed Neville the Victor Trumper of the cricket writing world and he thanked me for the compliment, saying he knew no greater one. As with runs from Trumper's bat, words just flowed from Neville's pen. I only once knew him stumped for a word. That was when the irrepressible Sid Barnes said to him in Brisbane: 'Eh, Neville, you and I write alike. What about me putting in a carbon for you one day and you doing the same for me the next? There's no need for us both to come down here every day.'

Cardus was a self-taught writer from the libraries of Manchester and he had the wit to study the styles of the great writers of the newspaper on which he worked with so much zeal. Many have tried to ape Cardus; none successfully. I don't think he was ever a good cricketer, just a very keen one. Once in 1936 I was batting in a Perth net when a ball, bowled by Neville, came over from the adjoining one. But no matter what his cricketing skill, he knew the game intimately. He had a love and 'feel' for it, possessed by few internationals. His knowledge of every facet of the game did not confine him, as it did so many, to a few gibberish phrases that many who cover cricket learn to bleat and repeat in the hope that they will get them by. He knew what was happening in the middle and had the lucid, limpid English to tell all about it. Most importantly, he knew how cricketers talked and he had the imagination to put appropriate words into their mouths.

He imagined conversations on the field. He never heard them, naturally, but he imagined situations and put the right words into his actors. He wrote once that for days he carried the bruise on his shins from a stroke played by Victor Trumper in his beautiful innings at Old Trafford in 1905, the ball scudding under the ropes where Cardus sat as a youngster. It might have happened but I would not be surprised if it didn't. Neville always allowed himself latitude in writing or telling his stories. I often wonder about the opening tale he tells, in his brilliant auto-biography, of his aunt and her activities. It could well not be true but that wouldn't concern Neville: it was a good story that gave him pleasure in writing, and that was the main thing with him.

He had the newspaper gumption to go to the south of England and be the only press-man on hand when Armstrong's team suffered its first and only defeat in England in 1921, although he wouldn't have had to see play to write about it. He knew every detail about the players and could write two columns at the drop of an ink-blob. Some of his best stories were written of games he had never seen.

*

I adored Cardus. Just to be in his company, chatting and laughing away, was bliss. I could feel my whole being light up when I saw him at Lords, with his brolly hooked over his arm and ready to bring it into sweeping action to illustrate one of his points or the deeds of the great batsmen of the past, cutting bowlers into small pieces. He would ape all the characters he spoke about. People around him never bothered Neville: he had his stories to tell and demonstrate, and bystanders might have been in another country. He would fall into their dialect when speaking of the men from his original north. He loved Archie MacLaren and was at his best when maintaining how that great Lancastrian would have reacted to bodyline had he seen all those men on the leg-side. 'Hi, Joe,' Neville would have MacLaren calling out to Darling, the Australian captain. 'What are you doing with all these men sitting on top of me on the leg-side? Take them away, Joe, take them away and let us get on with the game. None of your silly bloody nonsense, Joe.' Towards the end of his days he took little relish in watching what he called pedestrian cricketers. Nobody enjoyed his stories more than Cardus himself. He would cup a hand to his mouth and laugh behind it, his eyes sparkling behind his glasses, while his shoulders shook in merriment. Indeed, his whole frame would enter into the joke.

In the sixties I invited him to lunch with the Bedser twins at the East India and Sports Club in St James's Square. Neville came and dominated the meeting – no easy thing to do, as the twins are seldom lost for a word. At the end of the lunch I walked with Cardus towards Piccadilly and bade him goodbye. As he strode off down the street, his lips pursed in some tune, I looked after him sorrowfully, thinking I might well not see him again. But, luckily, he was on hand for several more trips and many more letters, though I did just miss seeing him again in 1975 when he died, aged eighty-six.

In 1972 I spent some most enjoyable hours with him in the Long Room at Lord's. 'My goodness,' he said, looking at his watch, 'I should, at this very moment, be keeping an appointment in the City.' We made extensive arrangements for our dinner date. He was to be my guest and we were to meet in Baker Street, where he lived. Nothing could go wrong. I arrived early, thinking he just might be there. The appointed time arrived and still there was no sign of him. I walked up and down in some perturbation. Had something happened to him, had he been taken ill? I now began to walk about in some distress. It was inconceivable that anything could go wrong, our arrangements had been so definite. Then, on an impulse, I looked inside the restaurant and there was my guest, sitting by himself at the table. I was so relieved to see him that I hadn't the heart to tell him he had broken every detail of our meeting. It was my dinner but Neville took it over completely. We were the last diners to leave. What matter if I knew all his stories, many times over? He got such relish in the telling and to listen to him was pure enjoyment. He insisted I tell several of my stories, which he had heard often enough before. He loved the one about Charlie Macartney telling me, when we opened an innings together once, that he always aimed the first ball at the bowler there (tapping his forehead) as the bowler didn't like it, it rattled him; and he rocked in delight when I told of the time I was felled at Birmingham and Bradman called from cover, 'Catch it, catch it!' in his high-pitched voice.

Neville had a deep admiration for Bradman and Macartney but he was never too starry-eyed to not know they were only human. He could look below the surface in most people and see their foibles and mannerisms. He told and re-told the story of Macartney coming down to breakfast on a sunny morning in his London hotel, the day a Test was to begin at Lord's, rubbing his hands together and saying: 'I feel sorry for the poor cove who has to bowl at me today.' And it was so. Charlie made ninety-nine in two hours and forty minutes.

There will never be another Neville Cardus just as there will never be another Victor Trumper. Cardus was a very modest man, though no encourager of one who had nothing to offer him. In his writings he was more than kind to me, and told me how he had made me one of the heroes of his book *Australian Summer*. I promised him once (I must often have bored him in the middle) that I would plan an innings especially for him in England in 1938 even though I trusted neither the pitches nor myself. However at Lord's one day (against MCC) I let myself go and really played my shots, making a century in some twenty minutes over even time. When I saw Neville, I told him that innings had been for him. 'I didn't see it.' said Neville blandly, 'I went home early.'

Neville had a soft spot for that Mancunian man of poetry, Francis Thompson, who died before he won fame. Like Neville, Thompson was self-educated in the libraries of the city in which he lived (Neville taught himself German) but he finished up one of those sorry derelicts who live along the London Embankment and come out of their hide-aways for the midnight soup hand-out. Thompson sold matches

and newspapers on the kerb. MCC appreciated Thompson
and once invited him to Lord's. He couldn't go: he had no
socks at the time!

*

Cardus never sought the opinion or support of former
players, as so many do before they begin writing their piece.
He never 'milked' others but wrote from his own knowledge
and experience. He was humorous and ironic, and depicted
characters so well. I should think of all those he loved and
admired, none stood higher than Emmott Robinson, whom
I never saw but imagine to have been a typically tough
Yorkshire man of steel and no nonsense. Neville described
him thus:

'He was a grizzled, squat, bandy-legged Yorkshireman,
all sagging and loose at the braces in private life, but on
duty for Yorkshire he was liable at any minute to
gather and concentrate his energy into sudden and
vehement leaps and charges and scuffles. He had
shrewd eyes, a hatchet face and grey hairs, many of
them representing lbw appeals that had gone against
him. I imagine that he was created one day by God
scooping up the nearest acre of Yorkshire soil at hand,
then breathing into it and saying "Now, lad, tha's
called Emmott Robinson and tha can go on with new
ball at t'pavilion end." Emmott cherished the new ball
dearly; he would carry it between overs in person to
the next bowler needing it after himself; and he would
contain it in the two palms of his hands shaped like a
sacred chalice. If some ignorant novice unnecessarily
threw the new ball along the earth, Emmott gave him a
look of wrath and pain. He was not a great cricketer in
technique; but by passion and taking thought he
became so. But for me he will be remembered for the
Yorkshire stuff in him. He had no use for the flashing
bat school, "brighter cricket" and all such nonsense.
He dismissed it with one good word: "Swashbuckle,"
he called it. Life had taught him to take no risks.'

Neville described how, on a cold, wet Bradford evening, a Yorkshire club committee-man was hurrying along when Emmott emerged from the fog, carrying a black portmanteau.

'Hey, good afternoon, Mr Houldsworth,' he said. 'Ah'm pleased to meet you.'

'Good evening, Emmott, How are you?' Neither had seen the other since summer.

'Hey,' said Emmott, 'Ah'm a bit poorly, Mr Houldsworth. Ah've got a pain.' He indicated a place in his stomach. Mr Houldsworth expressed anxiety.

'Now listen, Emmott,' he said, 'you mustn't neglect it. Go to the hospital. Find out what it is. You needn't worry about expense, if any is incurred. The committee will see to that.' Emmott pondered.

'Well, maybe you're right, Mr Houldsworth. It's been hurting me weeks now. Maybe Ah will try t'hospital. But ...' he paused, then announced decisively, once and for all, 'Ah'm 'aving no knife.'

Neville wrote that in time Robinson was obliged to go into retirement from first-class cricket and it was sad to see him passively looking on if Yorkshire happened to get into trouble. After he had been absent from the side for a year or two, some mishap unexpectedly deprived Yorkshire of two men at the beginning of the second day of a Lancashire–Yorkshire match; and Emmott was requisitioned as one of the substitutes; there, once again, we saw him taking the field against the ancient enemy on an August Bank Holiday. He had not been in the field five minutes before he yapped out a violent appeal for lbw. He was standing at backward-point and nobody appealed with him, not even the bowler, who was George Macaulay. The umpire who dismissed the appeal was the old Derbyshire cricketer, Arthur Morton. 'Not out,' he said decisively, and added, 'An' look 'ere, Emmott, tha's not even playin' in this match – so keep tha bloody mouth shut.' The Yorkshire team without him was never the same again.

*

Neville wrote too of Rhodes, the bowler, who went to work in devious ways. Nobody heard Rhodes appealing except the umpires (seemingly, a Yorkshire habit: Hedley Verity used to put his hand to his mouth and echo his appeal back to the umpire). Of Rhodes, Cardus said he 'had a throaty voice and the quiddity of him was expressed by the brass stud he wore in his cricket shirt. I would often come across Wilfred in my English travels. Ruddy of face, he was then blind and would look out across the field with unblinking, unseeing eyes. He would sit with cronies who would "tell" the match to him but he needed no telling of a good shot. He knew by the sound of ball on bat. "That were good stroke," he'd say. He had a deep admiration of Don Bradman. ... Rhodes lived in the Golden Age; he was the greatest slow bowler in the world when he was a youth. He bowled against Trumper, Ranji and Maclaren but he kept his head in spite of them. In conversation with him I once had occasion to deplore that in modern years the square-cut was seldom to be seen, much to the loss of the game's brilliance. He unhesitatingly answered, 'Well, it never were a business stroke . . .'

Neville wrote of how, against Australia at the Oval in 1902 when Rhodes went in last for England with 15 runs needed to win, he and George Hirst, another Yorkshireman, got them. The story goes that Hirst met Rhodes coming out and said, 'Wilfred, we'll get them in singles.' 'It was the most unnecessary caution,' wrote Neville, 'ever given a Yorkshireman, young or old. And it was at the Oval that Rhodes ended his Test match career in August 1926; he played a big share in winning the rubber for England. As he grew older, he naturally lost some of his spin. But, as he informed me more than once: "If batsman thinks ball's spinnin', then it is spinnin'."'

Of Rhodes, Cardus says he wrote one of the best pieces of prose of his life: 'Flight was his secret, flight and the curving line, now higher, now lower, tempting, inimical; every ball like every other ball, yet somehow unlike, each over in collusion with the others, part of a plot. Every ball a decoy, a spy sent out to get the lie of the land; some balls simple, some complex, some easy, some difficult; and one of them – ah, which? – the master ball.' That could well have been written of Clarrie Grimmett also. It was Neville who wrote that delicious line about Bertie Oldfield: 'He stumped one quietly and gracefully, the ball in one hand, an apology in the other.'

*

I have taken the liberty of quoting my great friend at length, in tribute to his memory and for many other reasons, to show how brilliant cricket writing can be. He would have liked to be quoted by me and, furthermore, his style of writing, his lovely expressive manner, should be read and studied by all who love the game and would write of it.

It is interesting to recall again the piece on Rhodes. It typifies the very art of bowling, craft against craft. In his later years, in conversation, he told me he rarely went to cricket. The multiplicity of seamers, fast bowlers with long runs and the like nauseated him. And he could have written little of the conversation and mannerisms of present players. I sat in the sun one day, near the Long Room, at an ordinary county match and I declare that as the players filed out beside me I heard two in earnest conversation about the City. 'I see,' said one, 'that the market was most "iffy" yesterday.' Such an attitude would have driven Cardus speechless, and he was not often that, praise the Lord.

He pondered on what true Yorkshiremen like Rhodes and Robinson would have thought of Sutcliffe, who conducted himself like a lord wherever he played cricket. His immaculate hair was vaselined down and I can hear again his imperious and euphonius 'Wait thar,' as he advised caution to his partner, the call suddenly developing into the broadest Yorkshire as he scented danger and fell into his best Pudsey dialect: 'Ee, noah. Go back, go back!'

Neville could see the 'times a changing'. The advent into cricket, and into the Yorkshire XI of all places, of Herbert Sutcliffe was a sign of those times. The old order was not changing, it was going, the pole was fall'n; young boys and girls level now with men; captains of cricket henceforth called 'skipper' by all self-respecting professionals, never 'sir'. Our Sutcliffes and Hammonds obviously have their tailors in Saville Row, have taken us far far beyond echoes of Billy Barnes and his rough horny-handed company of paid cricketers of the eighties and nineties – savages born too soon to benefit from Mr Arnold Forster's acts of education.

It was Billy Barnes who turned up late and more than tipsy at Lord's when Nottingham were playing Middlesex; but to prevent scandal – for he was a famous man and beloved by the crowds – his captain sent him in as usual, first wicket down. And Billy scored a hundred and more in two hours, banging the ball everywhere, powerful, safe, magnificent. Still, discipline is discipline, and behaviour must be attended to, so when the Notts captain returned to Trent Bridge he felt it was his bounden duty to report Barnes to his committee, composed mainly of Midland lords, squires and county notables. Barnes was called before them and solemnly reprimanded. He had disgraced Notts cricket, and at Lord's too. Billy listened patiently, and when they had finished, he spoke:

'Well, your lordships, Ah can only say Ah'm sorry, reight sorry, that Ah am. But begging your lordships' pardons – if Ah can go down to Lord's and get drunk and mek a century 'fore lunch, then I think it ud pay t'Notts committee to get mi drunk afore every match – begging your lordships' pardon, o' course.' Cardus observed that the modern professional cricketer does not get drunk at Lord's or often get a century there, or anywhere else, before lunch. Perhaps they are too busy thinking of what's going on in the City!

Reverting to Sutcliffe: he played many innings against Australia and scored many, many runs in his imperious manner. He was not often put off, as witness the day in Sydney when he played a ball from Bill O'Reilly hard into his stumps and the bails didn't come off. While we fieldsmen were going through the agonies of injustices and O'Reilly was offering up a few choice words, Herbert looked around at us all as much to say: 'Pray, what is all this fuss about?' He was then only a few and made 194. He loved the hook and I caught him out at Bramall Lane in 1938 at fine leg on the fence, in his very last of many productive innings against Australia.

*

I can't write of Neville's musical knowledge. (Roy Plomley once asked me on to his *Desert Island Discs* but I felt like a fraud.) In that period when he was in Australia, Cardus would play an hour of music on the ABC of a Sunday evening, and I never missed it. I would think that was the most enjoyable period of his life. The young female music-lovers made much fuss of him and he gloried in their adulation. He adored Keith Miller as a man and a cricketer. They lived in the same block of Sydney flats just after Keith was married. Keith was almost as great a music-lover as Cardus and they would compete with each other, whistling a tune and defying the other to name it. Whereas cricket bored him towards the end of his life, music never did and he was rightfully proud of his reputation in those circles. He learned his music by hard study and didn't like it when people thought he was better known as 'Cricketer' and Neville Cardus than Cardus the music critic. Hamilton Harty once wrote him a furious letter about his use of a stop-watch when attending a Halle Concert. 'Such mechanical aids,' wrote Harty, 'might be useful to a critic of Lancashire's batting but Beethoven and I deserve a judgement based on musical knowledge, not a time-test.' Neville replied: 'I do not attend your or anybody else's concerts supported by a stop-watch. But I must warn you, as man to man, that if you conduct the Ninth Symphony in the near future I shall bring with me – less for critical purposes than for those of personal convenience – not a stop-watch but an alarm clock.' It was impossible to get the last word with Cardus.

11

Laughing from Spinners' Valhalla

They don't come better as man, friend and slow bowler than Clarence Victor Grimmett, whom we put to rest in Adelaide in May 1980, aged eighty-eight. Attending his funeral were Sir Donald Bradman, often his Test and South Australian skipper; C. E. Pellew, almost a year his junior and one of only two survivors from the famous Australian Imperial Force side of the year after the First World War; Bill O'Reilly who, with Grimmett, formed the best spinning pair ever in Test cricket (they were basically leg-spinners); Len Darling and myself, two contemporaries of the 'Old Fox' as we knew him in his later Test days.

Clarrie Grimmett made tours of England in 1926, 1930 and 1934, and his biggest upset in life was being dropped from the 1938 tour. He did not make the first of his thirty-seven Test appearances until he was thirty-three and thought in 1938 that he still had another English tour in him. So did O'Reilly, who never forgave the selectors for dropping his mate. Darling may have had more than a little to do with Grimmett's omission. On one occasion against Victoria the Old Fox wanted a man on the straight-hit fence, but Bradman disagreed with him and wouldn't give him what he wanted. Twice Darling lofted him to the straight-hit outfield, a stroke he would not have attempted had a fieldsman been there. In between overs Bradman said to Darling: 'I think the old man's finished, isn't he?' Darling readily agreed because he didn't want Grimmett on. So Grimmett, much to his disappointment, didn't go to England again, and the very next Australian summer it was added gall to him when he was tossed the ball by Bradman in preference to Ward, who had beaten him to England. Grimmett took a record seventy-five Sheffield Shield wickets. There was still plenty of spinning cunning in him.

*

There's no place in modern cricket for his type now, although I feel bold enough to say he would get a manifold crop of wickets, because batsmen would be taken by surprise. Clarrie was born in New Zealand but filtered through NSW and Victoria before settling in Adelaide. He perfected his art on a pitch made in his back garden, and with the assistance of a fox terrier which he trained to bring the ball back to him. He was always experimenting with spin; in his prime he could have been awakened at midnight and still gone straight out to his pitch and put the ball on a sixpence (now, like spin, a thing of the past).

He was the first to use and perfect the 'flipper', bowled with a leg-break action but flipped with the fingers so that it scudded straight through and fast. Richie Benaud, Cecil Pepper and Bruce Dooland were later to acquire it. Succeeding batsmen told one another 'It's easy enough to pick. You'll hear his fingers flick.' Clarrie soon dealt with that. He flicked his left hand and bowled his leg-break with the other.

One day, on the old Wanderers ground in Johannesburg, Chud Longton hit O'Reilly for one of the biggest sixes ever. Clarrie waggishly sidled up to Bill and told him all about it. The light was very dark at the time, so dark that I borrowed a box of matches from the umpire and lit one over the stumps to show the next batsman the way in. Next over, Langton hit Grimmett for a huge six that landed out in the adjoining railway goods yard. O'Reilly couldn't get near Grimmett to tell *him* all about it: he went to cover and stayed there. Clarrie was a deep and long thinker. He would never bowl at one in the practice nets on tour: he never believed in giving the batsman a look at his wiles. Fielding up close for him and O'Reilly, I could see the furrowed and creased brows as the batsmen escaped from one end only to run into the other and similar trouble. There was no relief for them.

Grimmett considered himself a master of all spin, even at tennis and table-tennis. Stan McCabe used to challenge him at table-tennis on board ship and pull his leg unmercifully. McCabe would deliberately mis-read the spin and go the other way. Grimmett would double up in laughter. 'You old fox, Grum,' would say McCabe. He was a better bowler in England than Australia. He pushed the ball through faster. As Cardus put it, where Mailey bowled his slows like a millionaire Grimmett bowled his like a miser. His foxiness was best shown against Philip Mead of Hampshire. Mead had a strange ritual before every ball. He would left, right, left right, with his feet thrice and then turn to the square-leg umpire and touch his cap to him. Grimmett threw his ritual off-balance by wheeling quickly and bowling. It made Mead uncomfortable.

*

Neville Cardus spoke once of meeting him in Rundle Street when the war was waxing hot. Neville said what a terrible thing the war was, what it was doing to civilization and culture. 'I agree with you,' said Clarrie, 'but it is not that I am thinking so much about. I have found a new spinning ball and now I will never be able to exploit it.' He was then in his fifties.

He was almost blind near his finish but still came to the Adelaide Oval to see his old friends. He and O'Reilly would have a drink for old time's sake and though, as a batsman, I represented the type for whom they had no brief, they would invite me to join them. It was in the bar there that I heard Clarrie tell his last joke. He was playing in a club game and an umpire waited for him on the field to say how proud he was to be standing next to his great hero. Grimmett made sure he bowled at that umpire's end. More than that, he said he would run through his repertoire just for the umpire. 'Now, I'll bowl my leg-break for you,' said Clarrie, and, 'now I'll bowl a flighted ball.' Then 'Now the flipper and I'll get him leg before.' He bowled his flipper, hit the batsman on the leg and, turning around to appeal, saw the umpire appealing himself. That was one wicket the Old Fox got!

There wasn't a single member of the new generation of cricketers at his funeral to pay homage. Something tangible, I sensed, had gone out of the game. Immortals seem to count no more; names – unless there's money in them – mean not a thing. But Grimmett's name will live for ever more with those who know and appreciate the real verities of the game and value them. I can see him again, slumping to the ground and chewing a blade of grass when he got a batsman out. No back-slapping, no jumping up and down around him, no slobbering. 'I thought I would get him,' would say Clarrie modestly, nice little man.

There's bound to be a pitch in Valhalla and Clarrie will have been made right welcome. My bet is that he has already got Dr W. G. Grace lbw with a leg-break that was a 'flipper'. He once got Don Bradman's wicket quickly in the Richardson–Grimmett testimonial match in Adelaide and went up to Vic Richardson, expecting warm words of praise. Instead he got a blast. 'You've ruined our afternoon gate,' Vic told him. 'You have just robbed us of a thousand pounds.'

12

A Man Called Billy
– and Other Names

There were hundreds of press secretaries to the Right Honourable William Morris Hughes. They came and went like leaves in an autumn gale, and it was not until after they had left him that any of them had a kind word to say for the cranky, irascible, ruthless, gnome-like Welshman. He was a notable Australian in many ways and our country may never realize what it owed to him at Versailles when he fought the United States President, Woodrow Wilson, over the Japanese being allowed to infiltrate the Pacific Islands and, particularly, New Guinea. He threatened Wilson that if he didn't get his way on this he would come into the southern states of America and electioneer against him.

'What right have you got to speak to me like that?' asked Wilson.

'I speak on behalf of sixty thousand dead Australians,' snapped back the little Welshman. One other tremendous thing he did was to begin the Australian Navy. He shook everybody and everything up. Had Wilson had his way the Pacific war, and Australia, would have been vastly different.

Old Bill, as we called him behind his back, in addition to many other fruity names, was a crafty politician to his finger-tips. He revealed this early in life when he managed the affairs of the Wharf Labourers' Union, often fleeing from ugly scenes in which wharfies who opposed him wanted to flay him with their handling hooks; often he was chased back to the very door of his home, then at Balmain in Sydney. He showed his wiles best when he was secretary of a junior cricket association. He would often tell me, in the three tumultuous months in 1943 when I was with him as press secretary, how good he was as a cricketer. His team got into the Grand Final and Bill, as secretary, had to inform the opposition where the match was to be played. Bill didn't think much of his side's chances and, as secretary, sent the opposition the wrong information about the ground. When they didn't turn up at the proper ground, Bill claimed the match on a forfeit. He would have seen nothing wrong in this, believing it to have been sound politics. That is how he played the political game. No wonder he was turfed out of almost every political party he joined. He could have given tips to Machiavelli.

He knew many tough days, and nights, but probably none worse than during the Second Conscription Campaign in 1917. Bitterness and much sectarianism raged throughout Australia. Billy had lost one referendum and didn't mean to lose another. He had security guards travelling with him and conspired with them one night, seeking sympathy votes, to stage a mock assassination attempt on him as he came into his home at Wahrronga. At the last moment, Billy called it off. 'You —s,' he said, 'might be inclined to shoot too straight.'

He had a long memory; he knew many things about various politicians and never hesitated to throw his brickbats in Parliament. He was holding forth with great effect in Melbourne one day (when Parliament was there rather than at Canberra) and Member after Member rose to deny his charges. 'I deny it, I deny it, I deny it!' they yelled. Billy, who was a consummate actor, poised with one hand cupped to ear. The Speaker asked whether the Right Honourable gentleman had concluded his speech. 'No, Mr Speaker,' said Billy, 'I'm merely waiting for the cock to crow.' It brought the House down.

He was a magnificent spinner of yarns, especially of his early days in Australia when he came from London to North Queensland as a junior-teacher. He spent his first few nights in Brisbane, sleeping out under the stars in the Botanical Garden. He went north and west in his profession but soon found that teaching was not for him. He claimed he had gone deaf after sleeping on the ground in a heavy frost, but he heard much more than he admitted and when it suited him. Particularly was this so when some tart things were being said behind his back about his driving of a big Dodge car from Canberra to Sydney.

Billy was so minute that he had to be propped up by cushions behind the wheel to reach it. Pat Romans, his typist over many years, would sit in front with him and, as he would insist on driving on the wrong side of the road, she would warn him when a car was coming the opposite way. Old Bill would swing his car so sharply that all in the back, usually Bachli, his masseur, and his press secretary, if he couldn't escape on to the train as I used to, would be flung wildly across the seat. Outside Goulburn one rainy night Pat nudged old Bill and said: 'Mr Hughes, I'm afraid Morris is going to be sick.' 'Bloody cissy,' snarled old Bill. However, he pulled up, his press secretary got out and was violently ill. Then Bill drove on to Sydney; his press secretary had to trudge back in the rain to Goulburn and catch a train. Keith Waller, who later became Secretary of the Department of Affairs, and Percy Deans, were the only two press secretaries Hughes had of whom he spoke at all well. All the rest of us were 'blithering idiots', including the chap who walked back to Goulburn; he was Morris West, now one of Australia's most famous authors.

*

During my time with Billy I was fortunate in many things but for two in particular I will always be grateful. First, I was seconded to him from the army, so he couldn't sack me. The reason I was put with Billy was to curb the venom of his broadcasts. John Curtin, the Prime Minister, was getting a lot of flack from General Douglas MacArthur about Billy, who used to go on the air each week and give the American particular stick: in Billy's estimation, MacArthur was a dud who could do nothing right. The general, who was a very vain man, tired of this abuse and told Curtin that if he didn't shut the little so-and-so up he, Curtin, could get another Allied Commander for the Pacific and pretty quick too. Australia at that time was leaning heavily on the Americans for everything and General MacArthur would have been wrapped in cotton wool, so essential was he to the Australian scene. As luck would have it, Billy did tone down his mouthings somewhat, but I had absolutely nothing to do with it. The Old Master would scribble all his own words, standing up and writing at his table before giving it to Miss Romans to type. Luckily for me, he never found out why I was put with him or else there would have been another war; Billy would have torn Canberra and me to pieces in his fury.

I think the reason why he so hated MacArthur was because the general had dared to criticize Australian militiamen in action at Milne Bay. Anybody in a Digger's slouch hat was sacrosanct to old Bill. The militiamen who went to Milne Bay were in adjacent huts to us at Ingleburn military camp and were being drilled in a hurry, night and day. They were not ready for that tough action. Militiamen were often derided in the war by older soldiers, a few of them back from the Middle East with headquarter honours thick upon them, and these younger men in khaki were often denigrated and indeed even assaulted by some others. Insults were hurled at the 'Chockos', or Chocolate Soldiers, as they were known, and this in spite of the fact that Australia's two greatest soldiers, Monash and Blamey, were both 'chockos'. In the Second World War, there was a marked division between Duntroon men – those who came into the army as a profession – and those who rose through militia units. The winning of a Victoria Cross against the Japanese at Bourgainville by the late Frank Partridge, a militiaman, knocked that feeling on the head.

So Hughes let fly at the noble general. 'You know,' he said to me one day 'that bloody MacArthur chap. All he's done in life is lose the bloody Philippines.' That was a harsh judgement, but where Americans were concerned Bill was immensely harsh. Frank Browne ('He's an odd bloke,' Bill said about him) in his excellent book, *A Man Called Billy*, tells well the story of how Billy, as Prime Minister, sailed into anybody during the First World War who dared to oppose him. And he was never one to mince words.

Another time I was lucky was when I turned up at the Sydney Central railway station and found I had stupidly left my wad of train tickets at home. We were off to

Melbourne where Bill was to support a Loans appeal, but I would have needed support had he known what I had done about my ticket. I took my case straight to the Station Master. He told me that if I brought him my parcel of tickets later, he would ring down the line and make it right for me to pass at all ticket scrutinies and security blocks, and this at a time when the war was at its tightest. 'My goodness,' said he, 'Mr Hughes will blow my express off the line if he knows this.' I agreed, and I will always remember that Station Master with deep gratitude. He performed miracles for me, but the greatest of all was that Billy never found out. He would have loved to get his teeth into that and me.

One evening, during that Loan meeting, he had given Miss Romans, Bachli and me the most awful bucketing. He had roared and reviled us in his loudest voice, full of insults. Then he led us into the ornate dining-room of the Windsor Hotel and observed, in a friendly aside to me: 'I used to be a good cricketer, you know.' Little old ladies, who adored him, looked at him as he took his seat and murmured: 'What a lovely old man.' If only they had heard him five minutes before.

Bill would spend his Sunday afternoons on the Domain, Sydney's Hyde Park Corner, among the spruikers and it was there he met another brilliant orator, W. A. Holman, and also George Beeby, whom my father defeated in the 1914 NSW elections. Hughes and Holman began the Australian Labour Party. Billy was working very hard to become an orator and at his little Balmain shop would often take the floor, his squeaky voice resounding in the street outside.

In the first Sydney Eisteddfod in the 1880s, Bill entered for the impromptu speech section. As his name was called each competitor had to draw his subject out of a hat. Bill drew 'Myself'. He was hoping for one of the big topics of the day but he began by telling his audience that he was unlucky. Had he drawn the subject of the Woman Next Door, he told them, he would have been happy – there was enough talk about her for him to speak for an hour. That was the wit which was always to distinguish him; and Sir Henry Parkes, later the Father of Foundation, presented him with the first prize of a guinea and a blue ribbon. Bill, the orator, was launched.

Hughes became Prime Minister at fifty-one in 1915, after Fisher had cracked under the strain of repercussions about the slaughter at Gallipoli. He had studied law and become a barrister at thirty-six. Some thought he didn't have the constitution for the job of Prime Minister but Billy retaliated that had he possessed a constitution he would have been dead years ago. Yet, in his prime, he was a miserable specimen of a man. He was small, frail, bald, deaf and, because of his early hard days in the Australian bush, his digestion had been ruined. He had suffered in the Australian outback, almost starving to death on the track. By cycle, by buggy he traversed the bush, often being chased out of shearing sheds when he tried to organize unionists. Forsaking teaching, he came to Sydney and was in turn Shakespearean actor, knife grinder, umbrella mender, second-hand bookseller, and even posed as a cook. One day he took Pat Romans on a tour of the Wooloomooloo district and proudly pointed out the hotel where he started work as assistant cook at 4.30 each morning. There had been a huge vat into which all unused bread and such like were tossed and soaked. Bill's first job was to stand on a case beside the vat and fish with a net for mice and cockroaches that had fallen in during the night. At five o'clock the No. 1 cook would start work and toss in currents, milk, eggs and so on to make the hotel's *pièce de resistance*, 'Victoria Pudding', which, according to Bill, was tremendously popular and always eaten. Just as well the health inspector was not about, but Bill was very proud of his part in that culinary achievement. Queen Victoria might have had some thoughts about what was in her honour!

His first great triumph as Prime Minister came when he broke the monopoly which a German mining company in Frankfurt-am-Main had on Australian base metals. Thinking of post-war reprisals from the German firms, Australian companies were slow to make application to have their contracts annulled; moreover, the British Asquith government, even when thousands were being killed on French battlefields, had a policy of 'business as usual'. It urged Hughes to make haste slowly. He took no notice. He urged a retired metallurgist, John Higgins, to organize the metal trades and have Australian industries treat our ores.

The British Government, and some may have regretted it, invited him to England in 1916 and there he went with Mary and the baby, Helen, his pride and joy. When Britain went to war in 1914, most thought it would be over by the next Christmas. Hughes found it all unpleasant and he didn't think much of Asquith, whom he believed too 'perfectly civilized' for war. So brilliant were Hughes's speeches in their call for total war and an abandonment of 'business as usual' that the whole country responded to him. City after city gave him their freedom. Not since the days in 1757 when 'gold boxes' rained on the elder Pitt, says Browne, had the country seen the like.

The King invited him to Windsor Castle. He was cheered wherever he went. Newspapers paid tribute to him with leaders. A German newspaper commented: 'It shows the complete helplessness of England's cause that instead of Churchill, Lloyd George, French, Kitchener, from all of whom victory was expected, a loud-voiced man from the Antipodes is hailed as the saviour of the British Empire.'

Hughes sold wheat, he bought ships for Australia and all at a good price. Asquith tried to keep him from an Economic Conference in Paris and then tried to send him with no voice. Imagine that! Billy would have none of it and was such a success in Paris (the French loved him) that he returned a hero to London. He questioned the British command about the slaughter of so many Australians. He went up to the front line to see his troops. He spoke to them and had a few harsh words to say to the officers about the chaffing he thought he was getting from the troops in his rear. 'That's not our troops, Mr Hughes,' they told him, 'that's the German bombardment.'

In London the Australian troops mobbed him, put a slouch hat on his head and nicknamed him 'The Little Digger', which he loved. Every Anzac Day, 25 April, in Sydney, he would emerge from his office at the

Commonwealth Bank into Martin Place and stand at the
side while the march of Old Diggers filed by, many
breaking ranks to shake hands with him. One day Sir
Arthur Fadden went down and stood alongside him. Billy
wasn't pleased. 'This is my pitch, you know, brother,' he
said testily. 'Don't you think you ought to move further
down the street?' He was Prime Minister till 1923.

*

Old Bill was a sadist and gloried in terrifying people. He
had Miss Romans seconded to him and acted as if he owned
her. She was the daughter of George Romans, the chief
Hansard reporter in his time (and a good golfer who gave
me his copy of Abe Mitchell's book on golf). Old Bill would
expect Pat to spend her weekends at the Hughes' home, by
then at Lindfield. One night she was at the pictures at
Double Bay when a message was flashed on to the screen:
'Would Miss Romans ring Mr Hughes at once. It is urgent.'
The old villain wanted her to travel from Double Bay to
Lindfield and she did. All he wanted was a game of Chinese
checkers. 'It would not have been so bad had he not
cheated. He cheated at every game he played,' said Pat. He
certainly did at billiards.

Billy used to ring her to come up and give him his
medicine. He would not accept anything from Dame Mary,
his wife. Billy treated her shockingly and barely threw her a
word. She never went anywhere with him. Our staff knew
Dame Mary was a kleptomaniac. She couldn't help herself
and one of Pat's jobs was to return things Dame Mary had
taken. The Hughes family is now all gone and I see nothing
wrong in stating this about her. It was one of the loads Bill
had to carry.

After his daughter Helen died prematurely, Pat Romans
was his constant partner, though Frank Browne claimed in
his book that Dame Mary was a great comfort to Billy and
made life tolerable after his adored Helen died. Helen had
Queen Mary as a god-mother, and a trunk in the family
home at Lindfield was filled with clothes the Queen had
knitted for her. While she lived at Buckingham Palace,
Helen struck up a great and long friendship with the Irish
leader, Eamonn de Valera. They had met one day when she

was out walking and Helen felt sorry for him, believing he was lonely. He had come to London for talks on Home Rule. They corresponded for a long time in French. Helen was a rare beauty and Billy had a painting of her over his bed. 'However,' he would ask, 'did Mary and I produce a child like that?' She took ill in London and an operation was deemed imperative. Billy was away somewhere in Australia, electioneering, and couldn't be contacted. Stanley Melbourne Bruce, a former Prime Minister, was then High Commissioner in London and he gave permission for the operation. Helen died. Billy was inconsolable and always held it against Bruce.

A final word about Mr Bruce. I saw and much enjoyed the British television series on the abdication of King Edward but the portrayal in it of Mr Bruce was a calumny. He was more English than the English: he went to Cambridge, served in the Guards, always wore spats in Australia, and spoke with a cultured English accent. In the *Edward and Mrs Simpson* series he was depicted as a rough, tough Australian with the most pathetic Australian accent ever heard. When I did a lot of work for the BBC I always found it remarkable that everybody in that huge organization thought he could imitate my Australian accent. Most of them were woeful. The best of all, and perfect, were the two Ronnies. But the imitation of Bruce – horrific! One good thing is that Stanley Melbourne Bruce never lived to hear it.

*

Hughes was spinning a yarn in our room once to a fellow Member; he was at his best telling tales. This one had to do with nominations being called for his seat at Bradfield. The party was talking of getting young blood. Bill said how these chaps, all from the best schools, who came for the interview were well dressed, well spoken and were accompanied by their good-looking wives. 'And who have I got to set off against them?' wailed Bill. 'Only bloody old Mary.'

But there was one woman who worried him. He used to call her 'The Queen of Holland'. She was an evacuee from Java, as it was then, and she lived in Bill's constituency. She was a massive woman, towering over old Bill and she would give him stick. He used to be so worried when he knew she was about that he would get inside the wardrobe in his office and lock the door from the inside.

We all thought we could imitate the Master's voice. Artie Fadden and Alf Bachli were splendid and I thought I could do him well. At all events, one day I fooled Bachli. I got on the inter-com from Bill's room and barked: 'Is that you, Bachli?' and when Bach answered, 'Yes, Mr Hughes,' I knew I had him. 'I'll have another cup of tea, Bachli, and make it a bit stronger this time, will you?' 'Yes, Mr Hughes,' said Bach and bustled into the room a few minutes later with a steaming cup. His language steamed, too, when he knew he had been duped. It would have been bad luck had W.M.H. come into the room in the meantime but his staff were all good friends and hung together in adversity.

Bill had the habit of taking the sun in his back garden before he left for the city. He would sit in a chair in his underpants and dictate letters to Pat. 'It's no good you trying to see anything,' he would embarrass Pat by saying. 'There's nothing to see, anyway. They just look like a pair of ossified peanuts.'

He was always embarrassing Pat. He would take her out to lunch, up to Cahill's in Castlereagh Street, and make tart observations about the ladies and their hats that could be heard everywhere. He liked few people and disliked many. One man he took great exception to was Sir Percy Spender, possibly because he was Minister for the Army. Sir Percy went to visit Singapore and on to the Middle East. When he came back, according to Billy, all he could talk about was eating off golden plates in some sheikh's tent. 'That bloody Spender, you know,' said Billy, 'if he piddled on the Sphinx, he would think he was the source of the Nile.'

Such gems used to ripple from the Master's lips. One never knew what he would say next. Had he not been so cranky and irritable he would have been marvellous company. Arthur Fadden was in the room next door. He was friendly to me and I would often seek solace from him. 'It's no good, Mr Fadden,' I would whinge, 'I can't stick this old twerp any longer.' 'Come on,' would say Artie, 'you faced up to Larwood. You're not going to let this old so-and-so beat you, are you?' 'Larwood was different,' I'd say, 'he only came from in front of you. This chap comes from all round you at once.'

*

Bill disliked Mr Menzies with a hatred only he could muster, and he gave him no peace. In the Parliamentary dining-room one day, Mr Menzies was speaking to the Duke of Gloucester, then our Governor-General. The Duke asked him whether he had any problems. 'Here comes the biggest one now,' said Mr Menzies as Billy tottered into view.

Billy used to admire Eddie Ward. 'He's a fine type of man, that Ward, you know,' he would say. Billy admired anybody well built. When the going was even tougher than usual I would ring up Bill O'Reilly and say: 'You had better come down. The old bloke's being impossible again.' O'Reilly would always help out. Billy would look at him, click his teeth and say, admiringly: 'He's a fine type of man, you know.'

Anyone who knows the background of Canberra politics might think Alan Reid, the doyen of the Press Gallery, feared nobody; but Alan hated having to meet Billy. He quaked before him. He would um, ah, er and so on. One day he had to see Billy, when he was Leader, about a vote for the leadership. 'Look here, brother,' said Billy. 'The question of Jesus Christ as leader never arises in the midst of his apostles.' Another day when Billy wasn't Leader, we were waiting outside Mr (as he then was) Menzies's office, and Billy, passing by, addressed Alan. 'What's going on here?' Billy wanted to know, in his high voice. 'We are waiting to see the Leader,' said Alan. Billy pretended not to hear and barked in tones that could be heard as far as King's Hall: 'What?' 'We are waiting to see the Leader,' repeated Alan. Billy snorted. 'Him, the bloody leader!' he said. 'He couldn't lead a flock of homing pigeons.' One of the remarkable things about politics in my time in Canberra was the lack of loyalty in parties and, particularly, from Deputy Leaders to Leaders.

My near neighbour, Rupert Loof, who was Clerk of the Senate in less turbulent days, told me a Billy story that I messed up on the *Parkinson Show*, although I almost got it right. Billy was coming out of the Cabinet room, where he was in the process of arranging an intended Sugar Agreement. A mob of press-men converged on him. 'Mr Hughes,' they said, 'anything to tell us about sugar?' Billy was in his element. 'Oh, well,' he said, 'you see, the Arbitration Act . . .' 'No, no, Mr Hughes,' they clamoured. 'Sugar. Anything to tell us?' 'Well, the Navigation Act . . .' A burly press-man pushed in from the back. 'I'll make the old bastard hear,' he said. He cupped his hands to his mouth and roared: 'Mr Hughes, anything to tell us about sugar?' 'Oh well,' said Billy, enjoying it all, 'I have two things to say. In the first place, I am not an old bastard and in the second place, I have nothing to say at all about sugar.'

Doc Evatt, who did many such kind things, brought Bill back a hearing aid from the San Francisco conference in 1945, and the Country Party, up to its tricks, used to delight in putting blow flies in it. Billy used a hearing aid in Parliament and, when somebody was speaking he didn't care for, would have his machine make the most outrageous whistles and shrieks while he looked innocently ahead. He had a great habit in debate of pointing the fingers of his right hand. He had had some accident with the sinews and couldn't straighten his fingers.

He was incredible in that he never used glasses. Towards the end of his career he made one of his by then rare speeches one evening in the House, and one of his old cronies hurried after him down the lobby. 'Mr Hughes,' he said, 'I think it is wonderful. You don't use glasses at your great age.' Billy turned on him and raked him with blistering venom. 'Look here,' he said, 'I am bloody well deaf, you know: you don't bloody well want me to be blind, too, do you?'

*

It is the custom in King's Hall to hang paintings of Australian Prime Ministers. Billy, one of the least attractive of men, proved a hard fish to catch. Many artists tried to depict him but Billy was generally scathing of their efforts.

One, knowing the whip of Billy's tongue, was showing him his finished work and said, 'I hope I do you justice, Mr Hughes.' 'Ah, brother,' crackled old Billy, 'it's not justice we want, it's bloody mercy!' Near the portrait is a very good bust of him. When things were tough in the office Alf Bachli and I would go out and say a few well chosen words to it. It did help.

His photograph now rests on the Opposition side of Parliament House, among all the Labour leaders. Billy would have liked that and it was because of the kindness of a good man, Rex Connor, that it was put there. In fact, I think had Billy been asked he would have said he would have liked to die a Member of the Labour Party which he did so much to form and, indeed, to rend with his two Conscription referenda.

During the Second World War the Advisory War Council, of which Billy was a member, had had a tedious meeting in Melbourne at which nothing went right. The Pacific War was in a horrible mess and everybody was touchy. Billy tried to light a cigarette and the head of the match flew off into a mass of papers, private, confidential, highly secret. They caught alight. Billy leaned across and put his cigarette to the blaze. 'Any other silly —' he said, with an impish grin, 'would have lit another bloody match.' It broke the Advisory Council up. I apologize for so many rude words but one can't depict Blithering Blazes Billy without his colourful language. It wouldn't seem right.

This is a story Pat Romans told me that I didn't know before. On the night of the day that the Sydney Harbour Bridge was opened in 1932, Billy met Dr J. J. C. Bradfield, the designer of the bridge. The two girls, Helen and Pat Romans, were with the old-timers and the four set off to walk over the top of the span of the bridge. Height flummoxed the girls and they beat a retreat back to the pylon. But old Bill and Dr Bradfield kept going and got to the end of the span. And when they got there, they set out and walked back again. I find that delightful, two famous and aged Australians carefully picking their way over and back that immense height, holding on to the chain stretched in sections.

L

Sir Arthur Fadden made a dinner speech in 1950 to celebrate Billy's fifty years in Parliament. Artie played with the fact that although Billy belonged to the Labour Party, the Nationalists, the Liberals and the UAP, he had never been a member of Fadden's Country Party. The Welsh Wizard was sitting just near Artie. 'Blimey, brother,' he said, as he looked up with his elfish expression, 'a man has to draw the bloody line somewhere, you know.'

The afternoon in 1952 they put him to rest in Sydney at ninety, there was a blinding storm in Canberra. Hail pelted in over the hills, and the lightning and the thunder were staccatto and shattering. Frank McKenna, a top public servant who had served under Billy, telephoned Sir John Bunting, who had also known him. 'I say, John,' said Frank, 'you don't think the little bastard has come back already, do you?' It was a fair question. I'll bet somebody got a dressing-down as soon as he arrived anywhere.

· 13 ·

Sir Robert Menzies
and Me

How will history deal with Robert Gordon Menzies? Maybe it will claim he was a great statesman, maybe not, but no one will deny that he was an adroit politician, the best we have known in Australia. After being Prime Minister in the early period of the Second World War, after an immense schism in his own party which underwent several changes of name, he came back from backbench obscurity to reign as Prime Minister from 1949 to 1964, when he retired.

I knew him well, the best friend in high places I ever had. The game of cricket gave us a bond, of which he was not slow to avail himself when he wanted my opinion on happenings in the game; in my turn I, as a pressman, used to get background information from him to my great advantage.

Our first real contact was at Trent Bridge, Nottingham, in 1938 when I espied him sitting in a special grandstand, just over the ropes. Barnett, Hutton, Compton and company were giving us great punishment. He said my first remark to him was 'G'day.' It may well have been, in that off-hand manner Australians have, but I remember telling him that if he had any ideas I would be only too happy to convey them to our skipper, Don Bradman. 'It is not ideas you want, my boy,' he said chirpily, 'It's a miracle.' How right he was!

He thought my politics were Labour and he mildly berated me in his room once when I noted he had opened a building for a Finance Company in Sydney – I hoped he brought it luck as I had shares in the company. 'So,' he said, 'your politics are not mine but you try to take advantage of them.' 'Sir,' I replied, 'when a man has to live under a certain system, he has to take advantage of that system.' The biggest penalty a political journalist can suffer is to have his politics known, especially if he is unwise enough to show partiality in his writings or televising. Those who read and see jump to conclusions at the raising of an eyebrow – and with his dense eyebrows, Robert Gordon would have found life on television difficult.

I had a great liking for Sir Robert and his company, and a deep admiration for men like Curtin and, especially, Ben Chifley. Once when Prime Minister, Sir Robert declared he would love to have a man like Chifley in his Cabinet. He was most distressed the night he heard, during a function at Parliament House, of Chifley's death.

In politics, I was not one way or the other. I thought, like others, that politics was a dirty game and though I valued the comradeship of Members on both sides of the House, I never committed myself nor joined any party, as one or two of my colleagues unwisely did. During my long period in Parliament House, there were some I admired and many I didn't.

My mother came to Canberra on one occasion and, meeting her at the airport I also met Mr Menzies, as he then was. I introduced my mother. Ming, as we knew him behind his back, could be a little ponderous at times in his humour and he said to my mother, 'I suppose you are not proud of this chap!' In her loyalty to me, my mother gave Ming a terrific blast. I knew he meant to be humorous but she didn't. Anyway, she didn't think meeting him was one of the great events in her life. Ben Chifley she adored and I will not forget the look of adulation on her face when I took her in to meet him. As he shook hands he gave her a beaming smile. I left them together for a time.

While he was in power Sir Robert had a very good press, which for the most part, supported him solidly, especially the Packer press in Sydney which, if I may say so, supported him unctuously. Relations between politicians and press-men are always an interesting study. I was

attending one of John Curtin's press conferences one day
when he went off at a tangent and gave R. A. Henderson, General Manager of the *Sydney Morning Herald*, a
blast for something or other. Ross Gollan, then the *SMH*
political rep, summoned up his dignity and office patriotism.
'Mr Prime Minister,' he said, 'if you speak like that about
Mr Henderson, I will be forced to withdraw from this
conference and take the other members of the *SMH* with
me.' 'Mr Gollan,' said Mr Curtin, 'you are at liberty to
withdraw from my conference any time you like, and take
your staff with you. But I tell you this, Mr Gollan. If you
and your staff withdraw, neither you nor your staff will ever
come again to one of my conferences.' Mr Gollan stifled his
dignity and remained, but we thought little of his tart
obituary when Curtin died in 1945.

Prime Ministers have been known to contact a pressman's office when they dislike a particular article. I knew
Sir Robert to do this several times, and I didn't think much
of it; nor did I think much of his suggestion to me once, a
veiled one to be sure, that I might keep him informed of
'happenings' and trends in the press gallery. I didn't fall for
that one, though I could have ingratiated myself even more
with him. I know the chap who did; there are informers in
all newspaper offices, who keep the 'enemy' up to date.

*

I thought the incident that reflected least credit on Sir
Robert was the Petrov affair in 1954. Petrov was a member
of the Russian legation who defected and there were all
manner of innuendoes about spying, as if every member of a
Foreign Legation in every country is not expected to do just
that. The story broke one Friday evening when Dr Bert
Evatt, leader of the Opposition, was attending a dinner of
his old school in Fort Street, Sydney. Earlier in the day
Arthur Calwell, then Deputy Leader to the 'Doc', as we all
knew him, approached Harold Holt, who was in charge of
the House, and asked him whether it would be all right if he
('Doc') went to Sydney. Was anything expected to come up
in the House? 'No,' said Harold, 'tell the Doc he's in the
clear. Nothing is coming up.' That night Menzies broke the
Petrov story, and as Evatt was the one it was all aimed at

politically, he should have been in Parliament. I cannot
believe, knowing Harold Holt as well as I did, that he would
have misinformed both Calwell and Evatt. Looking back at
it I am inclined to think that Menzies did not even tell Holt.
On looking at it further, I think had the tables been
reversed the Doc would have pulled that swift one on
Menzies too, such was the hatred of one for the other.

The Doc could not pace it with Menzies as a politician.
He was too bluff, not adroit enough. Compared with
Menzies he had a poor speaking voice and, with his notes
strewn everywhere on the table, he rambled badly in a
speech and really bored people. Nobody could say that
about Sir Robert. Doc was a strange study for one so
academically gifted. He was suspicious of all people and had
little political 'nous'. I remember him saying in the House
once that he had written to Molotov about a certain matter in
the Petrov case and quoted Molotov's letter back. Nobody
rattled the communist can in Australia more over the years
than Menzies, and I can see again the gloating smile on his
face when he realized he had Evatt where he wanted him.
Molotov, indeed! Menzies called for a dissolution immediately. As I saw it, the Petrov case was a sheer waste of
public money, proving nothing we didn't know, and aimed
purely for the political persecution of the Doc.

Sir Robert took me much into his confidences during that
case. He told me that a certain journalist, mentioned in its
connection by Fergus O'Sullivan, the man on Evatt's staff
responsible for all the 'startling information', and described
as a cricketer, wasn't me. He also told me in advance that
Kenneth Street, my father-in-law, was to be knighted. One
needed convincing on several aspects of the Petrov affair. It
was not, I think, one of the outstanding events in Sir
Robert's reign and it was notable, also, how nearly
everybody associated with the case was knighted. I had to
be diplomatic to steer my course between him and the Doc
on cricket. Each was jealous of the other and would say to
me: 'Of course, he doesn't know anything about the game.
All theory.' It stuck in Sir Robert's craw that the Doc had
written an article for *Wisden*, the cricket almanac; but
R.G.M. later wrote several for the same publication. The

Doc, who was a great friend of Sid Barnes, was up to his eyes in all details of Barnes' court action over an alleged libel. I am not at liberty to divulge what Barnes told me of that case, otherwise I might have legal trouble on my own plate.

Sir Robert did me many good turns. The Sports Club in London made me an honorary member and, thinking I had some influence with Sir Robert, asked me whether I could get him to come there to dinner and address them, which they had often failed to do over the many years when he was in London. I wrote to him, telling him that members of the club were notable Tories, like himself; and how, through excise, they contributed in no small measure to Her Majesty's Exchequer. He consented and gave us a memorable night, telling at great length his many stories of Sir Winston Churchill, which the members loved. The club was ablaze, its flambeaux being lit in the square for the occasion, and Sir Robert stayed on late, yarning. Later that week he suffered his first heart attack. I think that was his last after-dinner speech and we were lucky to have heard it. He was on his best form. He was one of the best after-dinner speakers in the Commonwealth, of which he was so proud.

His ties with the Royal family were real and no one could doubt his fealty to and admiration of the Queen. This sometimes carried him away as when he quoted once in King's Hall, 'I did but see her passing by, and yet I'll love her till I die.' I think Her Majesty might have blushed at that. He was very proud of being made Lord Warden of the Cinque Ports and called a press conference to talk about it to an irreverent and cynical crowd of press-men. They were inclined to make light of it and somebody asked him whether he was entitled to the flotsam and jetsam. Sir Robert wasn't pleased.

*

Jim Killen, our minister for Defence, did me no good when he circulated the story that 'Father', as he irreverently called Sir Robert, would milk me for opinions and then circulate them in the Melbourne Cricket Club as his own. This story and one example of it even appeared in a book written on Tony Whitlam, and Killen was obviously the source. Killen said that I averred Neil Harvey held the bat wrongly with his top hand (his right, as he was left-handed) and that Sir Robert had put that forward as the reason for Harvey's failures (he did not have too many, by the way). I saw this in proof form and was aghast. I was assured it would be cut out. It wasn't and I wrote to Sir Robert saying that this was wrong and not to put any credence on the story. He wrote back a very nice letter, telling me not to worry my head about it.

My friend Killen had an inventive mind. In the sixties the fate of the Menzies government rested on the distribution of several hundred Communist preferences in Killen's seat of Moreton, in Brisbane. It was touch and go from day to day. Killen was asked by the press whether Sir Robert had been in touch with him. Constantly, said Killen. Sir Robert hadn't even rung him once. To him, to win government on Communist preferences was completely distasteful. All Australia knew how he had berated this 'ism over the years. When Killen finally just scraped in, the press asked him the inevitable question. Had he heard from Mr Menzies? 'Yes, I have,' cheerfully said the irrepressible Killen. And what did the message say? 'Just "Killen, you are magnificent",' – and the 'story' made big news. Menzies must have read that himself. When Killen re-appeared at the first Party meeting, Menzies said, 'Killen, you are magnificent.'

One day in the House Killen made a brilliant speech from the government backbenches (he was not then a Minister). He got a lot of publicity and congratulations. Oddly, he had based himself on 'Father's' oratory, and his vocabulary and delivery aped those of Sir Robert. I went to my room where I had many cables from overseas and in those days the Canberra Post Office was most liberal with its paper when it sent cables. I clipped the bottom off one and typed on it a lot of figures of dates and wordage, with the Cinque Ports on it, added 'Killen, you are magnificent. Bob Menzies', and sealed it in a cable envelope (even at this late stage, I will probably be interrogated for breaking all the regulations). I took it to an attendant I knew and asked him to give it to Mr Killen but to wait a few minutes until I got upstairs to the Press Gallery.

I saw the attendant walk across the chamber to Jim and his eyes almost popped out as he read the 'cable'. He began to show it to fellow Members, then suddenly looked up at the Gallery where he saw me almost falling off my seat in laughter. He shook his fist at me but I think I equalled the score on Harvey's top hand. When we catch the other's eye, we shape up with the top hand playing down the pitch. I think the Jackeroo from the Barcoo intends to tell the 'magnificent' story one day. I hope I have beaten him to the punch.

Killen once said Australia could not defend Botany Bay on a sunny Sunday afternoon. No doubt, as Minister for Defence, he thinks differently now. One of my best friends in the House, and I had many, was Josh Francis, later Sir Josiah. Josh established himself for ever in our eyes when he turned up one bitterly cold day at Manuka Oval where a group of politicians and press-men were playing a game of Australian Rules, with a bottle of Queensland overproof rum. In opposition, Josh used to give the Labour government stick on the buffalo fly and the ravages it was doing to his State's cattle industry. Every question, every speech on the adjournment by Josh was based on the buffalo fly – what was this inept government doing about this great curse? I asked Josh one day what had happened to the buffalo fly. 'A strange thing,' he said. 'When we came to power, the buffalo fly disappeared completely. Very odd.'

There were some great tricks pulled in Parliament in my early days there, mostly by the Country Party, who were up to all manner of dodges. They were led by the greatest humourist and story-teller in the House, Sir Arthur Fadden. I knew one Member, now a knight, who after a good dinner nearby told his guests that he would go into the House and make a speech for them. He often did this and boasted of it. Sir Robert grew to hear of it, and this Member wondered why he wasn't one of Sir Robert's bright boys; Sir Robert didn't like any fooling with Parliament.

*

Ian Fitchett, a fellow Victorian, was a great debunker of the Prime Minister. 'Fitch', as he was known to all, would sit on a chaise longue at the back of the PM's room and ask pertinent questions at a press conference. 'Was the PM going to appear in Bolte's Victorian elections?' 'I daresay I will make a speech or two,' said the PM. 'No show without Punch,' said Fitch.

Once the PM had been a long period in England and Artie Fadden had carried on the government here. Would Fadden join him to make a joint election policy speech, asked Fitch. No, said R.G.M. curtly and added the epitaph Dr Johnson wrote for Oliver Goldsmith: '*Nihil tetighit quod non ornavit*' ('He touched nothing which he did not decorate'). Fitch dredged this out for me. R.G.M. loved England, delving into bookshops, silversmiths', restaurants, antique shops and the like.

It was Fitchett who called him 'Ming the Merciless' after a character in a cartoon. And it was Fitchett, then with the *Sydney Morning Herald* and later with the *Age*, who delighted in some character assassination of R.G.M. when the *Herald* one year, strangely, but for reasons known in the Press Gallery, turned from Menzies to Calwell. R.G.M. was on his way to the Parliamentary rooms and passed Fitchett and some of his press friends yarning at Queen Victoria's table in King's Hall, a favourite place for pressmen.

R.G.M. looked across at Fitchett, whose piece had appeared that morning. 'Ho, ho, ho, Prime Minister,' chortled Fitchett. 'I'll make you eat humble pie, Fitchett,' snapped R.G.M. Fitchett was just as quick with a ready answer. 'As long as it is garnished with the sauce of your embarrassment, Prime Minister,' he called after R.G.M.

I knew the PM to be stumped for a ready answer only twice. Once was in Parliament with Jim Cope, later Speaker. Some Labour man had asked R.G.M. whether it was true that in certain circles he was known as Pig-iron Bob, a reference to the time when he allowed pig-iron to be sold to Japan on the eve of war. The PM agreed that in some places he was known by that name, but then he was known by many names. 'Only recently,' he said, 'I was driving down William Street, Sydney, in my official car and stopped at a light alongside a truck. The truckie put his head out of the cabin and said, "Good on yer, Bob".' Cope interjected. 'He should have been had up for drunken driving.' It brought the House down. R.G.M. put his hands over his head in salute to Cope.

On another occasion, in wartime when whisky was short and dear, Richard Gardiner Casey, Menzies' Foreign Minister, recommended a particular brand to R.G.M., a connoisseur who mixed the most pungent dry martinis known to man. Casey brought the PM up a bottle, poured him out a snifter and anxiously watched his expression as he drank it. The PM pulled a very wry face. 'You don't like it, PM?' Casey said. The PM said he didn't. 'It tastes like horse urine to me,' he said. 'I'm sorry, Bob, you have the advantage of me,' Casey said. 'I've never tasted that.' R.G.M. was lost for a quick retort to that, but he could be cutting for the most part.

A young journalist approached him at an airport and, hoping to get an interview, told him which newspaper he represented. 'You have my deepest sympathy,' said R.G.M. as he passed on. He was very critical of the slow progress of Canberra. 'On and on and on it goes, trespassing on eternity.' The Italian Embassy, opposite the PM's Lodge, was for a very long time an unsightly hole in the ground. Meeting the Italian Ambassador socially, R.G.M. told him: 'Now I fully understand the meaning of the old saying "Rome wasn't built in a day".' Soon afterwards the Italian Embassy began to shoot ahead.

Oliver Chidgey, mentioned earlier, was R.G.M.'s right hand man for a long time. He was Chidg to us all. He would often come to my room on the Senate side and say, 'If you are not too busy, the PM would like a word with you.' I would put aside whatever I was doing – I knew the PM must have some cricket matter to discuss and wanted my opinions. When that was over, I could always do my questioning. Or, sometimes, he liked the sound of words he had written in his book *Afternoon Light* and wanted me to listen while he read. Other times, it would just be a drink and a chat. He had any amount of acquaintances he could meet but I can't think of any real friends he had. Eric Harrison told me once in London that for a period he was worried about the weight R.G.M. was carrying and, being at the Lodge one morning he sent his car and driver away so that Sir Robert would have to walk to the House. 'He was furious,' said Eric. 'I never did it again.'

R.G.M., I'm sure, was a lonely man. He was a keen walker. He walked from the Lodge to my home in Forrest one day to take me to an Australian Rules game, which he loved. He talked all the time he walked. His big problem, he told me, was the high wages young people were making. At one press conference he and I wrangled for minutes about the merits of Rules and Rugby. I had asked him how he thought Rules could become the main football game in Australia if so few Christians, as I termed them, attended at the Melbourne Coliseum for the Inter-State carnival. He said the interest was in club games. How then, I countered, could Rules hope ever to become international? 'I'm not going to argue on the merits of games,' he said. 'All games are good.' It was on the eve of an election.

*

I made a note of a talk I had with R.G.M. in the Parliamentary Library on 1 February 1956, the morning of a Loan Council meeting. I was reading the latest edition of the London *Times* when the Prime Minister, wearing the Alec Bedser benefit tie, walked up to me and said, 'What's this about you picking a Sydney second grader to go to England?' (I was so impressed by the bowling of Martin in the Sydney nets against Keith Miller that I wrote he should be invited to England ... I was four years too early; he went next time.) 'This wretched Sydney press. They want twenty-two players out of seventeen for England. Carroll, Saunders, a world beater. Ugh.'

J.H.F.: 'Our Prime Minister should not be so parochial. Obviously you were sitting in the Victorian room in the recent game.'

R.G.M.: 'I sat in both rooms.'

J.H.F.: 'Parochialism hasn't always been centred on NSW. I remember in my time how your Victorian writers wanted their whole side in.'

R.G.M.: 'Who?'

J.H.F.: 'Millard, for one . . .'

R.G.M.: 'Oh, Millard . . . Anyway, in Sydney I saw the best piece of slow bowling in years. I tell you it was not only good. It was great. In the great traditions of the game.'

J.H.F.: 'Ian Johnson, of course, can be a good spinner. But what about batting against him? Any batsman who plays him from the crease will make him look good. You've got to get down the pitch to him. Freddie Brown told me he'd like him to be bowling both ends.'

R.G.M.: 'Yes, the batsmen did play him from the crease. But great bowling all the same.' (Frenzied public servants, off-stage, including Sir Roland Wilson, agitating for R.G.M. to come to the opening of the Loan Council, then past its appointed time of beginning.) 'You know, Sam Loxton is good stuff for anybody's money. I like Sam. He gives a game everything he's got.'

J.H.F.: 'I like him too. He'll work as hard at six as at eleven. But if you put him in you are taking a great lot of old players and the worst thing on a tour is having old timers who have decided it is their last tour.'

R.G.M.: 'I like Wilson. I think he's our best left-hander.'

J.H.F.: 'Yes, but he throws. And so does your friend, Johnson, every now and then. Burke I would never ask to bowl, or throw. He's a disgrace. Who are your keepers?' (Intense agitation now off-stage.)

R.G.M.: 'I saw Grout in Melbourne and he didn't impress me very much – though he took all those catches in Sydney.'

J.H.F.: 'Oh, those things happen. A day out with many snicks. What about this young bowler, Kline, in Melbourne?'

R.G.M.: (fingering the Bedser tie judicially): 'Yes, quite a good bowler.' (Wilson and Chidgey hopping like grasshoppers in the background.) Oliver Chidgey: 'Mr Prime Minister, the Loan Council . . .'

R.G.M.: 'I agree with you. We want to pick some young players. Coming, Chidgey.'

Later, through Chidgey, I sent in a note pointing out that of the Sydney critics, Mathers is a Victorian, Moyes and Whitington are from South Australia and Eddie Kann is a Queenslander. I got no reply. But R.G.M. was no great

lover of people from my State. Of his twelve Ministers at
the time, two were from NSW and five from his State.

*

His after-dinner oratory was brilliant and witty, although
he once told me he never made a speech anywhere without
getting 'butterflies in the tummy', which is something
known to all sportsmen before they face the moment of
truth. His manner, vocabulary, looks, suffused, so to speak,
by his intelligence and impishness, gave him a very high
position as an orator. At a dinner in England in 1938 he
came last on the list of speakers, a time when the listeners
had had their fill of everything and the speaker feels beaten
before he starts. Some of the preceding speeches had been
very heavy, so R.G.M. thought he would be fanciful. He
talked of what modern means of communication might
mean to the future ... Commonwealth conferences of PM's
by secret radio, television and so on. This was all prettily
played upon for ten minutes to the obvious enjoyment of
all. Going home, he said he hoped he had not been too
playful or overdone it. Next morning a press agency was in
touch with him wanting to know why they hadn't been
given a copy of this important speech, that it had been
scooped in India. They wanted details of the plan ... had
the engineers of the Post Office commented on the technical
aspects, would he write a special article on it?

He was often depicted as a yes-man for Downing Street
and his intrusion into the Suez crisis of 1956 would have
supported that. He had his own special way of urging the
doctrine of the indivisibility of the Crown. He gave me a
splendid interview on this once which the *Sunday Times*
highlighted: he believed that if the United Kingdom were
at war, Australia was automatically and totally at war and,
the evidence would seem to suggest, as far as Sir Robert and
some following Prime Ministers were concerned, this also
applied to the United States of America. We seem over-
anxious at times to follow them willy-nilly, to court their
favours.

In 1956, when Anthony Eden had been Foreign Minister
in the UK for only a few months, he gave a speech on such
affairs to a group which included R.G.M. and other

Commonwealth officers. According to R.G.M., Eden spoke for half an hour, from a well-prepared brief, in a smooth, well-rehearsed manner and used the term 'Her Majesty's Government', a term which infuriates Australians, as if Her Majesty had only one. At the end of it, Eden asked if there were any questions. 'Yes,' said R.G.M., 'just one [a pause], Anthony. Have you any policy in the Far East at all?'

At a dinner in London one evening, the Earl-chairman referred playfully to Australia having outgrown her very early humble origins of enforced immigration and the like. He meant convicts, a tag which has become even attractive to many Australians, who can trace their beginnings back to the First Fleet. R.G.M. was in rippling form as he replied. He admitted that Australians no longer remembered this except when studying history at school, but a few years before one Australian, who could afford it and for reasons best known to himself, employed two brilliant young research historians to spend a year examining original source materials. 'And do you know, my dear Earl,' – said with a bland smile – he was a great actor – 'what they found? For every person of a certain character, history and conflict with law who went to Australia in those early days, at least thirty-seven of similar character, history and conflict with law stayed in the dear old mother country. How far does your own family tree go back?' Our most famous early architect, Greenaway, was sent to Australia for life for forgery. These days he would probably be elevated to the peerage.

When I wrote *Masters of Cricket*, for which R.G.M. gave a splendid foreword, I showed him a few chapters of the copy. 'How long,' he said, when he found me one day in the library, 'did it take you to write this "tripe"?' I was a bit shattered. 'You don't like it,' I said. 'Yes, I do very much,' he said. He sometimes exhibited an elephantine sense of humour but he was always receptive to me when I wanted to discuss the 'politics' of the game, and would give me splendid advice. I valued that highly. I shared his love of England and all it meant. I have written how he liked to spend his spare time in London, and he would always fit in a long walk on his own at Oxford and Cambridge.

By contrast, Ben Chifley hardly spent any time at all in England. Curtin and Chifley, bosom cobbers, promised each other that when the Second World War was over they would go on a world trip in retirement. With the worries and rigors of war they each deserved it, but neither lived long enough. Ben Chifley came to England in 1948, taking his own money for the times he would have to return hospitality (R.G.M. entertained lavishly in England but not, I would think, with his own money). I tried to persuade Mr Chifley to come to Headingley to see some of the 1948 Test. He was keen on the game, knew it and had played it, but he would never dally outside Australia and especially not in England where he had the typical Australian attitude towards 'duchessing' – that is, being invited to some opulent home for the weekend and being made such a fuss of that he might be persuaded to agree to something he didn't want.

*

It was never the Labour party which came up with better slogans at election-time, although Gough Whitlam's crowd had a good one when he first came to power: 'It's time.' A good friend of mine, Frank McCaffery of Brisbane, who used to be private secretary to Artie Fadden, came up with a good one in 1949 – 'Throw out the government, and fill up your petrol tank' – and Chifley, who didn't deserve to be, was beaten. Chifley had kept rationing on longer than he should have done, politically and otherwise – people were tired of the exigencies of wartime – but Chifley's loyalty to the United Kingdom was his undoing. Chifley maintained that somewhere along the line, such was the stranglehold the USA had on oil, money for petrol had to be turned into dollars and the UK was very short of dollars.

R.G.M. had the slogan for one election 'Put value back into the pound' and that at a time when inflation was beginning to surge. He wanted very much that the basis of the new decimal currency (a change from the old was inevitable), should be called the 'Royal' but not even his most ardent disciples would swallow that one. I think it was his pre-election promise to put value back into the pound that prompted him to get rid of the pound so quickly. Pre-election promises are as pie-crust. Anybody who now believes in them would believe in fairy god-mothers. I should say that almost every promise Malcolm Fraser made went overboard in double quick time. Australians will be gullible indeed if they fall for pre-election gimmicks again.

As it would seem, I have no great faith in politicians. I have seen too many of them at work at close quarters. The Labour Party had the ball at their feet, but quickly kicked it into touch, trying to be all things to all people overnight. The great failing of the Labour Party is that, no matter what ability they have, they fight themselves much harder than their Opposition.

Yet I often wonder at the belief of the non-Labour parties that they have some divine right to rule. I often used to meet a former minister of the Menzies governments in Opposition, and he would almost cry on my shoulder at the fact that they were no longer the government. He almost suggested they had been cheated out of office. I met him at a Sydney shopping centre sometime after he had retired from politics, and he told me he owned about sixty units in one particular harbourside suburb alone.

Labour has one big difficulty in office. Its Ministers have not been used to being in business, yet they consider themselves fit to run the biggest business of all – their own country. The floodgates opened when Whitlam came to power. There was an obvious lack of discipline among most of the staffs of the Ministers. Jack was every bit as good as his master; and it seemed that a flood of sex, jobs for the girls as well as the boys, and bad language on most sides, took over in Canberra. There were exceptions, of course. Kim Beazley, Fred Daly, Frank Crean, Jim Cairns, and Rex Connor were Ministers who impressed me; but to go into some of the offices was to be impressed with the lack of general dignity and sound behaviour in the job.

And the hates of the Labour Party! Comradeship seems to go out the door (and it was one of the best things about Australian life) when advancement, trips or plums of office are in the offing. I met Arthur Calwell outside church in Canberra one Sunday and he proceeded to flay Gough Whitlam to me. 'Now, Arthur,' I said, 'that is not very

M

charitable of you, and considering the place from which you have just come. I recall when the Doc was leader and you his deputy, you weren't exactly too loyal to him.' (Whitlam was then deputy to Calwell.) 'The Doc! the Doc!' exploded Calwell, with heat. 'He was like John the Baptist compared with this chap.'

There were some outstanding hates in Canberra in my time, but I think the biggest hater of all time was the same Arthur Augustus Calwell. At the finish he didn't have a good word for anybody. It was embarrassing for his staff. I think the loss of his only son soured him. Yet Calwell was a classic example of how a man without great riches can't hope to get justice in law. The *Sydney Telegraph* once, in an editorial, called him a 'liar' and added the thought that this was worth money to him if he cared to go to court over it. Arthur went to court and won his case, but the newspaper continued the litigation in higher courts. Calwell had to drop it in the end. The legal costs were killing him.

I would often talk with R.G.M. and tell him of my doubts about the profession he came from and recite to him eight principles of law: a good cause; a good purse; an honest and skilful attorney; good evidence; able counsel; an upright judge; an intelligent jury; good luck. I have seen so many of his fraternity seemingly come into politics as a means of being elevated to the judiciary, and it is notable how many of that profession set out to get into politics. I always think with legal-politicians that they can argue to their brief. I think he got my point that one couldn't get justice except with a bountiful purse.

I first knew Gough Whitlam when he was associate to Sir Kenneth Street when he was NSW Chief Justice. Gough treated me very well and would always do his best to give me a story when I asked a question at his press conferences. Yet I was somewhat disappointed in him when he resigned from Parliament. I thought he should have stayed on and fought, as Sir Robert had done before him. But I think he realized, as Lord Butler once said and everyone in it knew: politics is a dirty game.

One never is surprised when politicians tell lies. They feel their calling entitles them to run for cover. I thought I sensed an irregularity in R.G.M.'s account at a press conference about the first time he came to know of the Petrov business; only a little thing, but suspicious. There was one occasion when I was in the House when Calwell told an absolute 'whopper'. He denied that any member of his department had ever done any political work for members of the Labour Party; and that very day I was in the House to get instructions from him regarding two political broadcasts I wrote each week for two not very bright members of his Party. 'Give 'em stick on the Depression,' said Arthur. 'That's always a good line.'

Once Calwell did a very foolish thing. Artie Fadden was making an important speech and through one of his informers Calwell had obtained a copy of the speech from the Press Gallery. He sat in front of Fadden at the Opposition table and quoted things which were coming next. Fadden was furious, as he had every right to be. I went straight to his room and said I hoped he didn't think I had given Calwell the copy of his speech (handed to the press to help them). My friend Fadden said I was one he would never suspect. Each member of the Press Gallery was called and sworn and asked whether he was the culprit. Nobody owned up but years later, when people had changed sides, Calwell himself told me who had given him the copy of Fadden's speech. I was not surprised.

As I have suggested, Gough Whitlam was very friendly and helpful at his press conferences. These seem to have gone overboard in recent years. Prime Ministers now shy away from them, rarely, if ever, hold them, and experienced press-men don't think much of asking their questions for the benefit of television. The whole show goes out 'live' and what it means, in effect, is that questions are asked for the benefit of viewers. When one asks what is perhaps a pertinent question, the answer is already stale news when it's printed.

Whitlam only once put me to one side. This was when an associate editor, John Pitts, of the Argus Group in South Africa, came to Australia to probe public feeling here on the visit, subsequently postponed, of the South African Cricket Team. Pitts got good interviews with premiers, sportsmen, union leaders, Lord Mayors and everybody he asked before he got to Canberra. I was able to arrange interviews on the spot for him with the then Prime Minister, Bill McMahon, and the just deposed PM, John Gorton. I left Whitlam to the last because I thought he would readily agree. I met him coming out of the House. Whitlam gave me a flat 'No,' he wouldn't even meet Pitts. I thought this rather petulant of him. People who have strong objections, on principle, to countries, should not trade with them. Whitlam was violently anti-South African, which was fair enough, but he did nothing about trade with them. We sold them $100 million of trade at the time and bought back $10,000,000. Malcolm Fraser had the same difficulty in wanting to boycott the Moscow Olympiad. He wanted the athletes not to go, but saw nothing wrong in continuing trade with the USSR.

*

My greatest 'wrangle' with R.G.M. was over his Prime Minister's match, which he loved. In the fifties, the West Indians were in Sydney with a clear week before their tour began. Ian Emerton, clerk of the Senate and President of the ACT Cricket Association, asked me one day in the library if I would suggest to the PM that he should hold a PM's match with them. I went to his room and put the proposal before him. He liked it immediately and on the spot, with me there, rang Sir Donald Bradman in Adelaide and asked if he would like to lead his side. Bradman didn't give the idea any thought. He said 'No' immediately.

Then the PM worried whether the game would be possible or would take on. I assured him it would and that he would love every minute of it. He tossed it about in his mind, with me urging him on. Then, one Friday night, he said he was satisfied the game would succeed and it was on. Next morning, Geoff (now Sir Geoffrey) Yeend, of his Department, rang me to say the game was off. 'But Geoff,' I told him, 'I saw the PM only last night and it was on.' 'Well,' said Geoff, 'it's off now.' I went on to golf and went into the Lodge on the way home to talk again to the PM. 'Are you sure it will go off all right?' he said. 'Certain,' I said. 'All right, it's on.' And it was on. It was a great success, the forerunner of many others and was much enjoyed by the PM, who entertained his team at dinner at the Lodge the night before the match.

At his last PM's match, against England, he asked me to make a speech. I said there was something nostalgic about this game as I felt it was the last of the line. There was intense speculation about R.G.M.'s retirement and he said (he made many speeches at his dinner) that he wasn't going to be trapped by me into announcing when he was going to retire. But it was his last and, remembering how hard I had to fight to get him to play at all to begin with, I wondered when he would say in a speech: 'When I first had the idea of this game ...' But that is typical of politics. If somebody gives the man-on-top an idea and it works, it is his idea; but woe betide the underdogs when something goes wrong.

Although Sir Donald Bradman turned him down for his first game, he afterwards led the PM's team against England and the biggest crowd known to Manuka turned out. I led that first side and we had some good players in Hassett, Martin, O'Reilly, Donnelly, Harvey and Paul Sheahan, who was the PM's choice as he thought, rightly, that he was a Test player in the making. A Minister, Athol Townley, was a big success and I thought we could well have chosen Harold Holt, who came to a net practice and lingered on the outskirts. He bowled a very good leg-break and I think would have loved to play.

*

R.G.M. was no great lover of certain United States Presidents. After making a speech which pleased him, to the Annual Liberal Party convention, a speech in which he said the Middle East was about as inflammable as the Balkans before the First World War, he opened up to me on the subject of Dwight Eisenhower. 'These Americans ...' he exploded. 'They don't know the first thing about it. If I were as poor a PM as Eisenhower is a President, I would have been out of my job eight-and-a-half years ago. Eisenhower is hopeless. Dulles is behind him. He's capable but Eisenhower ... Lamentable. Their policies. Ugh!'

He loved the Melbourne Cricket Ground and club and spent some of his happiest moments there, analysing the play. He did understand the game more than the Doc. Especially when he was PM, R.G.M. found many who tried to push their barrows at all times and would pester him during matches. He therefore protected his flank with Sir John Bunting on the end of the bench. One day he invited me to join him and told me something which nearly made me fall off the seat. It was something he had said to President Johnson about the Vietnam war that would have put the world in a mess, if indeed the world had survived it.

My second son, Grey, would have been eligible for that war if his birthday came out of the barrel. I had strong convictions about the war, into which I thought we should never have been gulled, and if Grey's birthday came out in the lottery I intended to refuse him permission to register. Boys of eighteen were not considered adults then and I would have offered to go to prison instead of him. One did not have children, nurture and educate them, for such an illogical war. That would have brought my friendship with R.G.M. to a sudden stop, but I knew many young politicians who should have been in uniform had their convictions been as strong as they suggested.

R.G.M. said to me that day at the Melbourne Cricket Ground: 'I told President Johnson: "Look, my boy, when you are in a war you have got to act as if you are in a war. You must drop the bomb. There's nothing else for it".' Military men to whom I have spoken on this aspect of the Vietnam war are horrified. Where could it have been dropped without damage to Russian, British and Chinese ships? And then the fat would have been in the fire, only the fire would have been too much for all of us.

It is for history to write on R. G. Menzies, the statesman, but the Petrov show and our entrance into the Vietnam war will count against him.

· 14 ·

Two Echoes
from the Past

Two of my most valued letters are from Syd Barnes and
Wilfred Rhodes. The one from Wilfred ('Am fairly well for
eighty-seven'), was dictated to his daughter and signed by
him. The one from Barnes was written in his own delightful
copper-plate handwriting. I had asked both of them
questions about happenings in their careers, and they
replied to me fully.

As M. A. Noble was reputed to be one of Australia's
greatest Test captains I could not understand how the
English took such complete command of the Test at Sydney
in 1903–4 when R. E. Foster made his brilliant 287. With
Rhodes, who went in last, Foster had a record last wicket
stand of 130; Rhodes remained 40 not out. Why, I asked
Rhodes, hadn't Noble taken more command of the game,
such as keeping the brilliant Foster away from the strike?
Rhodes replied almost with a tinge of sadness.

'My opinion of Noble is that he was a very fine all-
round cricketer and, I thought, a very good captain. As
regards containing Foster, Relf and Rhodes, may I
remind you that neither Relf nor Rhodes were tail-end
batsmen in the sense of the term, and Foster was in full
flight. I can remember hitting Noble's off-breaks from
outside the off-stump to the square-leg boundary from
a good-length ball. Did you ever know anyone who
could contain Bradman? And so it was in that match
with Foster, Relf and Rhodes.

'I can recall the running out of Hill in a Test match,

on the same ground, same tour and whether it was the same match you mention, I'm not sure, but I was lurking about the right-hand of the square-leg umpire. Hill played a walking shot on the other side of the umpire. I ran behind him, picked up the ball left-handed and threw it back to the wicket-keeper. Hill couldn't get back. From what I remember it wasn't an over-throw. I thought Bob Crockett [the umpire who gave Hill out] was a splendid umpire and quite unbiassed.

'As to my bowling, I did rely on length, flight and change of pace. I never expected anything from the wicket. The only thing was to hope that something would happen. Jack White was never a spin bowler. In England he used to bowl slow seamers and in England was difficult to hit past cover. I think fast bowlers should not be allowed to run more than a certain distance, it does waste time. As for captains of today, it is not fair to criticize if they haven't got the men to bowl. When I was on tour in 1911–12 we had three good men, including Foster and Douglas, who could captain. We were never briefed or told what to do on tour. They would let us do as we liked in our spare time, although we did not play golf on tour in those days.

'On containing batsmen, I only knew one bowler who could contain the Don in England in 1930 and that was Charlie Parker of Gloucester. I saw the marathon Test at the Oval when O'Reilly didn't contain our batsmen. I asked Maurice Leyland if he could pick O'Reilly's faster ball and he said yes – he ran faster up to the stumps when going to bowl it.

'Trueman would be a better batsman if he looked at the ball more. He's just been on the carpet again – he's a right showman. Any further trouble and he looks like being finished for Yorkshire. He is the best England bowler ever to play for Australia at Old Trafford – Benaud's benefit. [This an allusion to pitch-marks which Trueman left to be exploited by Benaud bowling around the stumps.] A bowler bowling three balls in front of the batsman and three behind him requires a few more fieldsmen. I may be old-fashioned but the off-stump was my target. I saw Woolley, Strudwick, Barnett and Leyland and a few more old ones last summer. The South Africans are a very interesting lot – drawing spectators and running about the field like greyhounds. I think Cowdrey has improved his technique.

'I still love my cricket and keep in touch as much as I can. Went to both Lord's and Leeds this summer. My best wishes. Dear Syd Barnes is improving.
Yours sincerely,
W. Rhodes.'

Written from Coppice House, Penkridge, near Stafford, on 17th July 1957, Barnes apologized for not having answered my letter of May that same year, but said he had been very busy at the office (he was with the Staffordshire County Council) and had not time to write private letters. He was at Lord's for the second Test against the West Indies and was pleased there to meet our Mr Menzies again, chat with him, and have his photograph taken with him.

'Your main question appears to be – what were my thoughts after the Test at Melbourne in 1911 [when he had the greatest spell of bowling to a Test player, with five wickets for six runs off eleven overs]. I was very pleased but, speaking truthfully, I did not consider that the highlight of my career. I knew it was possible to bowl well with little or no result; on the other hand, one could bowl not nearly so well and reap quite a crop of wickets – you know as well as I that there is a very small margin between success and failure. Still, I think I did bowl well that day.

'You mention "swing". I certainly learned a lot about the outward swing from Alf Noble – by spinning the ball as for an off-break. This, and body action, produced the desired effect. For the inward swing, I watched George Hirst and thought I could get this, although as a left-hander he had an advantage. But by perseverence I got the inward swing by means of leg-break action and again with body action. At the time I was able to bowl these I thought I was at a disadvantage in having to spin the ball when I could see bowlers swing the same by simply placing the ball in their hand and letting go, but I soon learned the advantage was with me because by spinning the ball, if the wicket would take spin, the ball would come back against the spin. It did not swing so much in Australia, of course, as in England. I must say I did not bowl a ball but that I had to spin and that is to my way of thinking the reason for what success I attained.

'Very pleased to hear of Vernon Ransford, a grand fellow. Thanks for your letter and all the best for your work,

Yours sincerely,
S. F. Barnes (Syd to you.)

Monsieur Bidet,
and Two Tributes

One of the happiest things in my life has been my friendly
associations with English journalists. They never resented
my presence when I worked for the *Sunday Times* or made
me feel that I was butting in and taking somebody else's
work. Their companionship in the press-box meant much
to me and I always relished the manner in which afternoon
newspaper writers would snap when morning writers would
begin the day chirpily and conversationally then, in the
afternoon when the position was reversed, the way morning
newspaper writers wanted peace and calm.

Some great practical jokes were also played there, mainly
by Peter Laker and Basil Easterbrook, and one had
constantly to be on the watch. Laker 'did' me beautifully
once at the Oval. He was a chap who would prepare his
jokes carefully and I never suspected anything when I got a
call to the Oval office to answer the phone. The chap at the
other end said he was a member of the French Embassy,
was very keen on cricket and wanted to know, if he called
up to the Oval, whether he might have a few minutes' talk
with me.

I expressed surprise that a Frenchman should be
interested in cricket but he told me a lot of it was played in
his province and he was a keen reader of mine in the *Sunday
Times*. I told him that I was always pretty busy in the press-
box but if he called up, I would have a chat with him for
several minutes. He told me his name was Monsieur Bidet.
I spoke to John Arlott on my return and told him I had had a
surprising call from a Frenchman. When I told John the

name he asked me if I knew what a bidet was. I said I did but still did not suspect anything, though John did.

Anon in the afternoon came a knock at our door and a call to me that I was wanted. The looks on the faces of most, who obviously were in on the affair, did not deter me as I went to the door. Sure enough, there seemed to be a Frenchman who grabbed me warmly by the hand and said he was 'very pleezed' to meet me. It was Laker and he had gone to great trouble to dupe me. He had on a black French cap, dark glasses and a black pointed beard. He had taken me in completely and I admitted it.

Laker enjoyed the success of his joke but he was a person I liked very much and I accepted with pleasure his Sussex phone number. He said to contact him before I went back home and he would have me to dinner. One morning I awoke, for a certain purpose, at 4 a.m. Armed with Laker's phone number I rang him. A very sleepy voice anwered and I replied with what I hoped sounded like a Pakistani voice.

'Mister Laker?' I said. Laker, very sleepily, admitted the fact. 'This is your early morning call, Mr Laker,' I said. 'But I don't want an early morning call,' said Laker, a little peevishly, I thought. 'Mr Laker,' I said, 'your name and number are on my list and you must take your early morning call.' 'But I don't want an early morning call,' protested Laker. 'Mr Laker,' I said, 'I have to ring the palace now with another call and I have many more on my list. I must go now.' Laker grumbled so I said, 'Go back to bed, you dope and apologise to your wife. This is Monsieur Bidet.'

In the press-box later that day at Hove Laker, looking a bit under-slept, freely admitted to his fellows that he had been 'done' by Fingo. He was good enough to contact me and say 'This nonsense must stop.' I had no more trouble with him in 1980.

There was one chap in our box who always wrote a regular article each tour, saying, 'Australians go home.' He was quick to see me next day and assure me he didn't mean me. That impressed me until someone said he approached all the other Australians he knew and assured them he didn't mean them, either.

But this is by way of saying 'Thanks' to all those I knew over the years and to apologize to 'Tiger' Smith, whose head I snapped off at Headingley. Once he asked me what it was like to make a 'pair' in a Test, some worthy just having achieved that; I called back churlishly: 'It's not so good, Tiger. Tell me, how many centuries did you make in Tests?' I got my 'pair' in Adelaide and, though it led to my quick dismissal for some years from our Test team, I never regretted the experience in later years. It taught me much about life and people. I noticed that those who were eager to know me when I top-scored in the Melbourne Test and when I foolishly thought I was on top of the Test world, used to cross the road when they saw me coming.

*

I would like at this point to introduce two articles published in England that gave me infinite pleasure. One is the magnificent foreword to my book *Fingleton on Cricket* by my late friend, Ian Peebles. I greatly admired Ian and loved his droll Scots sense of humour. I have had a noble line in foreword writers: Sir Neville Cardus, who did me proud in *Cricket Crisis*; Lord Birkett, who wrote felicitously for my *Brightly Fades the Don*; Sir Robert Menzies was another to do me proud, as did Bill O'Reilly, who wrote a piece for the Trumper book which I deeply appreciated. Michael Parkinson gracefully stepped into the breach for this one and I much appreciate that, especially as he gave the right to use any photographs of the two of us I liked. So I have been more than fortunate. I might ask Laker to do the next!

I am delighted to be able to reprint Ian Peebles' foreword, not because it speaks most generously of me, but because it comes from one of the nicest men I met in life, certainly in cricket, and it enables me to pay tribute to his memory. My daughter Belinda used to phone his copy to the newspaper office, and she said of him, 'Mr Peebles is a very dear and kind gentleman.'

'Some years ago Fingo and I, the joint representat-
ives of the *Sunday Times*, sat, gloomy and barren of
ideas, in the press-box at Lord's. The rain poured
down and what little juice the Test match had

produced in two days' play had been wrung from it by our daily colleagues. After a number of blank weekends we had already drawn heavily on the history of the game, and there was no convenient row or controversy to hand.

'In the midst of our agonies a letter arrived for me from a Scots friend, enclosing a cutting describing a match between Ross-shire and Elgin. This fixture had a special interest for me, as Ross-shire had been Walter Robbins' adopted county when on holiday and Elgin was at one time our local club for whom I had played on occasions. The point of this particular contest was that Ross-shire had been all out for nought. Having read it I passed the cutting over. "Fingo," I said, "you can have this Test match all to yourself. I'm going to write about Ross-shire." On the morrow Fingo's article started: "Ian Peebles has told me that I can have this dreary day all to myself as he is going to write about Scotland. Thus, while he sits smiling happily, I am biting my pen."

'This passing incident is not, to me, just a pleasant triviality. It is one of very warm memories of a very happy association. It was a joy to work with Fingo as an old friend with his humour, warmth and splendid company. It was a privilege and a revelation to work with a great and truly professional journalist. The incident I have quoted epitomizes his generous and positive spirit of co-operation.

'Amongst sports, cricket is extremely well served by writers and commentators of competence in their craft, and great love and knowledge of their subject. It is no belittlement of this devoted band to claim for Fingo a unique place in their midst. His chosen career as a political journalist was a very good training for his natural powers of intelligent observation and analysis. Armed with these he was ideally equipped to take full journalistic advantage of a distinguished and extremely varied cricket career. The result, so happily seen over the years, is the complete cricket writer and commentator.

'First the cricketer. Amongst many distinctions Fingo could fairly claim to have had the most exacting introduction to Test cricket of any man. As a very young man, after one respectable appearance against South Africa in the 1931–2 visit, he was heaved straight in to face the fury of Douglas Jardine's battery of fast bowlers in 1932–3. True, he got a most honourable pair in the third Test, but he had acquitted himself with such resolution against the thunderous bodyline attack that Lol Larwood was moved to say of him that he was the most courageous batsman he had ever bowled to. His disappearance from the confused and bitter scene of the bodyline series would seem to have been premature, but it is nice to record that between him and his chief opponent, Lol Larwood, there has, from that moment, been a warm and lasting friendship.

'Fingo was a cricketer of the best Australian school, which is to say well-tutored, fit, and a dedicated man of the team. I first saw him play at Oxford in 1938. Having expected something on the solid lines of his erstwhile captain, Woodfull, I was immediately and pleasantly surprised. True, his backlift was restricted by McLaren or Dexter standards, but the stroke was in every case crisp and, when necessary, forceful. Also there was such a grand, full range of shots directed to every point of the compass, starting from a very neat delicate slice which I should call a late and he a back-cut. It was in watching this innings, which ran to a century against an adequate University bowling side, that I was strengthened in a theory I had long pondered. It is that where, in general, English batsmen tend to make a clear distinction between the defensive and the scoring stroke, the Australian played every stroke with, at least, the intention of getting a run from some quarter. Thus a batsman as reputedly staid as Bill Woodfull, while ostensibly playing a defensive stroke, would constantly be pushing and deflecting with just sufficient force to make the fieldsmen move and, with the superb Australian running, this usually meant a constant flow of singles and a harassed field. Ponsford and Fingleton brought this industrious quality to a fine art.

'In after years Fingo and I took the field at various levels of club cricket. He loved to bat and play his strokes and, perhaps as a consequence, he always offered the opposition the ultimate courtesy. However lowly the standards to which they played he took them seriously so that where, on occasions, condescension and levity had become serious, he would provide a greatly appreciated measure of real entertainment.

'His record for Australia is remarkably good. Despite his "honourable pair" in 1933 and some disappointment in the English series of 1938, he averaged 42, having made three successive centuries against a good South African side in 1935–6. This, coupled with his superb fielding, marks him clearly as being in the higher bracket of Test Match cricketers.

'Although a very fast man in the field, with a sure hand and powerful throw, his great joy was to field very close at forward short-leg to a batsman bombarded by O'Reilly's beautiful and fiery variations. The friends made a deadly combination, for this was a key position. With O'Reilly's quality of bounce any mistake in judging or picking the "wrong-'un" almost certainly resulted in the ball popping up in the area of the short legs. So wide was Fingo's range and so swift and prehensile his grasp that, to the apprehensive striker, he must have appeared in the (very uncharacteristic) light of a voracious and sprightly spider in the midst of a comprehensive and efficient web.

'I promised to write this Foreword "warts and all". In honesty I find myself, after twenty years of friendship and association, hard put to find any suitable material in this direction. If, for the sake of keeping my promise, I was to say that he had a good Australian pugnacity it would hardly meet the point. For what in fact he has is the staunchness of a man who feels deeply about all the things that matter to him: his country, his religion, his family and his friends. Being, as Lol

Take that, Master Snow. In a pull shot that's never been bettered C. G. Greenidge, of Barbados and Hampshire, puts a bouncer from John Snow over the fence at Lord's for six. Intrepid Brian Close, possibly the best short fieldsman England has known, watches in admiration from short-leg, and is unhelmeted.

The two Richards, Viv and Barry, and this Chappell would have been champion batsmen in any era of cricket.

No hide, nothing. But hide didn't get the audacious Denis Lillee the Queen's autograph at Melbourne in the Centenary Test. Australian official Ray Steele and skipper Ian Chappell are amused.

Michael Parkinson, the well known journalist and television interviewer, saw the joke when I was appearing for the ABC for the first time. I did three shows with Parkinson inside a year, one for the BBC in London.

Larwood noted, a courageous man, he is not inclined to sit silently by should any person or thing near to him be disparaged within his hearing. This admirable courage and clarity is to be seen and appreciated in all his writings. In fact, the reader will find in the pages in this book clearer testimony to these qualities of the man than my few words can convey.

'The scope is very wide and affords ample space for the author's firm touch on every aspect of the game of cricket. This touch is so happy and sure in the lighter moments of personality or incident, as it is on the delicate matter of cricket and politics, a realm in which the professional training of a political journalist keeps emotion and prejudices in their proper perspective.

'. . . I would like to end where I started, with a footnote which is quite irrelevant, except that I think it would please the author. When Fingo and I parted at the end of that rainy but happy season, I went to Scotland. There I met the captain of Ross-shire, an erudite man with a twinkle in his eye. After some talk he said, "When you wrote about the match you did us a great injustice." Cricket writers have been known to drop clangers and I eyed him warily. "What did I do?" I asked. "You omitted to mention that we were one man short," said he. Should he chance to chance on this book I feel he will be amply compensated. – Ian Peebles.'

Under the title 'Fingo – friend from Down Under' in the *Wisden Cricket Monthly* (England) of April 1980, and with a photograph of me sitting at an improvized desk of beer crates on the roof of Cardiff Arms Park (the seats in the press-box were all occupied), Alan Gibson wrote this charming, if flattering, profile of me:

'Larwood said that he was probably the most courageous batsman he ever encountered; Lord Justice Birkett wrote that he had the courage in his writing that was found in his batting. He is acknowledged to have been a fine opening batsman, a brilliant fieldsman and a writer who has enriched our knowledge and appreciation of cricket.

'His was not a long career in the game. He played for New South Wales for ten years, from 1930 to 1940. For Australia he played 18 times, scoring 1189 runs at an average of 42.46. In 1935–6 he made three Test centuries in succession in South Africa and followed this with another hundred against England in 1936–7 – four Test centuries in a row. He first played for his country in 1931–2 against South Africa; then, in the notorious bodyline series, he was included in the Australian team three times, going in first and standing up to Larwood, Voce, Allen and Bowes with great courage at Melbourne, where he made 83. At Adelaide he was out for nought in both innings, but for NSW against the tourists he scored 119 "when we in Sydney had our first taste of bodyline from Bill Voce and didn't relish it". In South Africa in 1935–6 Fingleton enjoyed a great success, leading the averages with 1192 runs at an average of 79. He made six centuries, four of them in the Tests. In Australia at Melbourne he reached the century (136), partnering Bradman in a sixth-wicket record stand of 346 – Bradman 270.

'He was a sound, dependable batsman with a fine defence and mastery of most of the strokes. If he did not show the brilliance and the panache of Macartney or McCabe there were times when he demonstrated his ability to score quickly. He once wrote to me: "You missed nothing by not seeing me bat – but I could field. Loved it!" Tribute has often been paid to the magnificence of his fielding, either away from the wicket or in the close positions.

'Fingleton took up journalism as a profession and was a well-known and highly respected member of the corps of political journalists.

'His writings on cricket are authoritative, as befits one who has himself known the heat and burden of the play and, from the other end, often watched Bradman massacre the bowling. Shrewd and informative in his judgement of a situation, of a player or of the welfare of the game as a whole, he intersperses his cool appraisement with humour, always apt, never malicious. For over twenty years, he wrote for the *Sunday Times* and I, for one, turned the pages eagerly to begin my reading with "Fingo". I was never disappointed, for he always had something worthwhile and original to say and there was usually something to bring a smile.

'His standards are high, for he always thought cricket too great a game to be dishonoured by sharp practice, bad language, over-reaction and those manifestations of disapproval and bad manners which we have had to grow used to in recent years. He wrote, "It is all a matter of standards and what is acceptable ... I will turn aside from a modern novel which flaunts four-letter words in my face, which means that I seldom ever finish one. But I regard it as an insult to my intelligence that I should be asked to accept such gutterage and I hope it is given short shrift on the cricket field. How can modern players make abiding friendships, which is one of the rich gems of the game, if they slate each other unmercifully on the field?"

'He wrote often of Bradman, especially in his book on the 1948 visit of the Australians, *Brightly Fades the Don*. While he had the highest admiration for Bradman's batting, he did not always see eye to eye with him or admire the way in which the Don isolated himself from his fellow-players. But he wrote, after giving a list of "the greats" he himself had played with or against, "One, then, covers a glittering field, yet I have not the slightest hesitation in saying that Don Bradman was the most remarkable batsman I knew. Moreover, there would not be one of his generation who would not acclaim him the same way. He bestrode the cricket world as nobody before or since has done."

'"Fingo" has a number of very fine books on cricket to his credit: all are written with that blend of expert knowledge (which comes from experience in the very top ranks of the game), impartial judgement, and all-round competence in assessing the whole cricket scene. I have mentioned *Brightly Fades the Don*, which

combines an appreciation of Bradman with the story of
the triumphant 1948 tour. In *Cricket Crisis* he gives his
own summing-up of the bodyline tour. There is a book
devoted wholly to one game: *The Greatest Test of All*
tells the story of the only tie in the history of Test
cricket – the game between Australia and West Indies
in 1960. *Fingleton on Cricket* is a selection of the
author's best writing – and Fingleton's best is very
good indeed. His book on Trumper, published in 1978,
was a work of devotion. In a letter to me he said, "But I
felt inadequate to the task – that I would not do him
justice." Although the book did not meet with uni-
versal acclaim, I feel that he did do justice to his hero,
who was, and still is, hero to many Australian cricket-
lovers. "Carter, who was my first Sydney skipper, used
to say, 'Put Vic right up the top and then talk about the
rest.'"

'In all his books and articles there is a humour that
lights up the page, a feeling for the individual player,
and a deep awareness of the need to uphold the true
values and standards of cricket. He has insight,
understanding and a prose style that makes one want to
go on reading – and that is surely the best style of all.

'He has a link with the best-known of cricket writers
– Sir Neville Cardus. He wrote, "Neville Cardus, my
best friend in cricket I would say, and always an
inspiration to me in all ways, is always at me to write
more books."

'As a broadcaster he was a great success; that slow,
inimitable drawl gave us all we wanted to know of the
play and the players. He had no bias, and there was
always the wry comment to give point to his wordpic-
ture. In recent years he has been very much missed
from the microphone.

'I believe he is writing his autobiography. When it is
published I shall be at the head of the queue at my local
bookshop, for I know I shall be buying entertainment,
humour, good writing and the fascinating story of a
man who, by his ability as a cricketer and even more by
his contributions to the literature of the game, has put
us all in his debt.'

· 16 ·

Reflections on This and That

My worst driving offence in England was to go down Piccadilly the wrong way. Setting out for John Woodcock's home in the lovely village of Longparish in Hampshire, I asked a taxi-driver at Charing Cross how to get on to the A40. I don't know whether he meant it, or was pulling my leg, when he told me to go to Piccadilly and turn left. I did just that and was met by blaring horns and headlights. It is a one-way street. I couldn't reverse as the traffic was storming up behind me so, hoping for the driving luck I seem to have in England, I deemed myself a bus, crossed and went down the bus lane, ready to explain to any pouncing bobby that I was an ignorant Australian. Luckily I happened across neither bus nor constable, and I went under the Piccadilly tunnel to Knightsbridge and thus along the Brompton Road on to the A40.

I had a very close call one day in Nottingham, the worst of many bad one-way street cities I found in England. I found myself in the right-hand turn lane that led back to a city I had just left and certainly didn't want to see again in a hurry. Putting on my left-turn indicator, I bided my time and got into the main stream, heading north. In my rear-vision mirror I spied a police car which had done precisely what I had done but with a valid reason: the driver wanted to have a word with me. Realizing this and with him hanging on my tail, I indicated left into the scuppers and weighed anchor. Sure enough, a police constable was alongside me in a trice with a very polite: 'I wonder whether you would step into our car, please, sir. We would like a word with you.'

One does not refuse such an invitation so politely phrased, and I freely admitted fault. I pleaded that I was an Australian and rather ignorant of English traffic laws (Lord alone knows how many times I had done England by car!), that I wanted to avoid their city at all costs and that I was truly sorry. 'Who do you think,' asked the senior constable, 'will win the next Test?' I could see tact was needed. 'Why,' I said, weighing it up like a judge, 'I really think England will win the next, officer. With a little luck I think they might have won this one at Trent Bridge.' The answer seemed to be the right one. 'You have admitted your error,' he said, 'but in view of the fact that you will be back in Australia by the time the summons is issued, we will let you off with a caution. But in future, do what the signs say.' I thanked them both very warmly and at the next light gave the (still following) police car a merry wave and a toot.

On a previous visit to England I had bought a wretched car that would insist on giving up when most needed. I pulled away from our Altrincham hotel for Old Trafford with plenty of time to get ahead of a huge approaching truck. Sure enough, my car cut out and drivers of big trucks in England aren't very pleased when they have to slam on their brakes. At the next light, I wound down my window and called over before he could deliver his intended blast: 'Sorry, mate, I'm just a poor ruddy Australian driver.' He finished giving me a smile and wave.

I have found on all my trips to England that people respond quickly to a gesture of friendship. They want to be friends and always open up with a little sunshine. When I said a few tart things about the pouring rain at Nottingham, a woman asked me, 'Don't you like our liquid sunshine, luv?' I don't know what the Almighty had against Britain when he dumped it where it is. He could have put it a good thousand miles to the south. Low depression after low depression now leap-frogs the Atlantic to drench their loads on the Home Isles. But all the soaking does lead to a glorious spring and summer that is excelled in beauty nowhere in the world – if the sun shines!

Some London taxi-drivers are rightfully renowned for their wit, but I think they are the means of preserving an abject piece of snobbery. I am sure it is snobbery that makes everybody think it is the right thing to tip taxi-drivers. Tipping was once thought abhorrent in Australia but is now becoming the vogue. Why? They simply do a job. I have never yet seen one get off his bottom to open a door or help with luggage. I think they must have beds and coffins specially made in a seated position. In pouring rain once in London I took a taxi to the Sports Club and inadvertently gave some Australian coins among the fare. "Ere, wot's this?' said the driver. I went back to look at the coins and he was right. 'At least,' I tried to appease him, 'it is as good as your own.' 'Why, then,' he countered, 'do so many of you bleeding Aussies come over 'ere?' I had the answer to that. 'Well,' I replied, 'it's not for your bleeding sunshine.' One seldom gets the last word with a London taxi-driver.

I loved the London tubes, though they are now so pricey. Larry and I would often go into town to shop, and we once had an extraordinary experience. On our tube to Piccadilly we sat next to a young mother who had a beautiful baby girl, which we much admired. Shopping over some hours later, we had a drink and a meal and went underground again at Piccadilly – and sat down next to that mother again and her baby; goodness knows where they had been in the interval. And she got off, at our home station of Highgate, leaving us at Stanhope Road, 'our' road. I would have had words with her about the amazing coincidence but Larry hates me talking to strangers. It is, I suppose, the journo in me, the pro in him.

*

I got much pleasure during my last trip (1980) watching BBC television. I thought their coverage of everything magnificent, though it distressed me to see how far their ethical standards have dropped. One American film I saw would never have been screened in former years. It was full of violence, blasphemies and obscenities. Nauseating!

I began broadcasting for our ABC in Hammond's first trip after the war and found the technique vastly different from writing. An odd thing was that neither the ABC nor, later, the BBC thought it necessary to give lessons in the technique of talking on the air. They assumed you would know what to do and what to avoid. You were just thrown at the mike raw and learned as you went along in a world much less friendly than that of newspapers. The best lesson I ever received came from an anonymous listener in Australia (I suspect it might have been Percy Williams, a former cricket master of Wesley College, Melbourne; he once wrote a delicious satire on ABC cricket broadcasters, with them all thanking one another profusely) who suggested I repeat 'ring, ing, ping' over and over to bring out words which I had a habit of clipping.

Typical of him, Raymond 'Crusoe' Robertson-Glasgow moved aside from the mike for me on the BBC. Knowing I was struggling on my first trip, Crusoe said he had too much work and passed on some of it. I knew the gesture for the friendly one it was. So I moved into his seat, doing commentaries. Anthony Craxton took me on to television and he remains the best, by far, of the cricket producers I met. He knew his cricket and understood the men who worked under him. I didn't endear myself to one cricket producer by telling him I thought his commentators were too cock-sure in giving opinions about decisions, especially lbw ones, when they were replayed. The umpires, I held, were in the best position to judge, not people high up and far away, their views foreshortened by cameras. I think it wrong that umpires should be subjected to this ordeal. 'Must have been close,' is good enough. However, I gradually realized that broadcasting was making too many demands on my time and thoughts. Newspapers were my first love, and Denis Hamilton was right when he said I should have followed Crusoe's example and moved aside. Perhaps it was vanity.

*

On one occasion I ran into a difference of opinion with the Australian, Alan McGilvray, at the Oval during a Test. Ted Dexter came and went first ball, hitting the rankest long-hop from Ken Mackay, of all bowlers, plumb down Gaunt's throat on the fine-leg boundary. It was a ball Dexter could have hit down and anywhere on the leg-side. McGilvray had much to say about the bad luck of the shot. When my turn came to comment I disagreed with McGilvray and said it was bad cricket, that no one should play a loose shot like that first ball of a Test innings. To say the least, it was indiscreet. McGilvray came back and took issue with me. We were both in the wrong in debating the point on the air and should have left it where it was.

John Arlott now comes into the story. He came down late to breakfast one morning at Nottingham and, as I was on my own, he asked if he could join me. 'Sure,' I said, 'do join me, John, and tell me why you refuse to broadcast with me on the BBC.' 'No, no, no,' said John, in some perturbation. 'It was McGilvray who "did" you. Not me.' And John proceeded to tell me how, at a BBC dinner after the Oval play, McGilvray had been asked by Charles Max Muller, then Head of Outside Broadcasting, what had gone wrong down at the Oval that day. According to John, McGilvray put the blame on me and the great Max Muller pronounced the edict: 'Very well, Fingleton will never broadcast for the BBC again.' On the many occasions I have proved Max Muller wrong, for example by doing an hour-and-a-half stint for the BBC when rain held up an Old Trafford Test; I have felt tempted to give him a cheerio call, but have resisted.

It is ironic that earlier that summer I had given McGilvray a big boost: listeners had written to me and asked about him, wanting to know his cricket background as they had never heard of him. I thought laying the blame for the Oval exchange of views entirely on me was a bit thick. McGilvray can be very strongly opinionated at times but part of the fault lay with Max Muller who should, at the very least, have discussed the affair with me. Like Norman Yardley and Freddie Brown (who were former Test skippers), I was supposed to be an 'expert', the others 'ball-by-ball' men. If Muller knew the game intimately, he certainly concealed that knowledge from me.

At the time I never greatly appreciated being on the air with John Arlott. We had first tangled at Old Trafford in 1956 when he disagreed with me that the brown patch of a pitch in a green oasis looked a bit odd; he didn't think so at all. Arlott was supposed to relinquish the mike to the 'experts' at the end of each over for their comments, but John often had great difficulty in doing so. As I see it now, I was right with McGilvray; wrong about Arlott. I should have appreciated that he meant much to so many listeners. He was full of colour and chat and left no gaps. I should have realized that and let him have the mike – he always did! But there was no one on hand in my time at BBC radio who supervised and saw that the various people adhered to their work schedule.

Arlott had one final shot at me at the breakfast table after denying he was the one to get me banned. 'But you do,' he said, 'take the — out of me at times.' It was the only time I recall having the last word with John (whom I really like): 'And you do leave yourself open at times, John,' I said. When, later, I was invited to the mike at Old Trafford to 'fill in a few minutes', I had much pleasure yapping with Brian Johnston, Christopher Martin-Jenkins, Freddie Trueman, Henry Blofield and others. John walked into the box, saw me at the mike and walked out again. A pity, I thought, as I would have liked to reminisce with him in his final year at the Beeb.

Heads of Outside Broadcasting who have succeeded Max Muller have asked me to work for them, Robert Hudson and Cliff Morgan among them, and I do like an occasional radio chat. I have worked on the shows of Tony Lewis and Angus Mackay, and found Jim Swanton, Brian Johnston, Rex Alston and others easy to work with although, because of my writing commitments, I have seldom been able to accept BBC hospitality invitations. I played cricket once for Brian Johnston's side at Widford, and surprised myself and others by hitting five sixes off successive balls. It was a most enjoyable club game. At the supper afterwards I found myself in conversation with a chap who kept asking me questions about the game. I sidled away, and asked Brian who the chap was. 'That is Sir Charles Percival, in charge when Singapore fell.' I sidled back. A journalist can be full of humbug at times.

*

From the political viewpoint, I found the televised conferences at Blackpool and Brighton absorbing and beautifully presented. London newspapers were well out in their forecasts about our Australian elections (even at the distance I thought Labour had not yet lived down the years of profligacy under Whitlam, and had too much leeway to make good, to be in the running); they were also wrong in predicting that the American Presidential election, which had bored the world for twenty months of jockeying and ballyhoo, would be cliff-hanger; and the press was again wrong over the Healey–Foot tilt, tipping Healey.

Watching the Blackpool conference I sensed something that is prevalent in our own politics – the domination of the Labour party by the unions. The election of a leader surely is the prerogative of members, who know the contenders best, and it is bad for the party that pressures should come to bear from outside. In many countries now, and very much so in Australia, thuggery of one kind and another is coming into politics. My younger brother, Glen, made a trip to Russia in a union delegation in the early 1950s, but because he would not tread a particular line when he returned he was bashed up by the 'comrades' in a Sydney pub. I believe the ordinary person has been frustrated too much by strikes and now just won't wear a political party that is tied too strongly to the unions.

I took a bet with myself that Reagan would win the Presidency when I saw him on television. He called dramatically for a pause to pray and then told the world, and particularly Americans, that he never went anywhere without 'the good book'. Reagan might be a sincere Christian – I have no reason to doubt him – but he used a good ploy to get the Evangelical vote, which is not inconsiderable in the USA. In Australia, in the fifties, the press could not mention a politician without observing that he was either a staunch Presbyterian or a devout Catholic. I never knew what they dubbed Anglicans. Ardent, possibly. Catholics, with the press, were always suspect. Seemingly every politician was a church-goer, though few in fact bothered. Nor, I knew, did the men who wrote about them. Margaret Thatcher, whose standing in Australia and with Australian statesmen is very high, also indulged in some religious utterances, quoting St Francis of Assisi; but this was not until after the general elections and I believe it was the idea of her speech-writer, as was the line about 'the lady's not for turning'. A good speech-writer, who can produce the timely catch-phrase, is the best possession a leader can have.

I have to apologize to Sir Hugh Carleton Greene, former Director-General of the BBC, for a shabby trick I played him in Australia. He delivered himself in Sydney of the belief that 'A good politician should never object to hard questioning: it enables him to show off his strokes.' Still a bit nettled by Max Muller I told myself, 'Right, Sir Hugh. I'll be ready for you when you take block in Canberra.' He gave me first interview and I gave him some hard questioning. Yes, he admitted, there were 'queers and commies' in the BBC (in an organization employing some twenty-six thousand people there would be some of every type in it). Still the admission made a good cabling story. The *Sunday Times* cabled back and asked was I sure of my quotes; I said I was and they ran the story over four columns. Sir Hugh wasn't very pleased with me; he had complained to the next man in the interviewing line, Alan Fitzgerald of the *Canberra Times*, about the silly questions he had been asked. He didn't in fact play his strokes very well to the questioning, hard if footling, but my apologies to him, anyway, and the BBC.

*

Another television programme that absorbed me was the Richard Dimbleby Memorial speech by Lord Denning, Master of the Rolls. It was a brilliant, likeable talk but I was surprised that a person so high in the British judiciary should submit himself to a public debate that invited comment and criticism, and that he could propound the amazing theory that judges should be superior to politicians, having the power to set aside new legislation if the judges thought it unconstitutional, or if it offended against reason and fundamentals. It was a bold claim the noble law lord made, that in Britain every judge on his appointment discards all politics and prejudices, and deserves higher marks for impartiality, integrity and unfailing conscientiousness than any other group of the population. I doubt whether it is humanly possible for anybody to shrug off his background, his mind cleansing itself overnight, so to speak, of all the political beliefs he held before his rise to the bench. Judges may like to think this is so, but when they doff wig and gown and talk in their clubs, they immediately assume the conversation of an ordinary individual. If Lord Denning believes in the perfect world in which a judge 'discards all politics and prejudices' he must believe, as I do, that a lawyer who enters party politics must forfeit any chance of being elevated to the bench.

Lord Denning described earlier editorials in the London *Times*, criticizing a decision by the Court of Appeal as well as one by the Lords, as 'restrictive, reactionary and clearly against the public interest'. One expected the Thunderer to boom, but apart from a splendid account of the talk, the *Times*, editorially, was mute. Harry Evans, then editor of the *Sunday Times*, went into bat. He said that Lord Denning was a great man but that in his Dimbleby lecture he had reached the apogee of his second career – after the Master of the Rolls had come the populist leader. 'Denning probably is the only man alive who could command a peak-time television audience in order to advance the proposition that among human types, judges are the most superior beings of all: not only above kings and politicians and trade unionists and, of course, journalists, but above the laws themselves.' The *Observer*, another good newspaper, also tore strips off Lord Denning. The Professor of Public Law at the London School of Economics, John Griffith, thought the good Lord was arrogant and short on humility (though he did not appear so to me), thereafter taking the same line as Harry Evans.

Lord Denning did speak of possible abuse of power by judges. He admitted that if they diverged or departed from their responsibilities they would be guilty of misuse of power, but gave no suggestion of how they would be dealt with. He asked a question with a quotation '*Sed quis custodiat ipsos custodes?*' (Who will guard the guardians?) but his question seemed only to address the possibility that a future Prime Minister might seek to pack the benches with judges of his own political colour. He spoke of a political decision so to pack the House of Lords in order that they should vote themselves out of existence, and wondered whether Parliament could lawfully abolish the second chamber. I saw his talk, in itself, as a threat to democracy. Parliament is answerable to the electorate, judges aren't.

I don't know what the position is in Britain, but in my own country it would seem that some politicians enter Parliament simply as a step towards the bench. So many have become judges by that route; our present Chief Justice of the High Court, Sir Garfield Barwick, is a case of a once-busy Minister and keen advocate of Liberal party policy who must have found it extremely difficult immediately to cast out of his mind all the political ideals he had previously held and expressed.

Judges can be the very epitome of charm when it suits them. I was the only press-man once in a certain court when proceedings broke down. His Honour let fly a blast about his time being wasted, the time of counsel and litigants being wasted, and all at huge cost. He left the bench and in a minute his associate was beside me, asking me to come to the judge's chamber. 'I would not, of course, run the story. It would only cause trouble.' The judge was very persuasive but what he was asking me to do was put my job on the line for him. Les Herron, later Chief Justice, was one of the barristers that day and he, or anyone would be free, later in his club, to say how so-and-so blew his top in court that day. The story could have got to my editor, Frank Ashton, who would have been justified in sending me a 'Please see me' note, asking why I hadn't written the story. Had I the nous I should have made the judge no promises, written the story, sent a memo to Frank and said the judge had asked me not to write this story. I think the judge had tee-time booked at an adjacent links; it might have meant him missing a few easy putts that day, but he was notorious among us for that type of behaviour. As it was he did not realize he had made a good story into a rip-snorted 'Judge blasts court then asks our man not to write it.' I would have been *persona non grata* in his court in future, if he still had a court!

Bill O'Reilly tells a story of a district court judge named Sheridan, his friend, who told his court one morning he had

had an anonymous letter in his mail dealing with the case in progress and how seriously he, Sheridan, viewed the offending communication. 'It ill behoves me,' he said, 'sitting where I am now, to say what I did with that letter, sitting where I was then.' Judges like good publicity; one in Sydney, named Curlewis The Elder ('Curly'), was always good copy – he took a delight in dressing-down any cringing member of the bar who committed a grammatical slip.

No judge was less pompous than Lord Justice Birkett, formerly Sir Norman, who was an outstanding barrister before he moved to the bench. In 1948 we thought him the best after-dinner cricket speaker we had heard. I ventured to ask him to write the Foreword to *Brightly Fades the Don*, which he did magnificently and from that we formed a firm friendship. Lord Birkett was a natural charmer and dined me twice at his club, the Athenaeum, to talk over his foreword. His love of cricket was the kind that many people once enjoyed in England. He spoke feelingly of how, as a lad, he saw the miracle of Archie Maclaren's cricket bag on the Piccadilly station in Manchester and, making sure he was not being watched, touched it! Once we were together at a garden reception given for Australian cricketers. The face of his host puzzled him: he was certain he had seen it somewhere. Then it dawned on him; he had sent him 'down' some years before! I recall him talking of American hospitality: of somebody claiming that where she came from in the States the hospitality was so lavish that they had drinks between drinks; and of the blond who was enjoying herself so much at a party she said she felt much more like herself now than when she first came in. It was Lord Birkett (and it would be difficult to receive more authoritative views) who told me one London morning during an Authors and Players match that I had been libelled by a gossip column in a certain newspaper whose view it was that I could well be playing for either side as the books I had written had been 'ghosted'. As I got a century in the match and had made many from the same column source I did not accept Lord Birkett's magnificent free advice.

Gough Whitlam, who can be most splenetic, didn't

forgive Chief Justice Barwick for dismissing him. Though I must beware of contempt in speaking of Barwick the Judge I think it fair to discuss him as a Member, and the general opinion was that he didn't cut a resplendent figure in politics, being irritable in debate, a bit pompous in declaring his stout political beliefs (he, too, was a Cabinet Minister), and rather peppery; he and Whitlam used to swap words on the floor of the House. Nor did he leave an imperishable memory as a Foreign Minister. Whitlam, who didn't miss such things, wrote how Barwick and Kerr had both crossed the tracks, developing a similar love of royalty, panoply, honours and form. He pointed out how on 10 November 1975, without telling the Prime Minister or his own judicial colleagues, Barwick advised the Governor-General how to dispose of the Prime Minister (Whitlam). 'When I was discussing the situation at Harvard Law School,' wrote Whitlam in May 1980, 'one of the professors exclaimed, "He should have been impeached!" ' Whitlam would have agreed although, as the elections showed, Kerr-Barwick interpreted the feeling of the electorate correctly. A Labour member who had the pre-election job of estimating the vote told me there would be a ten per cent swing to Labour!

Dr Herbert Evatt was certainly one judge who didn't put aside his politics and prejudices when he went on the High Court bench. His brother judges, Starke and Rich, showed their displeasure by sitting on the bench side-on to him. The profession could never forgive Evatt for going into politics, although I think their dislike was mainly because one so distinguished in law chose the Labour party.

Evatt hoped to become Prime Minister but, although brilliant and gifted intellectually, he didn't quite possess the talent for that job. He thought intrigue was an essential part of politics and, although I agree there must be a certain amount of wheeling and dealing in the game – even Chifley acknowledged that – the Doc overplayed his hand. He was a born schemer, always thinking people were plotting against him. I doubt if he trusted anybody. He frequently instructed Albert Grundyman, his factotum, to 'Go down to the bar, Grundyman, and listen to what they are saying

Denis Lillee, the famed Australian, at the moment of delivery and decision. A perfect follow-through.

Viv Richards, batting against England. One of the all-time greats.

Off to meet the Don. Ian Chappell, with a big beer and cigar, goes to front Sir Donald Bradman, a member of the Board, on a charge of misbehaviour. Ian was 'warned'.

This could rank as the stroke of the century. Kim Hughes of Australia hitting a miraculous four past point off Mike Hendrick in the Centenary Test. The photographer, Patrick Eagar, should get as much commendation as Hughes in capturing a genius of a stroke for posterity.

about me,' giving him 2/– for a beer. When Evatt made a big speech he did so in a flat, monotonous voice, no rise or fall, with his notes and paper scattered on the table in front of him; he was the untidiest politician in the House. Chifley used to refer to him as 'my learned friend': 'I must put that to my learned friend down the corridor,' he would say.

So, as far as politics and lawyers in Australia are concerned, I could not see eye to eye with Lord Denning in his television talk; and if they do ascend the bench judges who have been politicians, and high ones at that, must not object and mutter 'contempt' if their actions as politicians are recalled. No, I think the solution is that those who participate actively in politics should be debarred from elevation to the bench. I wonder which political side would complain most about that? The most boring legal cliché I know is that one about justice must not only be done, but must be seen to be done. Probably that is why Justice is depicted as being blindfold! Until the bench is barred to politicians I won't line up with Lord Denning in his high opinion of his fellow judges. As Harry Evans wrote: 'Their talents are not yet godlike and nor should be their powers . . . I think Lord Denning has weakened rather than increased support for the case he was arguing. Still, being apparently indestructible he may have other peaks of populism to scale. Given his life of luminous achievement it would certainly be a pity if the Dimbleby Lecture, which was most people's first sight of him, should also be what they remember him for.'

*

I began this chapter writing about English traffic and people I met, together with various sayings I heard, particularly in the north. Now I have indulged myself by reflecting on the BBC, Lord Denning, the judiciary and politics. Reverting to Australian affairs and writing as an observer rather than an expert, I know my view on the constitutional crisis is of no importance, though I think a government elected for a certain term of office should be given that chance. The manner in which Rex Connor was vilified over the Khemlani affair was a disgrace. In my time Rex was one of the outstandingly honest men around. I

P

think Whitlam brought much of the trouble on himself (when the Senate stubbornly refused supply to him) when he tinkered with the Senate by making Senator Vince Gair Ambassador to Ireland. Still, politics is a dangerous game for a pressman; he has too many to please and if his copy does not meet with the beliefs of the reader he is immediately thought to be 'biassed'.

· 17 ·

A Brilliant Editor
and his Feats

Harold Evans, till lately editor of the London *Sunday Times*, is known as the glamour boy of Fleet Street. He neither denies it nor is ashamed of the tag. He assumes that he is so described because he learned to ski at forty. A further distinction, of which he has many, is that he is the only Briton to write a best-selling book on ski-ing. Moreover at university, where he went after leaving the RAF, he had a small BSA!

At one stage London's *Private Eye* gave him the title of Dame Harold Evans. This was a take-off based on the famous English actress, Dame Edith Evans and, Evans thinks, has some connection with the name of his wife being Enid. He recalls going up in the lift at the *Sunday Times* building with a lot of blue-suited print workers and an advertising manager. The advertising man said, 'Dame Edith Evans? Are you a *bit* queer, then?' Posterity does not record what Evans said but, knowing him, it would have been terse and to the point. Evans is never lost for a word.

*

Evans began his brilliant newspaper career as did so many famous men who have risen to the top of the tree – at the very roots. I had always thought he was a Geordie but he isn't – only his university was. His father drove steam engines out of Manchester. Harold, or Harry as he seems to be more generally known, began his newspaper life on a weekly in a cotton town of Lancashire, and his first job was as film critic. This consisted of searching out grubby film magazines, hoping to find in them the film that was on at the local flea-pit and then summarizing the film for the benefit of the cotton-workers. The magazines he consulted used phrases like 'good thick ear', meaning there was a lot of fisticuffs in the film. Evans duly translated this into something like 'unedifying scenes of violence' or something suitably pompous. For the rest of the time, Evans put on his size 9 walking boots and called on vicars, tea-party ladies, undertakers and, on one occasion, a suspected murderer, collecting paragraphs which added up at the end of the week to something like eleven columns of print. He was getting plenty of experience, if not money, at the base of the tree.

The proprietor of the newspaper used to breeze into the office on Friday night, smoking a cigar and with a milk bottle in his hand – Evans remembers him as somewhat of a health crank who hadn't given up smoking. In those early days Evans was keen on table-tennis and his playing companion was Ronnie Allerck. They played tournament doubles together for some time while Allerck was an international going down to the English open championships. Evans admits he wasn't quite in Allerck's class and never made the English standard – although he thinks he might have made the Australian one!

Entering the RAF, he found himself clerk to an air commodore but, being a man of intense vigour, Evans organized a magazine for the boys. He ran into problems, the first and a considerable one being that the man drawing the front cover was put into clink; Evans had to use his influence with the air commodore to get the man allowed drawing paper and pen so that he could continue to draw covers. Evans admitted the magazine had a bad start because he didn't know what the air force men wanted. He made the mistake of putting aeroplanes on the covers, which were the last things they wanted to see. Harry nutted it out and secured a photograph of a partly-clothed local lady named Diana Fluck, sitting on a stile. She later became the filmstar Diana Dors. That issue, Harry was happy to report, was a sell-out and he realized he had struck the right note for the boys.

Before the magazine, Evans and his staff had tried to produce a paper and this gave him a unique insight into type, something which aids the working life of all news-papermen. Evans would stay on late, week after week, hand-setting body type, and finally rushing out copies just as the camp broke up. Learning to hand-set type was his introduction to typography and one of his five newspaper books, all required reading now, is about type. The others are on English, lay-out, and his latest is on photo-journalism. The wonder is that one who never spared himself on his main love, the *Sunday Times*, should find time to write so many books for budding journalists.

*

I think he used to go through his Sunday newspaper with a fine tooth comb. Harry always encouraged his men in far-off countries with much-appreciated cables. I once wrote an article from Australia depicting for those lying in their warm beds on a cold Sunday morning in England what it would be like facing up to the hostile Lillee and Thomson at their fastest, and supported by yelling thousands in Melbourne. I got a cable back from Harry: 'No thanks. I'd sooner stay in bed.'

Evans is a difficult man to interview, mainly because he has so much on his plate in limited time. He is reticent about the really great and successful campaigns he has run, to get money for the thalidomide children, and in defying the government censor on the Crossman papers, though he considers that 'quite a thing'. He took his case on the banning of the thalidomide articles to the European court in 1973 and contending there that it violated his rights to free speech he had a famous victory, culminating the work of six years. He thinks that this will have a profound effect upon the laws of England and considers that would be the biggest achievement of his newspaper life.

Evans is a modest man who realizes his capacity and prefers to let his triumphs speak for themselves. A recent book, *Suffer the Children*, tells the whole story of the thalidomide children. There was a time when even the affluent *Sunday Times* thought his campaign was costing a little too much. So the Evans victory in that was doubly sweet. He also rates highly the investigation into the spy, Philby. He sent Murray Sayle to Moscow; he returned with quite a few stories about Philby, for whom he waited at a post office. Harry gives much credit to his staff, saying it was the result of teamwork.

*

What appeals still to the newspaperman in Evans was the famous Evans–Christie saga, which took place when he was editor of the *Northern Echo*. Timothy Evans (no relation) was hanged for the murder of his wife and baby on the testimony of a wartime policeman named John Christie. A few years later it was discovered that Christie was a mass-killer – there were bodies everywhere, including a human bone propping up the garden fence. Christie was arrested and later hanged. Many people were horrified at the thought that Evans had been hanged for a murder he might not have committed. Michael Eddowes and Ludovic Kennedy both investigated the mystery and proved to the satisfaction of many people that Evans had indeed been wrongly hanged. But nothing happened.

Harold Evans was in Darlington and read that Sir Frank Soskice, then Home Secretary, had just turned down a demand by Eric Lubbock, the Liberal MP, for an enquiry. Harold Evans was enraged by Soskice's refusal, because he recalled that when Soskice was in Opposition he had demanded the very enquiry he was now refusing. Harold Evans teamed up with a fascinating local businessman named Herbert Wolfe, who had come to Britain with only a few pence and stayed to make a fortune in chemicals. Together they started a national campaign for an enquiry and in the course of it one of their main helpers, Michael Eddowes, arranged for the press to be shown around the house in Rillington Place where the murders had taken place. It was a big event for the campaigners. The idea was to convince the press that the physical lay-out of the place made it impossible for the mass murders to have taken place in the way Christie said they did, i.e. that Timothy Evans must have been innocent. Unfortunately, everything went wrong. Hoards of press-men turned up and Eddowes let them all into a house which he had sub-let to West Indians.

After about half an hour, as the pressmen were being shown around the backyard, a huge West Indian lady bellowed at the press from an upper floor, clearly conveying the impression they were not welcome. Then she rushed to the front door and turned the key; and they were all locked in. Harold went to the door and conducted a lengthy conversation with a policeman through the letter-box, explaining he was the editor of the *Northern Echo* and how imperative it was that he catch a train back to the office. Eventually, the West Indian lady was cajoled into unlocking the door but she clearly gave the press to understand that she was, very naturally, fed up with their investigations.

Christie was a necrophiliac and Evans treasured a letter which Bernard Levin of the *Times* wrote to him next day saying, 'It would have served the lot of you right if Christie had come down the chimney and necrophilized the lot of you.' Anyway, out of the comic disaster the campaign got an enormous amount of publicity; and Evans got back to his editor's desk on time.

*

One never got the impression with Evans that he pulled rank as editor of the world's outstanding newspaper. He is always on good terms with his staff and takes an interest in them; but I would imagine if the need arose to say a few curt words to any of them, they would remember it. One of his greatest disappointments in his newspaper career was when a newspaper strike hit both *The Times* and the *Sunday Times*, so that his own paper was out of circulation for eleven months. It came back bigger and brighter than ever, the lapse giving it added stimulus. But for one who had risen from the lowly ranks to his high office, that dispute hurt Evans more than he cares to admit.

I was having dinner one evening at one of London's most publicized hotels with Evans and Graham Perkin, the editor of the *Melbourne Age* but since, sadly, deceased. It was Perkin's dinner party and if Evans had one disciple in newspaper work it was Perkin, who fashioned his own remarkably successful editorship on that of Evans. Thanks to him I also wrote extensively on cricket for the Melbourne newspaper. The fourth member of our party was Percy Beames, then the *Age*'s cricket correspondent. I was in mid-sentence when a very strange thing happened: I disappeared completely from view under the table. The leg of my chair had collapsed and a waiter, coming up to sympathize, said that was the second chair which had so collapsed that week. The unctuous head waiter, full of smiles, arrived bowing and scraping and I sent him off, saying he would hear from my solicitor on Monday. That particular hotel would not have appreciated publicity about the black watch beetle, or such like, infecting their chairs. I could not have had two better witnesses than two editors in pleading some sort of whip-lash but, with my dinner, I swallowed the indignity.

Evans once took a rise out of me. It was a Saturday when rain had washed out play at Lord's and I returned to my hotel to write letters. I left the room momentarily and, on returning, saw a stranger going through my overcoat pocket. Thinking I had mistaken the number of my room, I went outside and checked. It was my room all right. This chap was obviously pick-pocketing. I chased him down the passage, missing him with my diving tackle. I cried, 'Stop that man' and he fled down the long broad staircase, but people just looked up disinterestedly. Belinda, my daughter, had the foresight to phone the front desk and George, the doorman, put his large boot in the revolving door. The policeman came in from Charing Cross station, and we all set out for Bow Street in a Black Maria. The man, known to the police, as they say, got three months. I wrote what I thought was a humorous account of the event and they ran it on the leader page. Harry sent me a nice note about that but staggered me a little by adding, 'This is the type of story we would like more often from you.'

I had joined the *Sunday Times* back in 1948 when Pat Murphy ('the Big Man'), then Sports editor and later editor, engaged me, for which, and for all Pat's help and friendship I shall always be grateful. On Friday, 3 October 1980, the *Sunday Times* gave me a farewell lunch in the board room, at which Harry Evans presided and said a few words. His cheerful and friendly spirit ran through the whole newspaper and that lunch was one of the nicest things that happened to me in my newspaper career.

· 18 ·

Farewell to Old England
For Ever

It was just after midnight on Thursday, 27 November 1980, that the Australian Container line ship, *Australian Endeavour*, slipped out of Liverpool docks and headed down the English coast. I looked through the cabin window: the rain was coming down in sheets which was fitting, because that English summer had been the worst of many I had known, wet and cold. So I said a final goodbye to England from Liverpool, a city in which I found much to admire, the city of the Liver Birds, of two of the finest cathedrals in the world and, surely, the friendliest of people in shops. And two champion football teams into the bargain. It was to nearby Blackpool that George Duckworth took me in 1948 to meet Harold Larwood again, who was running a small sweets and cigarette shop there. From that meeting grew a warm friendship that certainly never existed on the cricket field and which was to lead to him migrating with his family from Liverpool to Australia. This he has never regretted. He came not so long ago as a visitor to my golf club in Canberra, and when he was signing his name in our visitors' book I told him to put his residence as 'Nottingham'. 'What ruddy rot,' said Harold, 'I've been in Australia now longer than your Dennis Lillee.'

I had been in Liverpool a week before it dawned on me that David Sheppard was bishop there. He had been friendly to me when he played cricket for England and I thought it would be nice to give him a ring and chat, but I couldn't get past the tight security at Bishop's House. No, they wouldn't give me his number, he was ex-directory, but

if I left my name they would get him to give me a ring. I
wanted to pull his leg about the fact that I had come into his
diocese without first getting his permission, and I told them
if I left my name that would be giving the game away. So I
missed out on having a chat with the bishop, though I had
met up with him earlier in the year at that renowned
Taverners' dinner at the Grosvenor, the outstanding social
event of the disappointing Centenary Test at Lord's. I first
came across David at Canterbury in 1938 when, as he
subsequently told me, I trod on his toes as we were going
out to field. He was always a most pleasant man to talk to.
He told me the story of when he was having a good slice of
luck against the Nottingham character, 'Bomber' Wells.
When he got down to Bomber's end, that hero snarled at
him: 'You must have said your prayers this morning, Rev.,
with all the luck you are having.' 'Yes, Bomber, I did,' said
David, 'did you?'

The bishop has a really remarkable cathedral, magnificent
in conception and execution. I was toiling a hard-slogging
two-mile walk up the hill to go to mass, and passed the
Anglican shrine. A chap in the street told me to turn left
when I got to the top of the street and I couldn't miss the
Catholic cathedral. 'It looks like a ruddy space ship about to
take off' – and indeed it did. It is described as daring and
revolutionary, and it is all of that. It is said to be the most
modern cathedral in the world and I can well believe it. The
windows, by Margaret Traherne, are unbelievably beautiful
and must be more so when the sun shines which, not
surprisingly, it didn't while I was there. The archbishop
stood at the exit to greet people after mass and I said, as I
shook hands with him, 'Greetings from Australia.' He asked
'What part?' and, when I said 'Sydney', said he had just
been with the Sydney Cardinal, Jimmy Freeman (no doubt
at the Synod at Rome). I said I knew him well. I strolled
then to David's equally beautiful church and on the way
passed a man with a copy of the *Sunday Times*. On being
asked if he would direct me to where he got it he said:
'Certainly not on Bondi Beach,' with a big grin. I wandered
through a very derelict part of Liverpool, which seemed like
a bomb site, with raucous clusters of coloured and white

children, and got the last copy of the newspaper I wanted, and the last copy I would buy in England. It is more than sad to do accustomed things for the last time, and realize it won't happen again.

I wrote to David from the *Endeavour*; he replied to me back in Australia and said he was sorry he missed me in Liverpool. He was pleased I saw both cathedrals; he thinks they do a lot for each other and believes that the remarkably good relationships which have been developing these last few years are in a real sense because both are able to meet from strength in the Christian communities.

'And the two cathedrals stand for that. When you have had enough of one style you can go on to the other. We have had some very good occasions together in each cathedral and had one particularly great day on the Sunday of the Queen's Jubilee, when some four thousand people came first to crowd into our cathedral, then to walk along Hope Street together to complete the act of Thanksgiving and Dedication in the Roman Catholic Cathedral. Relationships were very bitter in Liverpool, the nearest to Northern Ireland in every way. It has been one of the most exciting experiences to come very close indeed personally to Archbishop Worlock and at much more than a personal level.

'You recognise something of the struggles of Liverpool. Unemployment here is not part of a "dip" in a bad economic cycle. It is something which has been chronic for many years. It seems to me one of the real callings of the Church to try to be a bridge across some of the divides in a very polarized society, and to allow people from both sides of the divisions to have their say properly within the Christian family.'

I have had some delightful encounters in life through cricket and though I never considered myself above the ruck of Test cricketers I was fortunate to possess an unusual name, as I have been more than fortunate to go thrice on Parkinson's show, twice in Australia and once in England – but more of that soon. In the early thirties I was a Royal

Australian Navy reservist and we used to do a three weeks training course at sea. My first trip was on the ill-fated *Canberra* and our trip that year consisted of a voyage from the buoy at Farm Cover to the dry-dock at Cockatoo, just up ahead in Sydney Harbour. Also on the *Canberra* at that time, was a fellow reservist named Jack McNally. Jack swam in the much publicized tilts with Arne Borg, the champion Swede, and Boy Charlton, an Australian folk hero.

It was my reservist friend, 'Buck' Jones from Paddington, who got me a game of cricket with the ship's crew at Brooklyn on the Hawkesbury. He told the officer of the watch that there was a reservist who played a bit of cricket. The reservists didn't quite appreciate the awesomeness of the quarter-deck and would often saunter out to go straight to the man who counted, instead of going through an intermediary. Generally, we were snapped into our place.

So, lent a pair of sand-shoes and in naval singlet and bell-bottom trousers I turned out for the ship's crew and was put in last, where I got a few not out. Our captain was an English lieutenant and he said to me, 'I see you have played this game before. I must put you in higher up at Jervis Bay.' The ship made its way down to Jervis Bay where the naval college was. We reservists didn't play much part in that voyage. The cook had put on beef for lunch and I recall he didn't drain the fat very well, so we were all sea-sick.

I was put in higher up, in fact I opened, and got a century. It was a superb pitch and a friendly attack. The captain-lieutenant patted himself on the back when he said to me: 'I knew you had played this game before. Tell me, have you ever played for any good teams?' 'Well, sir,' I said, 'I played for Australia last summer.' He took it very well and I'm sure it was for cricket and not for seamanship that at voyage's end I was promoted to A.B.

I haven't yet told the story about the Duke of Norfolk, who came to Australia with an English team in 1962 and was certainly the only Duke ever to do so. Moreover, Bernard (the Duke) was the premier Duke of Britain. Our cricket people got themselves into a terrible state about doing the Duke homage, but what put him off his ducal beat most were the women who would insist on bobbing curtsies to him. Bernard wasn't used to that. As we were flying to Adelaide, Woodcock nudged me, at thirty-five thousand feet above the Nullabor Desert. The Duke was making his way down the back with an obvious intention. 'There goes the highest peer in the land,' cracked Johnny, whom the Duke liked immensely. When we arrived at Adelaide the cricket establishment there waited at the first-class end of the plane for the Duke to emerge with his boys. The Duke came off the tourist exit and the establishment had to beat a hasty retreat to new positions.

*

I really think that after my cricket and even my political writing days were at an end, the best thing that happened to me was meeting up with Michael Parkinson in Australia. I have written at some length of Parkinson in this book but must explain how I first came to meet him. It was at one of those protracted business lunches in London when the *Sunday Times* sporting editorial staff assembled to confer on the coming summer. We were all invited to say a few words. I can't recall Michael saying anything at all, which is rather unusual for a Yorkshireman. Henry Longhurst spoke at length on golf and life because Henry was a philosopher. Others spoke spurred on, no doubt, by Lord Thomson's hospitality though his Lordship was present in name only, perhaps so that the name could be put to the bill. Michael Parkinson asked me to come on his show in Australia in 1979, and I went on with Bob Hawke, our number one trade union leader, and Kate Fitzpatrick, a charming Australian actress; I could not possibly have had better or nicer foils. If you go on television you submit to the public gaze in more ways than one, and that is fair enough. You get pleasant letters and abusive ones too. I got one of the latter after that appearance from some twit in Adelaide who accused me of being drunk, as if one would touch a drop of liquor before such a show. The adrenalin flowed, not liquor. The next time I appeared on the *Parkinson Show* was also in Australia, with John Watters and Maggie Dobberer, two well-known Australian actors; the third time in London I shared the show with Katie Boyle, well known in England, and the blind pianist George Shearing.

The appearance in London with the BBC was an

education, so highly-toned is their technical and production work. In London I kept my appearance a secret from my son, Larry, who was working there at the time. He had been in the audience at my first appearance and it was good to know he was there; but I thought he might tell me I was stupid to go on again, and I would probably have agreed with him. I got home to Highgate in time for us to watch the recorded London show together. I had had the horrors before it. Foolishly I had consumed a piece of BBC fruit-cake and a cup of tea beforehand, and they sat so ponderously on my chest I was sure I was due for a heart-attack. The chest pains were acute but Chris Greenwood, one of Mike's staff, sat by me, holding my hand, so to speak, and I thought, 'To hell with it. I might be doing Mike a good turn by croaking on his show.' The words of the poet Keats came to me, with a little variation: 'Now more than ever seems it rich to die; to cease upon the Parkinson with no pain.' I walked down stage steps very carefully, not trusting a 'dicky' right rugby knee, and the show seemed to be over before I was aware it was on. Being with Parkinson is like that, he puts one so much at ease. On all three shows I was the last to come on; this is a test, for you have to sit beneath the level of the stage, in a dingy dungeon, watching the other guests go through their paces on a set placed there for the purpose. Waiting to appear is like waiting to bat in a Test match; the clangour of butterflies in the stomach is deafening. After sitting in the pit, imagining the worst, you emerge at last to come down the steps into the dazzling glare of all the arc-lights and tiers of spectators, who might or might not be friendly. Fortunately I had family and friends in the Australian audiences, so I was sure of some support. In all three programmes Michael could have slapped me down at any time, as I took many liberties with him, but he is much too kind a man to do that. It was early in our journalistic careers that we struck up a friendly rapport. He says that at first I had refused to come on his show, but my memory of it is that he asked me when the show was running, I think, at Ipswich, and as a cricket tour was beginning next day in Worcester I couldn't see how I could fit both in.

I think his shows are popular because he has such a natural talent and is, as we say in Australia, a fair-dinkum person. I have heard some critics say he is a 'professional Yorkshireman'. It is true, he *is* a Yorkshireman and he *is* professional, to the tips of his fingers. Parkinson is the successful professional that he is because his family life is a happy one. His wife is a peach, Mary Agnes, of Irish descent, his three boys are manly and full of character, and he lives in an idyllic world at Maidenhead where his lovely garden is full of roses. His luscious lawn, complete with a piece of Bramall Lane turf (he is nostalgic by nature) runs down to the very brink of the Thames. Verdant trees surround it all. Nearby is the village of Bray and the local cricket ground he loves so well and where he and his three boys perform with his own team. There, too, are the local pubs where he drinks and yarns with several self-exiled Yorkshiremen. One pub, in particular, has a stupendous restaurant where the Queen once invited an army of guests, taking it over completely; the guest list from that occasion still hangs on the wall. To reach that pub from the Parkinsons', you have to pass through the ancient churchyard of Bray where the celebrated Vicar changed his religion as he pleased. Set in the walls of the church, upright, are the two tomb-stones of the lovers who committed suicide by jumping from the top of the tower. What a story that must have been! My son Larry and I are much indebted to the Parkinson family for the most generous hospitality we have known there, especially as Mary, a bubbling attractive woman of great intelligence and wit, cooks the best Yorkshire pudding in all England. Nor must I forget Freda, Michael's lovely Yorkshire Mum.

*

I have come so often to England and returned by many and various routes, but never by such a comfortable and enjoyable way as on this last occasion, the *Australian Endeavour* gliding over the bluest of Mediterranean seas and under a beautifully radiant sun. It was a time for reflection. I was traversing a passage I knew so well in former days: it was along that route I made my first trip to England on the *Orontes* when I met my wife, Philippa. I have come in other days on other ships but the voyage which gave me most pleasure was on the *Orcades* in 1953, when I had my wife and four children with me (the family later grew to five with Jacquie).

Travelling has given me tremendous thrills. One occasion in 1965 I remember in particular, when my daughter Belinda and I went one Sunday morning to St Peter's in Rome for a mass celebrated by Pope Paul VI. I had tried to get tickets from the *Sunday Times* man but he told me that I had left it too late: our best chance was to go down and stand in the nave, adjacent to the altar. So we did and watched the diplomats, the rich and all the rest being guided into their special seats in an enclosure by the altar. I saw a chap whom I named Private Garibaldi – for he seemed to have no rank at all in the drabest of khaki – taking the tickets and showing the invitees to their seats. I got his attention once, motioned to Belinda, gave him an assessment with my hands of the midship beam and pointed to the enclosure. Sure enough, Garibaldi was back in several minutes with a ticket which he passed to me and I in turn passed to Belinda. She sailed past smiling, and Garibaldi said something to me in Italian. A chap nearby asked if I knew what he said. I didn't. 'He said to wait a moment.' And sure enough Garibaldi came back with another ticket. I slipped him some lira, which I called 'Peter's pence' to square my conscience. (This was the term given to a collection made yearly in our churches for the aims of the Pope.) We had ringside seats, if one may so describe them. 'Somehow or other, I thought you'd get up to the front,' said Belinda. The adulation the Italians have for 'Il Papa' is amazing, though I must confess to some surprise when the onlookers began clapping as he entered the basilica, borne in on his Papal throne. It seemed out of place to me. I hope Garibaldi got the promotion in the Italian army we thought he deserved. What he had done, quite simply, was to take two tickets out of the box into which he had previously slipped them as the invitees came in. Ave Garibaldi!

*

One who admires and loves England as much as I do could

not help but leave it this time with sad feelings; so many unemployed, so many just out of school with no prospect of employment, such high inflation, such wide discontent. Pound notes seem to weigh as much as a piece of confetti, and to buy as much. The buying power of the pound in October 1980, was equivalent to about ninety per cent of the buying power of the post-war non-silver 'white' half-crown when it was first introduced in 1947, and about half the buying power of the 50p when it was introduced in October 1969. Doleful thoughts, indeed, but I will finish this chapter on a happier note. It might be recalled how, in an earlier chapter I wrote of Charlie Chaplin and Mary Pickford, and my abortive attempt to tell of an imaginary picture. I tried to visualize what my fellow-urchins, squatting along the kerb at night, would have said had I told them that some day I would meet both Mary and Charlie in my travels.

It was at night that I met Charlie – in 1964 in Khartoum of all places. He was travelling up through Africa with his wife, Oona, and his two young daughters. News quickly spread on the plane that he was aboard and, as a journalist, I tried to see as much of him as I could. Once landed, he went in to have coffee and sent his daughters into fits of laughter as he imitated his wife dropping off to sleep on the plane. I thought how wonderful it was, the greatest mimic the world has seen, and in action at midnight in darkest Africa. The females left him momentarily and Charlie sauntered out under the stars. I sauntered alongside him. We came to a sign-post pointing in all directions, one indicating that Australia was, I think, some four thousand miles to the east. As nicely as I could I interrupted Charlie's thoughts, and asked him whether he had ever been to Australia. No, he hadn't; and we chatted amiably for a few minutes until his women-folk returned. Before that Charlie had given the huge negro who had served them with coffee the biggest tip he had ever seen, or so his bulging eyes seemed to suggest.

Mary Pickford I met at Bibury, on the river Coln, in the Cotswolds. We stayed at the same hotel, the Trout, near a big hatchery, and had adjoining rooms. We met simply as fellow-guests, although Mary did not appear until the day

Q

was well advanced. She insisted on buying me a beer and I reciprocated, chatting along in great style. Her husband, Buddy Rogers, was with us and he couldn't fathom me. 'You don't seem much like an Australian to me,' Buddy told me. He was reproved by Mary. 'Oh, Buddy,' she said, 'you mustn't think all Australians are like Errol Flynn.' Probably just as well. As to Mary and Charlie, Michael Parkinson, who seems to have met all Americans in the acting game, had not met either!

It's mighty sad to think that England, for me, has gone for ever. I have so many friends in London and in all the home counties. Life has been richer for knowing them. I've driven hundreds and thousands of miles by motorways and other ways and, luckily, have never had an accident, though several close calls. I've been lost many times and don't think I have ever been given directions without the final admonition – 'You can't miss it.' I often did.

Instructions generally run by the pubs. 'Turn right at the Fox and Hounds, left at the Duke of Wellington, right at the Queen Bess and there it is in front of you – you can't miss it.' The best guidance I got over many tours was when I was seeking a public telephone to ring ahead to Lymm, to say I would be arriving late. I was given intricate directions and then I would find a hill with a public telephone on it – 'Only they took it away last year.' So I missed that, as I will miss Great Britain and all my good cobbers.

· 19 ·

Time to Pull Stumps, Gentlemen

'Well, now ...' as friend O'Reilly has a habit of saying before he sets out to sum up a situation as he once summed up batsmen. He did the latter with such success that he was the quickest bowler in Test history to get a hundred wickets against England, when a Test wicket really was a wicket; Tests then were mostly between the two 'enemies' and not a League of Nations with some easy pickings to be had. O'Reilly got his 102 wickets at an average of 25.36 and never once shirked an urging from his skipper to 'Go on, Tiger, and see what you can do about it.' He often, too, yielded to Clarrie Grimmett, great little fellow that he was, who could smell from afar a spot on the pitch, even if O'Reilly had found it, and wanted it.

Mention of Bill O'Reilly enables me to pay tribute to our greatest cricket mate, Stanley Joseph McCabe, who played three of the immortal innings in Tests, at Sydney (against bodyline), Johannesburg and Trent Bridge. As Bill never forgets to remind me, the two of us are now the only two alive who saw all those unforgettable innings. The power, the strokes, the grace of McCabe, typifying the character of a noble friend, will remain with me vividly for ever.

So I put it to myself again: 'Well, now ...' Here I am on the last chapter of a book I have written chiefly with the help of memory, a few clippings and a cuttings-book of some of my articles for the *Sunday Times*, the *Times* and the other papers I have contributed to. I am writing on the Indian Ocean from the comfort of the *Australian Endeavour*. There are many aspects of my life which I have not touched on. But before concluding this book, there are a number of important matters concerning the game of cricket that I want to write about. For a start I want to revert to 1934 when I experienced the bitter pill of not being chosen in Woodfull's team for England. Had I got that trip I would have been a much better batsman: one needs experience of English pitches to make a big success of a first tour. Though Bradman is an exception, there were those who thought English pitches would floor him; but he took them in his stride and vaulted them. Most modern Australians get an early taste of them in the various Leagues and so are well equipped for them when a tour begins.

On this subject, I was sad that our selectors did not choose the talented Peter Toohey (O'Reilly will agree with this) for the short Centenary tour. On the whole I would think it worth the gamble of including him on the next tour, even without the experience. Another I would have chosen in our best team was Ian Chappell, on merit and possibly as captain. Not knowing the modern behaviour of some members in the Long Room, the selectors wisely reasoned that Ian would not be welcome because of the many disturbing things he has done in cricket. I have always found Ian a warm, generous friend and a straight-shooter, if a stranger to tact and diplomacy. He can be his own worst enemy; he tends to speak as he thinks and often charges around like a stung bull. Early in his career in Adelaide he found himself at loggerheads with the prince of cricket power, Don Bradman, and the contumacious Ian is not one to pull his punches. Even his grand-dad, Vic Richardson, would often have been tempted to give Ian a well-directed kick in the pants, particularly when he allowed them to drop once on Adelaide Oval.

But back to 1934. I had not fully recovered from the several thrashings I had taken against Jardine's men. I was jittery when the year began but I was getting consistent runs and thought my prospects for England good. I felt I had to make a special effort in the final game in Sydney against Victoria, after which the team would be chosen, but I badly over-trained for it. I used to jog around Centennial

Park several times a week but stepped it up to several times daily. I came to face Victoria taut and tight, retired early with an attack of cramps, and then Bradman gave Fleetwood-Smith the biggest hiding he knew in cricket.

I think it was when I returned to the middle that I was dropped in the slips off Ebeling, a fast-medium bowler who used the angle of the bowling crease. A little embarrassed at the dropping, I moved up the pitch to pat it and Ben Barnett, as he was entitled to do, took off my bails. I left for the Pavilion but had only gone about twelve yards when Woodfull ran to me, took me by the arm, and asked me to come back: 'We don't want wickets like that.' I said, 'No, Bill, the umpire has given me out, I must go.' Woodfall said 'I will ask him to change his decision.' Kippax told me in our room later that I was wrong to argue or seem to argue with Woodfull, but it was an awkward situation for me. I thought I was out and had accepted the decision. Woodfull did induce Borwick to change his decision and, rather flustered by the commotion, I continued batting. Ben Barnett had been right in what he did. It was my responsibility to keep my crease just as it was that of Hogg when a similar thing happened playing against Pakistan in Melbourne. Hogg's ill-tempered response was to send his stumps flying with the bat, as several have done since. A stiff fine on Hogg would have taught him and others better, but our Board did nothing.

I went on against Victoria to 135 or 136, I've forgotten exactly, and in the course of my innings hit Ironmonger for six over the off-side fence, near John Snow's pickets where he was to tangle with spectators years later. I remember it because it was the only six I hit in Shield cricket, and it came so easily I wondered why I had not tried it before. I hit two sixes against West Australia at the WACA the following year and two far hits over long-off towards the Seigal clock at Durban off slow bowler Murray, who was later to come to Australia as manager of his country's soccer team. But Murray, like all bowlers against whom one gets a score (and my 167 that day was my highest in first-class play), didn't remember the sixes, only the times when he thought he should have had my wicket. Or so he said. Like golfers with their 'might haves'.

I think Woodfull made that gesture towards me because he already knew I wasn't going to be in the team to England. Anyway, I didn't make the team; a pity, as with Larwood and Voce both on the shelf, out of favour, it would have been a much more comfortable series than the bodyline one. No more than three openers were ever taken, and Woodfull and Ponsford were obvious choices; also it was too much to expect another NSW man to go. My chum, Bill Brown, had a splendid season and, showing much promise, deserved his place, though he had never faced bodyline. Perhaps I should have scraped another 17 runs to my 83 in the Melbourne bodyline Test, because it is hard for selectors to overlook Test centuries. Still, Bradman and Oldfield had both spoken against me, as I found out later; and it was possible that the belief that I had leaked the Warner–Woodfull story from the Adelaide Room didn't do much for me. Woodfull, Ponsford and Kippax retired after the tour. I sensed I was not liked personally by Bradman, and Oldfield would have his own special reason for not wanting me in the side. Though he could be most charming and was generally liked, most of us regarded him with suspicion. He had a habit of asking mighty personal questions and we considered him a leaker of dressing-room gossip. He told me when I first played with NSW that he knew my father at the Waverley tram depot, from which I assumed that he must, originally, have been a Public Service clerk. The non-selection was a blow to me but I think it did me good in many ways. Those who felt it most were my family, my mother particularly, and I didn't think much of that.

I had no trouble in being chosen in the Australian team for South Africa the following year, something I regarded as giving me the chance to answer the 1934 selectors. I think – in fact I am sure (none of this mock-modesty) – I did earn my place by the end of the tour. I may be forgiven for quoting the figures:

TOUR OF SOUTH AFRICA. 1935–6.
TEST MATCH AVERAGES.
AUSTRALIA.
BATTING.

	Matches	Inns.	N.O.	Highest Score	Total	Avge.
S. J. McCabe	5	7	2	189*	420	84.00
J. H. Fingleton	5	7	1	118	478	79.66
W. A. Brown	5	7	—	121	417	59.57
L. P. O'Brien	2	2	—	59	107	53.50
L. S. Darling	5	6	1	62	229	45.80
A. G. Chipperfield	5	5	—	109	196	39.20

AUSTRALIAN AVERAGES—ALL MATCHES.
BATTING.

	Matches	Inns.	N.O.	Highest Score	Total	Avge.
J. H. Fingleton	15	19	4	167	1192	79.46
W. A. Brown	15	19	2	148	1065	62.64
A. G. Chipperfield	14	15	4	109	655	59.54
S. J. McCabe	13	16	2	189*	800	57.14
L. P. O'Brien	12	13	2	113	523	47.54
L. S. Darling	14	16	1	108	711	47.40

As I had got three centuries on the trot in South Africa and another in the first Test of the series against Allen's side in Brisbane, this gave me four successive Test centuries, something which hadn't happened before. Alan Melville, of South Africa, joined me later with four against England, a splendid feat, and Everton Weekes beat us both with five against India. From what I read of his fifth innings it was a pretty lucky one. Weekes was a lovely batsman but suspect against bouncers. Though I made only 12, my best innings in the Allen series was in Sydney on a 'sticky'. I saw Badcock, Bradman and McCabe go the other end for ducks but the merit in my 12 was that I stayed there for seventy-five minutes while the pitch improved. It rolled out into a beauty in the afternoon when Bradman and I looked like a big partnership. We did not carry on next morning.

Things looked good for me for England in 1938 and they looked even better when Don Bradman invited McCabe and me out to his lovely Kensington home to dinner and a game of snooker, at which McCabe excelled. Don's charming and capable wife, Jessie, was a lovely hostess. The only cloud hanging over the 1938 tour was the threat of war which continued through and culminated in the downpour of 1939. The fact that Don Bradman, a selector, invited me to dinner was as good as an invitation to England on official Board letter-head. Yet with hindsight, I could well have exploited my selection by negotiating with a London popular newspaper to write about the tour instead. It was the sort of gimmick which would have appealed to many London newspapers of that time. 'Aussie turns down tour to write for us,' they would have screamed and, if properly handled, a writing tour would have been worth twenty times more than the meagre £800 we then got in lieu of wages lost. However, I doubt whether a popular London daily would have suited my writing style, and in those days there was still glamour in being an Australian Eleven player on tour in England. It bought lustre and acceptance in high places where money couldn't.

Although I had a moderately successful tour of England it came nowhere near my South African tour. I was never really suited to English pitches and it was only after I retired that I worked out why. I couldn't play the pull shot. Once in Sydney, a ball was so short that I could put my *back* foot up the pitch and across to get my body well positioned and played a lovely, lusty pull. That should have told me what the solution was, but still I didn't reason it out. Frank Conway and I had worked out as youths how Wally Hammond played his glorious shot through the covers off the back foot: his body was locked and thus the horizontal pull to a short ball was beyond him. I never remember him playing the pull, nor did Gubby Allen or Bob Wyatt when I asked them one day. Wally got many runs off his famous cover-stroke off the back foot and he was a delight to field against at cover; but he disregarded the most paying stroke on English pitches which got Don Bradman many runs.

To go to England without the pull shot is like touring without a pair of pyjamas. I asked Sammy Carter to stand behind me one day at the Lord's net and tell me why I didn't play the pull. Sammy, whose head was full of cricket knowledge, couldn't tell me what is now obvious –

footwork. Instead of going *across* the pitch with my back foot and so opening my shoulders, I was closing them by going back *towards* the stumps to force. Only a little thing, which I could have remedied with some careful thought. Small, but of the utmost importance. Looking back, I should also have gone further up the handle with my top hand for a more fluent swing, making sure both hands were together. So much is clear in retrospect, although a fluent swing is not a good thing against a new ball. In addition I didn't think too highly of being an opener on English pitches, where the new ball did much it couldn't do in South Africa or Australia. Two of the Tests were ruined on me – the non-game at Old Trafford and that at the Oval, where I didn't bat. I kept thinking I would come good in the later Tests but didn't reckon upon getting no chance.

Charlie Barnett, a magnificent stroke-player, commiserated with me at the end of the series, saying neither of us had any luck in dropped chances. Charles deserved luck with his approach; I didn't, although I got four satisfactory centuries at Oxford, Cambridge, Lord's and Southampton, and a near-miss in the nineties at Old Trafford (I was bowled for 99 at the Old Wanderers) where Dick Pollard and Bill Phillipson on a green-top turned Bill Brown and myself inside out. They also had a favourable wind. Over lunch Don Bradman asked us 'What's going on out there?' Bill and I told him we were lucky to be still there, let alone to get quick runs. Don makes a point in a book of how, after our slow start, he tore the stuffing out of the attack; but I don't think he would have done so in the morning.

I don't know whether they inhabit English grounds any more but in our time there were many of that club-like type who knew all about cricket and never hedged their opinions in any company. I read once where Charles (later Viscount) Cobham, Plum Warner; Charles Fry and Gerry Weigall were all together at Hagley Hall, where Charles lived and where he had them all to stay during our Worcester game. They talked about cricket before dinner, during dinner, after dinner and until three a.m., when somebody mentioned bed. 'Bed?' said somebody else. 'Bed? Why, we have only just begun to talk about cricket.'

Charles Cobham, when Governor, made me a life member

of the Izingari, a high distinction. With Len Hutton, Keith Miller and Charles, I yarned for hours one night after a Lord's dinner and although I can't recall one pertinent point anybody made (apart from Len tapping me on the chest and saying mysteriously, 'I'll tell you for why'). I do wish I had been wired for sound. It was talk that only cricketers indulge in. Lord Cobham is buried at Hagley and, typical of him, has this epitaph over his grave: 'Here lies Cobham beneath this hump; bowled as usual, middle stump.' He was a tremendous character who gave the press something to write about at Worcester in 1938 when he won the toss for his side and put us in. Bradman had made his usual double century. Charles was asked why he had put us in. 'The crowd came to see Bradman bat, not us,' he replied in his usual blunt way.

I must expand on Gerry Weigall too; as far as I know he had no accreditation in the game apart from being a pavilion pundit, a role often adopted by loquacious sons of famous cricketing fathers. I was riled on this tour at missing out at Canterbury on a peach of a pitch. I knew it for exactly what it was as soon as I saw it – full of runs. I started off, too, like an express train and thought, 'This is the day.' Sadly, Watt got one to snip back and some umpire (rightly) raised his finger for lbw. I had not got over my disappointment when I ran into Weigall, who always demonstrated his point with a walking stick. 'What I like about you most as a batsman, Fingleton,'* he said, 'is that you realise your limitations.' If I had had the stick I think I would have wrapped it around Gerry's head.

But I enjoyed the tour on the whole, although perhaps I missed a chance of furthering my writing career and earning a marriage-bank at the same time had the thought of renouncing it come to me. Had it done so, I don't think I would have behaved differently but, with hindsight again, I

---

* Australians generally, and Wally Grout in particular, resent being called by their surname. He would literally want to fight if called 'Grout' or 'Groutie'. I never minded. If the English call you by your surname it means you are accepted. Bill Brown and I spent a weekend with J. R. Mason, the Kent and England player, with his family at Cooden, a Kent-side beach. At the end of the weekend, J.R. said to me, 'I feel I know you well enough to call you Fingleton, if you don't mind.'

wish I had known as much about batting techniques then as I do now. So many opportunities are missed in life. It is natural to look back and reflect with the knowledge one has now – things would have been different but what a perfect world that would make it.

*

Those who should look back and reflect are those who were in charge of the Centenary Test at Lords. It would have been impossible for it to have equalled the Melbourne Centenary of 1977, so perfectly conceived and planned by Hans Ebeling was it and with cricket, luckily, worthy of the occasion. It must be said that there was a civic community spirit there that no other city would have matched. For hospitality the Lord's one was excellent, but as a cricket spectacle it failed badly. High officials of the MCC now think both teams, and particularly the captains, should have got together before the Lord's game and should have been told exactly what was expected. I don't agree. If the modern player is so highly professional, as we are led to believe, he should know his job. But, as a gesture, the MCC president, Billy Griffith, should have been invited to the centre with the captains and umpires to stress on behalf of the paying public what was due to them. There certainly appeared to be a desire to fill the ground daily without seeming to worry whether those who paid got anything for their money. I hope to see some day an itemized balance sheet of that game. It seemed to be regarded by those running it solely as a means of money-making. Along with others I was invited to write an article for the Centenary Test Book and offered a very minimal sum for the article 'as it is for charity'. At Lord's I found the book selling for £1 a copy. Some charity! I think Billy Griffith might have reasoned with those who didn't want to play to start by saying, 'Look, chaps, we have a full house. Let us give them some value for their money. This is not a typical Test between the old "enemies", with nobody yielding an inch.' And with what delight the bored crowd would have welcomed an amplifier announcement that 'MCC have arranged for a service helicopter to arrive in five minutes and dry out the patches which have stopped play.' The reception given the helicop-

ter would have been resounding and brought Father Time
down from his pedestal near the score-board to give his
blessing. So many MCC members, service chiefs, would
have been pleased to give permission for a helicopter to dry
up, and it would have been good publicity for the service
concerned. At the very least, one could have been flown in
from Heathrow – then there would have been no need for
MCC members to go on a tie-pulling jaunt.

It would have been great publicity value for the game
and, my word, does the game need that now. People have
always been pessimistic of the future of cricket but never, I
would think, with more reason than now. Kerry Packer,
whom I like, has done cricket more harm than he knows and
I am certain that that was not his intention. He has
Americanized cricket with gimmicks, in disregard of the
history of this gentle, peaceful English game, redolent as it
is of country villages and meadows. It has been re-
volutionized for money and the television screen, which is
so often demeaning to those performing and those
watching.

The true game doesn't lend itself to television gimmicks
and I foresee only a dismal future unless cricket quickly
regains its English character by returning to its grass-roots.
It has a charm all its own and a culture that is only acquired
over a long apprenticeship. I don't see one-day cricket
contributing anything to this – rather the opposite – though
I see some merit in a game that insists a batsman be forced
to play his strokes. Most can play better than they believe.
One-day cricket, with its slather-and-whack and non-
sensical field placing, appeals to the public, a certain section
of it at least, and it is popular with officials because it brings
in revenue. But the price in the long run will be horrific
because it holds cricket up to ridicule. I read nothing better
in my tour of England than Alan Gibson's article in the
Times; and as Gibson is one whose friendship and cricket
intelligence I value, I take the liberty of quoting it
extensively:

'England played the Rest of the World at a game
purporting to be cricket last night on the Bristol City

ground. I had been warned that I would find it a repellent spectacle, but the half had not been told to me. I felt bitterly towards our cricket correspondent [John Woodcock] who had been unavoidably prevented from attending by a previous sporting engagement (boating on the Thames with Brian Johnston). Not since I played for Yorkshire against the Rest of the World on a rough common outside Smolensk have I seen a more gross caricature of the game, but the competitors at Smolensk were a coachload of tourists and here they were some of the best cricketers in the world. In this was the tragedy.

'No doubt floodlit cricket has a future, for this is the age of the sporting stunt, and it is only fuddie-duddies who remember it was once the meadow game with the beautiful name. I did meet one or two regular cricket followers among the crowd – about nine thousand it was estimated – and they muttered shamefacedly things like "a bit of fun" and "does no harm".

'I suppose the harm has already been irredeemably done. But how any cricketer with any feeling for the game at all can regard the sight of the best players in the world bashing monotonously into the stands on a narrow football field passes my comprehension.

'Never mind, in ten years, mark my words, we shall have the pylons go at Lord's and the riots to go with them. They have had a promising trial run for rioting already.

'The emetic-yellow pads, the umpires dressed in red nightgowns like Chinese mandarins, the black sightscreens, the indiscriminately yelling crowds (I imagine the things they like most about soccer are sudden-death penalties), the artificial pitch, combined to make it all a hideous nightmare.

'It was just the game for Botham, able to mishit as much as he liked and still score sixes. Boycott, whose inner soul must have shrunk from what was going on around him, could not resist the temptation to play a cricketing shot now and then. Doshi showed that even in such conditions bowling a length could still bring a reward. The fielding was of high quality, even in the difficult period when daylight gave way to floodlight. These are the only polite things I can think of to say.

'The English innings ended for 214 in the thirty-eighth over. The rest of the world scored 220 for two. The players and Bristol City both made some money and Bristol City, at any rate, need it. But the end does not always justify the means and I would have thought it much better to see Bristol City in the third division than survive by such tales "told by an idiot, full of sound and fury, signifying nothing".'

Saying that such cricket bears no comparison with the real thing, John Woodcock suggested that it should be called Flashit, Thrashit, Nickit or Kickit and until it is, it must be known as 'Night Cricket'. He hit the nail on the head when he wrote: 'The whole performance will resemble the night the circus came to town. For as long as it lasts though, the players, if not the game, will be that much richer. It has the makings of a nice autumn bonus for them.'

Two days ago, my friend Jim White came with news that floored me: some forty-six thousand spectators watched the one-day game in Sydney between India and Australia. I must now, grudgingly, accept the inevitable and dip my flag. This, indeed, must be what the masses want, a constant clamour, bash, beer and fights on the Hill. Cricket, like England, has gone forever for me but nobody can take my memories. No longer can I come around the old Members' Stand, now replaced by the M. A. Noble Stand, to see the great Macartney twirling his bat aloft as he surveyed the field, like a Field Marshal about to attack. Not even Charlie would be welcome now. He wouldn't be appreciated or understood; the noisy masses would not even tolerate Don Bradman and his glittering double centuries. It is a new world to which the culture and charm of cricket have been sacrificed. It is sad, very sad, but it is covered, I daresay, by that all-enveloping word of progress – which, I note, has the same number of letters as pressure and pleasure.

But I still think sport, generally, wants to take a good long look at where money and television – often inseparable

– are leading it. They put boxing on at midnight and 2 a.m. at Wembley now to aid a trans-Atlantic hook-up; and tennis, thanks again to money, has been taken from Wimbledon to the desert at Dubai where the lure is $680,000, provided by the petrocratic government of sheikhs. The first prize, with only sixteen men contesting it, is $125,000, a fatter purse than Wimbledon, the US Open or Roland Garros. The grandstand has three floodlit courts cut out of the surrounding desert, and American Bud Collins, of the *Boston Globe*, said that except for the interminable azure sky and 90° heat, one could very well have been in England – oil money had brought thirty officials over from Wimbledon, so English voices were calling the scores just as they do there. Strawberries and cream were to be had, and fish from Iceland. The Bucharest Buffoon, as Collins called Nastase, actually won an argument with an umpire, but I fancy Nastase is like so many cricketers: he puts on a show for the lens and if spectators come in howling and helling – why, that is a better show for the camera again. The lens can't get enough of that. Collins wrote an excellent piece which was reprinted in the *Observer*; I guess the tennis press of the world were also guests of the sheikhs. Oil is selling well at the moment and at a good price.

There is now so much advertising ballyhoo about world sport. Boxers, who thrive in a cruel, unnatural sporting world, fight each other harder with words and insults before a bout than they may do in the ring. It is good publicity. A cricket captain makes vainglorious promises as a tour starts but rarely keeps them. Tom Kemp told me one day at Twickenham that his Rugby men had to watch sponsorship. 'If we are not careful, they will take our sport away from us. They will want to run it if we let sponsorship in.' That is what is happening in cricket. Sponsors for this, sponsors for that, rewards for this and for that. It is an advertising world. One English County Club gets £24,000 yearly for advertisements strung around its boundary fence.

That's the kernel of it all – more money for players and too bad whether the game of cricket is mortally hurt in the process. Such 'cricket' would not produce a star in a million nights; the only thing that actuates the play and officials is money, the curse of the age. I sympathize with the Packer players wanting more money, although it dazed me that they should sign an agreement with our Board for an English tour and its after-commitments when they had already signed an agreement with Kerry Packer. I thought the crunch would come one day before play in a Test in Melbourne when, with the ground filling up, the players announced their wants – or else. I remember the Big Ship of Cricket, Warwick Armstrong, once put his anchor down in the MCG dressing-room when he wanted an allowance of £6 for the match instead of £4. Warwick usually got what he wanted, but he delayed the start of that game by thirty minutes and didn't add to his list of friends, of whom he had few among officials.

As long as I have known the game there has always been tension in Australia between players and officials; but now that the players have got their way (the Board could not hold out against Packer's money-bags) they must accept that it is not all take; there must be a certain amount of give – value for money. We didn't get value from them at Lord's. From what we saw, it would seem that players were willing to accept what came their way when the game ended in a draw, with both sides sharing the winning and losing prizes. I wonder whether Cornhill Insurance, who sponsored the game, thought they got value for the hefty sum it must have cost them. Let me warn intending sponsors and spectators of the future: I still see no real value for them or their money while modern players, over-keen to turn out anytime for financial reward, are shuttled all over the countryside to provide incessant fodder for television. The players are in no fit mental or physical condition to lift themselves for Tests as we once knew them, and this is what was basically wrong with the Lord's Centenary Test. The players could not lift themselves; also the inexperienced Ian Botham, England's captain, must accept some blame: he seems to have developed a 'one-day' mentality with his field placing.

The ABC had sent a big team of commentators from Australia to London for the occasion, this being a chance, as they saw it, of getting back some cricket television rating from Packer; but what viewers in Australia saw of what was built up as the 'Test of Tests' was mostly sheer boredom, with England seemingly never giving a win a full look in the face. It was Kim Hughes, a cheerful young man spurned by Packer's agents, who alone redeemed the game. Well as Wood, Border and Boycott, in his usual back-to-the-wall style, batted, it must have been very pleasant for Hughes to get within a whisker of a century in each innings. Greg Chappell would have set England a target they could not have refused (350 in 370 minutes was the ultimate and not unreachable target) had he not wanted to give Hughes a chance at his second century. Time and again Kim has sacrificed an innings when well away, but he showed in that game that he could apply himself. In a one-day match at Edgbaston he twice played a reverse drive for four, smack through the deserted slips, a gifted shot which I have seen Greg Chappell play. But Hughes's stroke in the Test off Hendrick, a drive in front of point for four, was the shot of the match and could well have been the shot of the century. To catch it for posterity, as Patrick Eagar did with his camera, was almost as good as the shot itself. Hughes went yards down the pitch apparently to drive straight, but finding the ball just suited for the most unusual drive past point, changed his back-swing and follow-through and did just that . . . a genius of a stroke.

*

Two of our oldest players at the Centenary Test, or ex-players, were 'Stork' Hendry, who headed the list aged eighty-six, and Bill Ponsford, on the verge of eighty. 'Stork' agreed with me about the pleasures of Somerset, not least the delectable vegetables and berries out of the garden. He remembered, in 1921, when he took ill with glandular fever and spent his recuperation with a family at Curry Rivel. 'Stork' was so thrilled with the hospitality he received that he decided to repay it by playing in a village match. He had grown a beard during his recuperation and thought he would not be recognized. He was clean bowled first ball! I did a good turn for a friend at Yeovil (also in Somerset). He asked me to give him my opinion on whether Bill Voce

was a fast or a spinning bowler – he had a bet on it. I did
better than that; I sent him written and signed testimony
from the Test, from Bill Ponsford, Bill Brown, Bill
O'Reilly, Artie Chipperfield and myself that Bill Voce was
not only fast but ruddy fast. I had put it to Ponsford one
day that he had often got to 300 and 400. Had he ever
thought of trying to get 500? Bill's eyes twinkled. 'Not yet,'
he answered.

Don Bradman didn't accept his invitation to the
Centenary Test and he showed good judgement in that; he
would not have liked what he saw. He would have known no
peace either, being pestered to visit and make speeches.
Those many who still revere his name would have lined up
in a long queue between Q Stand and the dining-room. It
was only a distance of twelve yards but meeting fans
invariably took nearly an hour for even the near-
nonentities. I had a lovely talk with Bill O'Reilly one day as
we signed for the most polite autograph-seekers I have
known. We were too busy to talk about much and Bill said
to me, 'You're pretty monosyllabic, aren't you?' And I
replied, 'Yes,' which came in nicely. We both liked that.

*

I have written much of my newspaper work but not yet on
how it nearly cost me my life. For years, as I have said, I
had written for a multiplicity of papers, building myself a
neat and profitable little empire. But I was over-doing it
and I felt dizzy pains at Edgbaston in 1961 when I used to
dash around the ground like a peanut-seller on the way
from the press-box to television and broadcasting posts.

The crack-up came in the mid-seventies after Perth and
its Test. I did a BBC talk with Christopher Martin Jenkins
when Doug Walters got his century between tea and
stumps. The Test over, I set out for Melbourne. We were
called on to our plane long before it was ready. In sizzling
heat we waited for some twenty minutes in space not
enough for sheep, let alone humans. Arriving in Melbourne
I had to wait several hours for my connection to Canberra
and I was pretty exhausted when I got home. Next morning
cables arrived from almost all my newspapers, demanding
specials for Sunday, on various aspects of the Test series. I

quailed at the prospect, especially as there was a Press Gallery Christmas drinks party that day for Parliament House employees. Still, work never frightened me and I slogged at those specials all day and well into the night. I did the job but it was a Pyrrhic victory.

That night, in the house on my own (the family were all in Sydney), I felt dizzy and fell over repeatedly. I couldn't raise my neighbours so I rang Sue Willoughby (now Phipps), a friend of my daughter Belinda's; her husband, Don, came round. A doctor inspected me, then Don drove me off to the Woden Valley hospital, where I was admitted to intensive care and into the excellent hands of Bob Mitchell. I was, as we say in Australia, 'pretty crook' and might indeed have snuffed it if, when I regained consciousness, I hadn't seen the ever-loyal Larry, my son, sitting at the end of my bed. He had flown up from Sydney immediately and that decided me – I wasn't going to throw my hand in. I had had a CVA (central vascular accident) – in other words, a stroke. I had no power on the right side and, as in such cases, I was affected by a palsy. My mouth was drooping on the right side and drooling with an inability to speak clearly. Bob told me that I had been foolish not to watch my blood pressure, and I pass this advice on to people who lead an active life and think they are as good as they were. Bob told me that my writing career was over – I wouldn't be able to spell, for a start. In fact, the stroke hit me most in the right rugby knee and in the voice-box, so that my singing – and I loved to warble – has gone to pot and my voice is now weak. When I try to sing the hymns at mass, it is not unusual for children to turn round and gaze at me in wonder. It was not always so. My golf is affected, too: I have had to restrict my backswing; if I go back too far I unbalance and make a proper mess of the drive. But in spite of all I am fortunate in that I can play nine holes comfortably, and even eighteen if I get a lift on a buggy. My medical friends at Royal North Shore, Sydney, want me to write a paper on my experiences and that is the next job after this book. I think my 'experience' was interesting, if that is the word for it.

*

The time has now come to tell the story of Fuserium

Fungus and the tie which I gave Michael Parkinson at our first interview. I never got around to saying what the tie represented and as many people have asked me, 'What was that tie all about?' I must tell the story. On the tie in front of three stumps is a donkey with four pads on and nibbling Fuserium Fungus. It is the tie our press party had struck in 1972 when Bert Lock came to look at the Headingley pitch and said it was infested with the fungus. The tie is in the Yorkshire colours of blue and white.

I asked George Cawthray the day before the Test if I could have a look at his pitch. The pitch belongs to the caretaker until he hands it over to the umpires. I have always observed the ritual of looking at a pitch and to do so I ask in the right quarter for permission. So many journalists just walk on to a ground with no invitation or 'by your leave'. On this occasion, while George and I were looking, Ray Illingworth, the English skipper, walked out and joined us.

'This pitch,' Ray said to George, 'is not your Test pitch.'

'Yes it is, Ray,' said George.

'I remember the Test pitch here,' said Ray. 'Every time somebody walked out of that bar in the stand we had to stop play.'

'Oh, it is the Test pitch all right, Ray,' said George.

I had a sensational story on a plate. I could see the headlines: 'English skipper says it's not the Test pitch,' but, as I was still George's guest, so to speak, I really was not free to write the story for the papers. However, I made mental notes and remember the incident and the details. The pitch was funereal, nothing like the fast one we had expected for Lillee and company, though it was apparent that it would suit Underwood and Illingworth. I requested an interview with caretaker George and also asked that the county secretary, Mr J. Lister, be present. Mr Lister took an active part in the discussion, though I only wanted to ask George about the pitch's preparation. 'We will see what the English batsmen make of the pitch,' said Mr Lister. I said they would not have Illingworth and Underwood as spinners to contend with and Mr Lister said he resented my interference. We got nowhere. The game finished early on

Saturday afternoon, two playing days untouched and gates sacrificed. That evening I was asked to speak at a big dinner. Ian Chappell criticized me in a yarn for being too trenchant about the Headingley pitch, but Ian didn't know what I did. Nor did I tell him.

Bert Lock, curator of curators, had been called in to examine the pitch and it was then that he diagnosed Fuserium Fungus, caused by the pitch sweating. The fungus had come up under the plastic cover during heavy rain before the game, and I could believe that. Before our tour finished I gave up a precious Sunday in London and caught a train up to Leeds where Yorkshire was playing Leicestershire a one-day match. I made more enquiries and it was then that I found Ray Illingworth had been correct: it wasn't the Test pitch. The club had sold a certain number of reserved seats behind the pitch which was used, and as they had been sold for big 'brass' it was decided the Test would be played on that pitch, and not the Test one. My investigations and the train trip were well worthwhile. I would suggest that any team going to play a Test should always, on arrival, send an official to those grounds where the Test is to be played. There the pitch should be pointed out to them and its preparations discussed. I hadn't the heart to tell Michael Parkinson the history of the tie, but retrieved it from him and gave him instead an Australian cap of mine, with no fuserium in it.

An old friend of all of us, Jim Manning, now alas no longer alive, spoke some good words about sport; when Jim spoke and wrote or broadcast people sat up and took notice. 'I'll tell you what sport is about,' Jim once declared. 'Sport is play, so that life without sport would be unplayable. That is why people who dislike sport are a menace and those who think of nothing else are a nuisance.' Jim never pulled a punch. He gave Yorkshire and Headingley absolute stick after our Test there in 1972, pointing out how Lord's and *Wisden*'s had attacked Yorkshire for years over the pitches they were presenting. In an article headed 'Murder Most Foul', Jim said England in 1961 had beaten Australia more quickly than in 1972 on a pitch less unfair. The Yorkshire representative then told Lord's that Yorkshire realized their pitch at Headingley was not up to Test standard and that the county would do all in its power to see this was not the case in future. Brian Sellers, famous captain of Yorkshire, once joined in the general criticism of a pitch at Lord's, the ridge one, and said 'We know how to make pitches in the north. We will show them up here.' The pitch turned out to be a shocker. Many counties fiddle with their pitches in England, making them to suit their own particular bowlers. The English thought we fiddled with the Melbourne one in 1932-3. After hearing a well-known English cricket personality talk one evening about how pitches are fiddled in the Bradford League, I rather feel they not only fiddle pitches in Yorkshire but cello them also.

*

As I write, the Australian coast is off our port beam. We are only two days out of Melbourne, our first port of call since Liverpool. We have stopped only twice, once outside Port Said and once in the Big Lake in the middle of the Canal in which I saw wondrous things.

On this trip I have sunbathed each day, with ten minutes extra for my son Larry in London where, we hear on the air, there is now snow. My sunbathing won't do Larry any good but it is pleasant for me to think of him and the other four children – Belinda, Jim, Grey and Jacquie. If I don't mention them all (and I do) I will be in trouble.

David Patterson, cardiologist of the Whittington Hospital in London, gave me a comforting report to leave England with but, the Australian coast now in sight, I have no fears. It would be a nuisance to my ship-mates, I know, but I think dying at sea has much to commend it, especially now we have reached Australian waters. They sew the body up in canvas, with weights at either end; departing this life in such a way would delight me: it would mean beating the undertakers who get themselves a free ad. at the expense of a bereavement. State Minister Syd Einfeld was going to do something about this some years ago but nothing has happened as yet.

*

It is high time to move on. Only six months ago, just before leaving Australia for England, I had a most enjoyable bush lunch in golden autumn sunshine with my brother Wally, his great mate Ken Francis and our friend Mary Savnik, at that rustic ground of lovely memories, Brooklyn. Much water has flowed under the nearby Hawkesbury Bridge since then. We sail into Melbourne on another lovely morning of glowing sun. That's it, gentlemen, time to pull stumps.

Postscript

As a final act of audacity I propose to choose four sides that I think would worthily represent the West Indies, South Africa, England and Australia in a series of Tests (have you noticed how an extra Test has been wriggled in now to make it a series of six?). These imagined sides would make for magnificent cricket – or war! Fearing the latter between South Africa and the West Indies, if somebody could ever induce dark men to take the field against white, I would unhesitatingly choose Frank Worrell as captain of my West Indian side – the reader can pick his own. That is the main reason for this postscript, to make you think, argue and disagree.

Frank Worrell was a credit to his country. He was a beautiful batsman, who played all the delicate strokes as well as the ones of gusto, and he brought a great charm to the game. He was always smiling and moved with grace on the field. In his rich Barbadian voice, 'Move dem hips, man' he would chortle. These are solid reasons for making him my captain. What he possessed more than anything else was the ability to get on with his white fellows. It could have been that attending Manchester University, where he obtained his law degree, broadened his mind. But he would have stamped down quickly if his fellows, as I think they have done in recent years, were inclined to let their dislike of white men degenerate into spiteful bouncers and a complete disregard of whether the batsman hit suffered an exceptional injury.

I have known serious allegations in my time of white men being accused of racism but the reverse also sometimes seems to me to be the case. So Frank Worrell walks into my

West Indies team as skipper; and to make sure that any
nonsense of not playing against white South Africans is
scotched before it starts – this is a game, not politics – I
would make Dr Ali Bacher captain of South Africa for the
reason that he attacked apartheid in a practical manner,
working as a surgeon in a coloured hospital in the
Transvaal. Many who do a lot of spruiking don't put their
beliefs into practice in that way. Another reason for
favouring Bacher is that he proved a wise and thoughtful
leader at a time when South Africa could easily have been
the best Test side in the world had they not been blacked
out, so to speak.

It will surprise many that I include (Lord) Learie
Constantine in my team. Learie was also a great leader of
men. I saw him bowl his last few balls in cricket in
Canberra, of all places. He had come to a Parliamentary
Conference and some cricketers in the House asked me if I
could induce Learie to come to their pitch on the Senate
side and bowl a few balls. Learie took off his coat and
obliged. I noticed that each time he delivered the ball he
looked up at his arm. Why? 'My father taught me to do
that,' said Learie, 'to make sure I wasn't throwing the ball.'
I know of a few Australian players who could have done
with that advice. Many will argue that Constantine's Test
figures don't entitle him to be chosen in the best West
Indies team of all time. They may bowl me out on figures,
but Learie in all departments of cricket – batting, bowling,
fielding – was capable of unforgettable deeds. This is my
team and as things apart from cricket count a lot Learie goes
in, to aid Frank Worrell, if need be, in keeping things in
perspective.

Many of the West Indians choose themselves – Sobers,
Walcott, Viv Richards: no better batsman than he would
appear in any of the sides. It will surprise many that I don't
include Everton Weekes, one of the famed 'three W's'. He
showed a weakness against pace in Australia and I have
preferred George Headley to him. Bert Collins, the
Australian captain, once told me that Headley was the most
accomplished batsman he knew – and Collins played with
Trumper and saw a lot of Don Bradman too. It might

surprise readers that I have chosen Rohan Kanhai, but at his top he was a superlative batsman. Wes Hall gets the fast bowling spot with me because Wes was a cheerful, big-hearted man who also brought distinction to a cricket field. I thought long of Roberts, at his best a tremendous bowler, of Holding, Croft and Charlie Griffith; but for varied reasons I pass them by for Wes. Many may disagree. As the West Indies have attacked through fast bowlers only in recent years, so I reverse the policy and commit them to several of the best spinners known to cricket – those two old spinning pals of mine, Ramadhin and Valentine. Worrell will have to wear his best skipper's cap because I have also included Gibbs, the off-spinner, who has taken most wickets in Tests. On second thoughts, I reluctantly leave out my friend, Alf Valentine, and put in Roberts, at his best.

I have been somewhat inconsistent in choosing this team: I had decided that figures would not sway my decision, that I would think first of the make-up of a cricketer and what he has to offer. And in these days of instant Tests, so to speak, Test records aren't as good as they look. This, then, is my West Indies team: Frank Worrell (captain), Sobers, Walcott, Headley, Kanhai, Viv Richards, Constantine, Ramadhin, Roberts, Gibbs, Hall.

*

Now to South Africa and another Richards, Barry this time. A glorious batsman who has spent the last few years twiddling his thumbs because of the apartheid embargo. He could well have equalled the feats of his West Indian namesake and this is the highest praise.

South Africa has known two batsmen fit to rank with those of other countries – Graeme Pollock and Dudley Nourse. Herbie Taylor, too, was another of world stature, as he showed against the great Englishman, S. F. Barnes, on the mat in his home country and in England. I would essay a guess that Herbie is the only winner of the Military Cross in the four teams; he was also a pronounced theorist on the game. Heine and Adock were a pair of fierce fast bowlers and I would separate their speed with the splendid off-spin of 'Toey' Tayfield, so called because of his habit of tapping his toe before bowling. Jock Cameron was a splendid wicket-keeper and a fine, forcing batsman. Purely on Bert Collins's word again I have chosen Blackenburg, a right-hander who swung and spun the ball. Bert thought him the finest slow bowler he ever faced.

It has been hard to overlook Percy Sherwell. He was a distinguished captain and wicket-keeper, but we have only one of the latter in a team. Early South African teams were famed for their slow spinner, Schwarz picking up the art at Oxford from the originator, Bosanquet. Ian Peebles, another whose opinion meant much to me, was an ardent admirer of Aubrey Faulkner, at whose nets in England, where Faulkner settled before his tragic death, Ian bowled and coached. So I have chosen both Schwarz and Faulkner. The world of cricket has missed much with no Test cricket from South Africa for far too long.

So my South African team is: Dr Ali Bacher (captain), J. Cameron, G. Pollock, Barry Richards, Dudley Nourse, H. W. Taylor, H. J. Tayfield, P. Heine, J. M. Blackenburg, G. A. Faulkner, R. Schwarz.

*

The English and Australian teams are difficult. I would not hesitate with my openers for England: Jack Hobbs and Len Hutton. There will be a big outcry from many that I have omitted Geoff Boycott, who now has become most popular in England after his early eclipse in the fifties. Nonetheless I do so, though I may receive a writ from his solicitor who, I believe, scans very closely everything written about Boycott. I would reply that I have overlooked another famous English opener in Herbert Sutcliffe. No, I don't think there will be any complaints about Hobbs and Hutton.

I surely must place Dr W. G. Grace in my side on many counts, and I nominate him skipper. This would give him the chance to match his well-known sharp wits against those of other generations. I choose him as skipper mainly because he would twiddle his famous beard when the press, as is now their custom, flock to the dressing-room for quotes after a match – particularly the Australian press.

'What's this?' would squeak the doctor in his high voice. 'The press were never allowed near a dressing-room in my time.' 'But we want quotes,' would say the spokesman. And here I might add that it was Richie Benaud, when he was Australian captain in England in 1961, who got the press into this particular habit. Richie was a journalist and a very good one too, and was adept at giving morning and afternoon angles to those newspapermen who depended upon them. Once, as the press so often do, they over-stepped the mark and his newspaper, the *Sun* of Sydney, rang him direct to England for a story. The Board of Control, not always the strongest body in sport, demurred and ordered that Benaud no longer talk to the press. Instead, all quotes would come through the manager, Mr S. G. Webb, a rather talkative QC. The press had to work harder for their stories.

But back to the great Grace. He is one whose figures you can look up and gasp if you believe figures, as most cricket society people do. 'Quotes, quotes,' would say the doctor, 'what are they?' 'How do you think the game is going – what do you think of this and that incident?' 'In other words,' would squeak the Great One, 'you want me to write your story. Like all doctors, there will be a fee for that. But I will relent and give you one quote.' 'Yes?' would say the anxious press. 'Buzz off,' would say W.G. Yes, Dr Grace would be the man for the press. He would send them scuttling. Peter May was a captain who went out of cricket before his time and I think he rightly resented the hounding he got from his own press. Peter would say that he retired because he had to think of his business future. In any event, he gets into my English side, a batsman of lovely strokes. Hammond must come in, also, and Denis Compton, if he promises to turn up. I might be light on bowlers here and might have to tack a bit to fit Jim Laker in somewhere. Jim was no great performer on Australian pitches; he used to look at them, think back to Old Trafford in 1956 – and sigh.

Woolley just misses out and that saddens me. I would have him on hand because Compton, despite his promises, could easily fail to materialize. So my English side is:

Dr W. G. Grace (captain), Hutton, Hobbs, Hammond, Compton, May, Evans, Larwood, S. F. Barnes, Rhodes, Hirst.

*

Now, only my Australian side is left. Bill Ponsford would open with Victor Trumper and there is no doubt who would follow. And he would also be skipper. Stan McCabe played three of the greatest innings seen in Tests and he gets in on many counts. He played cricket in a cavalier manner, though he hated the intensity of Tests. Greg Chappell also gets my vote. There have been many laments in Australia about selectorial bungles in not choosing various players to tour. I would think the non-selection of Greg Chappell to go with Lawry's team to South Africa, the last team of ours to tour there, was the biggest howler of all. Tom Trumble, who twice got hat-tricks in Tests, comes in and so does Don Tallon as keeper.

O'Reilly and Grimmett were the best spinning pair I knew in Tests, although I noted both delivered full-face, with the front foot pointing down the pitch. They might have spun the ball more had they delivered side-on, an interesting thought. Lillee and Lindwall get my nod and I don't think any side will have a better pair of speedsters. So my native side reads: Bradman (captain), Ponsford, Trumper, McCabe, G. Chappell, Tom Trumble, Tallon, O'Reilly, Grimmett, Lillee, Lindwall. I would like an all-rounder to boost this team, somebody like Keith Miller.

*

Possibly many won't agree with me for selectors have odd quirks in choosing sides. Plum Warner, who became very friendly with me after the bodyline Tests, told me once that he wanted a certain batsman in an English team for Australia – because he had won the Sword of Honour at some military academy or other. 'But Bob Wyatt is as stubborn as those mules I used to drive in the West Indies in my youth,' Plum wrote to me. I think I would agree with my friend, Bob Wyatt. I couldn't see what the Sword of Honour had to do with batting. Nor did Bob. Plum's favourite didn't come.

Two umpires – Frank Chester in his early years but not

later days, and George Hele (of Australia); they would keep
bouncers in check. Three writers – Cardus, Peebles and
'Crusoe' Robertson-Glasgow, a lovely man of delicious wit –
and the rest of the world's press to run their messages and
bring them sandwiches.

Acknowledgements

I am indebted to many people for help with this book and would like to express my thanks to them: William Noonan (NSW) and Jon Cleary (NSW) were helpful with sound advice, as was Gilbert Mant (NSW) with early newspaper reminiscences. For help in many ways I must mention Bill O'Reilly (NSW), Dr Larry Fingleton, Dr David Patterson (London), Sid Herbert (London), Quentin Lindsay (Scotland), John Luff (Somerset), John Woodcock (London *Times*), Dennis and Christopher Martin-Jenkins (London), Tom Conway (NSW), Peter West (Camberley and BBC London), M. Gemmell (NSW), M. Jarvis (NSW), David Frith (editor of *Wisden's Monthly*), Harry Evans (London), John Lovesey (London), Ian Wooldridge (London), Brother A. I. Keenan (NSW), Ned Wallish (Victoria), the London *Observer*, Walter Brooks and John Malone (Australian Government) and Merv Agar (Adelaide). Most helpful with statistics were George Franki (NSW) and Cliff Winning (NSWCA); Alan Reid, Ian Fitchett and Miss Pat Romans (all Canberra) helped in various ways. Patrick Eagar, friend and prince of photographers, provided some of his splendid action pictures, as did Ray Blackburn (*The Age*, Melbourne) and Brian Bassano (South Africa). I should like to thank Captain Barry Powis, Chief Officer Jim Snow, and their crew, for making me so welcome on their ship, *Australian Endeavour*. The two Pats, Mrs Harrison and Mrs Rawlings (both Canberra) were generous with their typing help, and aid during a crippling communications strike in Australia; the Misses June Griffiths and Roxarne Burns of Collins Publishers in Sydney were helpful and reliable. Thanks are due to the *Sunday Times* and *Times* of London for permission to use their material and to

Collins Publishers for permission to quote from my old friend, Neville Cardus. Finally, my sincerest thanks to friend Michael Parkinson for his generous foreword, and to the editorial team at Collins Publishers in London – Mark Bonham-Carter, Robin Baird-Smith and Gillian Gibbins.

Index